LOOKOUTFORSHORTS

A PRISON MEMOIR

GARRETT PHILLIPS

Disclaimer: I have tried my best to accurately recreate events and conversations based on both my memory and by consulting my extensive journal entries from the period. All names have been changed to protect the anonymity of subjects.

© 2020 Garrett Phillips. All rights reserved.

ISBN (paperback): 978-1-7348575-0-4
ISBN (hardcover): 978-1-7348575-2-8
ISBN (ebook): 978-1-7348575-1-1

Designed by Euan Monaghan
Author photograph by Garrett Phillips

For information about discounts for bulk purchases, permissions, or to report errors please contact Garrett at his website: lookoutforshorts.com. Also visit for links to more story-related photos and blog posts about his self-publishing experiences.

This book is typeset in Bembo and Univers LT. The publishers are concerned with and committed to protecting the galaxy by using environmentally sound printing practices. This book was printed with soy-based ink on recycled paper. Printed in the U.S.A.

Second Edition

To the memory of my dear mother Beth, lover of words.

"I don't want to pull any more time, but I wouldn't take anything in the world for the experience I had in prison. It's not a waste of time there, it's good experience."

— NASCAR legend (and notable bootlegger) Junior Johnson

CHAPTER ONE

When the Whip Comes Down

Even on a mild ecstasy high, I should have known the jig was up. Perhaps sensed something was off as I reached my hotel room door, but I was starving. I'd forgotten to eat in the midst of ten hours of dealing drugs and seeing a Widespread Panic rock concert. I slid my key card through the lock eager to devour a to-go barbecue dinner I'd just purchased. With the swinging open of a door, hunger became the least of my problems.

Four Asheville city cops gang-tackled me and introduced my face to the nearest bed surface. Handcuffs then dug into my wrists, but I felt lucky anyway. If I *must* be subdued by burly police, a pillowtop mattress in a luxury hotel was a pleasant place for the indignity. I cooperated with the cops, so the tension in the room dropped and they loosened my cuffs a little.

I felt an immense relief, bordering on gratitude, of all things. What awaited me was certain to be awful, but at least the stress of living a lie might end, and my failed life plan could be corrected.

The cops who threw me on the bed were soon dismissed from the room by John Thornmartin, a plainclothes officer for North Carolina Alcohol Law Enforcement. This oddly-named agency probably chased Junior Johnson around many decades earlier.

"Sorry y'all had to wait around all night, fellas," Thornmartin told the officers as they left.

Hearing this pleased me. Better the police waste six hours in my hotel room than harass my fellow concert fans as they partied around town. I'd taken one for the team by accident.

Officer Thornmartin, a mellow guy, proved to be a credit to law enforcement, although at first he refused to let me eat.

"But I'm *starving*," I whined. "Who knows when I'll be able to eat again?"

"Okay, fine."

Thornmartin directed his sidekick plainclothes cop to move the handcuffs to my front. I sat on a bed and endured questions as I ate.

"Where'd you get the drugs?"

"I plead the fifth."

"Are you working alone?"

"I want my attorney."

My mouth was full for every response, trying to talk while inhaling hunks of slow roast pork. I started just shaking my head to reply instead. I felt lucky for my molly buzz, which kept me in the moment and amused. Otherwise, I might've broken down and cried as reality crashed down around me.

"Hey, thanks for letting me eat," I managed at one point. "Mind grabbing me one of those waters there?"

Thornmartin glared as I nodded towards water bottles in a cooler. "Now you're *really* pushing it!"

The cop grabbed a bottle anyway, probably more to prevent a captive from choking than to be nice.

My eyes drifted to a large Tupperware container next to the cooler, which held roughly ten thousand dollars worth of drugs. Forty-five grams of MDMA powder (aka molly), which is over four-hundred doses, and twenty bags of high-grade pot. Also seized were an ounce of smokable DMT, non-prescribed Xanax, and various tools essential to the drug-dealing trade like a digital scale and baggies. *I might want to find a lawyer who has compromising photos of the local DA.*

Thornmartin soon lost his patience, realizing I didn't plan on talking. He halted my greedy chow session and cuffed me behind the back again.

"But I'm not done," I protested.

"We've been here for six hours," he growled while nudging me towards the door. "We need our own fucking food."

We passed through the plush hotel lobby, my first of several serious *w*alks of shame to come. Bystanders gawked, and I felt like each of them saw me as the shit stain I had become. Thornmartin shuffled me to an unmarked SUV and dismissed his sidekick cop for the night. I headed to jail for the first time in twenty-five years, since a bullshit disorderly conduct charge in college.

Thornmartin and I began a two-minute drive, me riding shotgun. Upon my arrest, they failed to search my back pockets so I started unloading several zip-top packets of molly from them while the cop kept his eyes on the road. My long arms and fingers allowed me to fish out the contraband and stuff it into the seat crack, possibly lessening my charges and definitely giving me an adrenaline rush like I'd stolen something. I truly hoped the inmate who cleaned the SUV next found it all and enjoyed the best week in the history of incarceration.

I tottered into Buncombe County Jail intake area around one o'clock, and into the modern hell of trying to remember a phone number. I had two for my lawyer memorized, you know, on the off chance I ever got arrested. Calls to them went unanswered and leaving a message on a collect call wasn't an option. I gave up and just stared at the phone, joining two other detainees in the same predicament.

Under the pressure, snippets of cell numbers and those of old landlines bounced around in my head, but none worked. The cops refused to search a directory, and each use of the phone required begging. My fading molly buzz made my disjointed thoughts even foggier and worrisome. How long would I be locked up if I contacted no one? The countdown began.

I had to be sprung fast. My hotel room was full of belongings to retrieve, and I needed to get home to clean up my apartment in case the Feds raided it. My car in the hotel parking lot had $6,500 stashed in it, too, in case I came across a good deal for LSD or weed while in town.

Oxygen seemed hard to come by. I may have heard a panic attack in my head, personified: "Hop in, I'm taking you for a ride!"

With my fingertips freshly ink-stained, a cop barked and pointed me to the next stage of booking. There, as I watched my belongings being cataloged, a phone number finally came to me. An Atlanta restaurant owned by one of my best friends, Jamal. I'd worked there years earlier and knew someone might answer the phone even around 3:00 a.m. My heart soared.

"May I please, please, please use that phone over there, officer?"

"After I'm done booking you in, you can," she mumbled. Minutes passing suddenly seemed like hours as I pictured the restaurant manager killing the lights and locking up for the night.

I finally placed the collect call and spoke my name at the tone: "Jamal's friend, Garrett."

Eons of silence passed, followed by the sweetest voice I've ever heard: "Garrett, it's Laura."

I knew her well, my favorite of all the managers. I spat out my dilemma.

"Damn! Okay, I'll call him right away. I know he's still awake."

In theory, I'd walk out in an hour or so because Jamal just gets things done.

In the meantime they stuck me in a holding cell. They call it *the cooler* since it's colder than the milk they serve there. Hours passed as I sat with teeth chattering and my t-shirt pulled over my bare knees, confused by the delay. Had one of my best friends forsaken me? God knows my dealing partner Joe had. He'd ratted me out to the cops. My thoughts ran to killing Joe and to other dark places, including suicide. Dwelling on my string of poor life choices tortured me.

Eventually they moved me from the holding cell into the general population. I ended up with my own cell, so at least a menacing cellmate didn't add to my worries. I also finally received a little bit of padding for my bony ass, in the form of a foam jailhouse mattress.

The first time I entered the common area for a meal my eyes widened and my jaw dropped. There sat Joe, munching away. He saw me, dropped his plastic spork, and skittered back to his cell, leaving his tray sitting on the stainless steel table.

I felt like attacking the rat, but this would only worsen my problems. I could whine about how he broke the rules of The Game, but ultimately the blame was on me. I should have kept my circle close and never involved him. Joe not knowing the best way to sell the product without getting caught was my fault. My stupidity and greed created the problem; Joe's betrayal was a side effect.

Sitting in my cell, I marveled at how great life seemed a mere six days earlier.

The music group "Further," an offshoot of the Grateful Dead, played Atlanta in April of 2011. I joined the pre-show party, a traveling bazaar that spanned several parking lots and brimmed with recreational drug customers. "Shakedown Street," as it's known in the scene, mixes local concert-goers with fans of the band who follow them from city to city. These travelers funded their lifestyles by selling the likes of clothing, drugs, and provisions to those milling about. My drugs sold well in this environment – a modern-day version of Ken Kesey's Merry Pranksters as described in Tom Wolfe's *The Electric Kool-Aid Acid Test*s.

Happily, Atlanta police mostly ignore these events. Big city cops have more pressing matters than fucking with pseudo-hippies who are "harming" no one but themselves. As a result, drug sales were wide open compared to many other cities.

I ran into old friends this day, both locals and people I'd met over three decades of my own jam band travels. One of these was Joseph Warren Johnson.

Joe and I met in the late '90s Phish scene and attended a couple of concerts together before losing touch. He appeared friendly and intelligent, just as I remembered, but claimed to be down on his luck. He asked to help me sell my molly that afternoon and allow him to pay me afterward. I was happy to front him this way to both help him out and move more product.

I ended up re-supplying Joe three times that day, selling out of product with little effort. My buddy and I made a ton of cash, and dozens of concertgoers rolled through the show while enjoying my high-purity recreational drug. Everybody won.

Next up on my concert-drug-vending schedule: Widespread Panic, in Asheville, a counterculture town in a sea of red state conservatism. At first, I intended to travel solo and meet old friends when I got there. However, a day before leaving Atlanta, Joe suggested he come along to do more business with me. This idea appealed to me initially, but second thoughts about it kept me from sleeping well that night.

I once knew Joe well, but not so much anymore. He wasn't connected to any social network of mine. But he *was* familiar with selling drugs at jam band concerts. I could trust him if he got popped, which he probably wouldn't anyway. In retrospect, I should've listened to the voice that suggested otherwise. Unfortunately, the Xanax I frequently used at the time squelched such useful noise in my head. In this case my typical unease would have helped. I also got sloppy in other ways.

Indifference to my legal jeopardy from dealing kept me from even researching mandatory minimum sentencing laws in case I got arrested. I always held less than an ounce at a time anyway – under the weight threshold for a trafficking charge in most states. But then my supplier started trusting me more. Her most recent shipment was *four times* the usual.

"Pay me when you can, no sweat," she said.

So instead of my typical inventory, I brought over twice as much MDMA as usual to Asheville in case a bulk-sale opportunity arose. My exposure to serious consequences was redlined. The selling weed to friends business I started eighteen months earlier had mushroomed out of control, just like my entitlement complex.

I felt the world owed me something, despite my chronic

procrastination. I allowed no place in my life for patience, persistence, or postponing gratification. This approach deserved to collapse and I did my best to hasten the fall.

None of this occurred to me on the three-hour drive to Asheville with Joe, a fortyish redhead of average build. Had I been thinking straight, I would have spent this time planning a sales strategy that avoided cops. Instead, I figured a liberal town awaited us – how risky could it be?

I'd learned that wandering around nice hotels is the best way to sell drugs on the road. The commotion of arriving guests lends perfect cover. Jam band fans – my customers – were easy to spot. They wore wide grins and colorful clothing, and usually pulled large coolers in addition to their suitcases. I'd usually hang around the elevators or roam hallways to make contacts, then move to guest rooms to make the sales and socialize.

The front desk clerk might as well have told guests: "You're in room 318. The elevators are to your right, and the tall guy wearing the Phish hat sells a full selection of mind-expanding chemicals for your weekend. Enjoy your stay!"

I failed to confirm that Joe knew this hotel process when I supplied him with molly and weed to sell that afternoon. As a result, he solicited buyers in the parking lot of the concert venue, which turned out to be under surveillance.

After working the hotel, I set up shop at a pizza joint to make mostly prearranged sales with previous customers or people I'd "met" from internet message boards. The afternoon was safe, lucrative, and fun for a while. But soon something seemed off. A couple hours in, no word from Joe. I operated as if everything was cool. Shut down mode never entered my mind, but a booze and molly buzz did.

I moved into the concert venue to commence full-scale partying, despite no word from my partner for four hours. I should've sensed police problems, but figured at worst he skipped town with the drugs I'd fronted him. Joe eventually texted, twice in a row.

[In room. Need to re-up. Where's the stash?]
[Got two girls with me who want to party.]

Even *this* didn't alarm me, probably because I was high as fuck. Joe already knew where the stash was and knew Widespread Panic concerts involve *thousands* of girls partying. Why the fuck would I *leave*? I didn't recall Joe being this stupid. Not to be denied a good time, I met up with some friends and enjoyed the whole concert.

Afterward "Joe" repeatedly texted, urging me to hurry back to the room to party. Obscenely hungry, I grabbed some barbecue at a food truck and headed to the hotel, wondering how hot these girls with Joe could be. The night was still young and life was good. Molly doesn't help spot red flags.

As I said, my pal Jamal just gets things done. I expected to be bailed out in an hour or two. Instead, I logged nearly a full day in lockup. Turned out that out-of-state detainees with serious charges like mine require full bail – thirty-three thousand dollars in my case. Worse, the bail bondsman didn't take AmEx, the only card Jamal carried that had a high limit. He eventually convinced the bail guy to spring me anyway, essentially promising the check was in the mail.

I got released after about twenty hours, which seemed more like twenty days. In the jail lobby on my way out I met my folksy bail bondsman.

"I'll tell you what, fella, you got one helluva persuasive friend!" the big guy whooped. "I ain't got his money yet, but I can tell he's good for it."

I appreciated the websites for Jamal's restaurants in a whole new way.

My hotel was a short walk from jail, yet a world away. The room was still under my name despite the whole *multiple felonies committed here yesterday* thing. All of my legal possessions were still there, and my car (and the cash) remained untouched. Evidently the cops found sufficient evidence against me without searching it.

My drive back to Atlanta the next day was a slow, surreal freakout. I never even turned the stereo on. The sound from my flipping brain kept me occupied. *How many years will I do in prison? How much will this cost? How will I ever pay off my massive credit card debt?* Any relief I felt upon my arrest became a distant memory.

Once home I cleansed my apartment of incriminating evidence and grabbed a suit to wear to court. I tried to focus on the upside. At least my arrest came before I became a dealing kingpin. A federal case hadn't been launched. My car wasn't impounded. I didn't have children to support. I always wanted to author a book, so this could be my research for it. I can find bright sides anywhere.

After driving right back up to Asheville the next morning, I encountered Joe at our arraignment, before I found peace with his role in my life correction. I first saw him slinking in the corner of the lobby. "Do you have that ten bucks I lent to you?" I asked.

He looked away and said nothing.

"Thanks for ruining my life, asshole."

This was the extent of our interaction, He avoided my glares in the courtroom. He deserved a beating, but his end punishment will be worse. Joe has to be *him* the rest of his life, and I wouldn't wish that on anyone – except him.

I pleaded not guilty, in case my highly touted lawyer could work miracles. Afterwards I met with this new best friend in his penthouse office and assessed my ruins. I felt good about my lawyer, but my cash flow did not. I explained my fingerprints were everywhere and refused to incriminate my suppliers for reduced charges. Snitching wasn't a favor I wished to pay forward.

My attorney suspected search warrant shenanigans by the cops, but I lacked the additional ten grand required to investigate it. Worse, I learned the district attorney was an anti-drug crusader who harbored a particular distaste for dealers. Lawyers knew of him joining DEA agents in the field to bust people when jam bands came to town. Looking back, perhaps he'd been sent to straighten out my crooked life.

Along those lines, my only reasonable strategy was to enter rehab in hopes the DA might reduce my charges. My prescription pill abuse needed addressing anyway, so all the better. I spent the next ten weeks calling in debts and selling possessions to pay back Jamal and raise the money for rehab. A saintly group of family and friends donated to my cause. My "front" job, as a courier, kept me occupied in the interim, but not always smoothly.

One time I exited an elevator while still in tears over my predicament. I faced a receptionist to make a delivery.

"Good morni ... are you okay, sir?"

"I ... Well, no. I mean, there's been a death ... it's just hard."

The receptionist signed for the package and I left, not mentioning I felt like the one who'd died. I gobbled the opioid and benzo stash that remained from my bad old days, but even that couldn't kill my pain.

The weeks following my arrest had me constantly on the verge of tears. A deep fear for my future made me want to drop to my knees in agony. Any laughs I found while staggering through days were tempered by dread. My mind became a self-torture chamber.

I scraped by financially. I used loose change for gasoline, which I'd also buy using a debit card, knowing a check may bounce because of it. If my car wasn't on the road, I had no income. Overdraft fees were the cost of doing business. Instead of paying for expensive suspension work on my decade-old Mazda Protégé, I changed out twenty-dollar used tires instead. New rubber was out of the question.

In Asheville for a morning court appearance, a $6.99 hotel breakfast proved too pricey, especially with the tip. I paid for a cheap meal on a date and winced because my companion's order was nine dollars, roughly ten percent of my net worth. After that I might as well have been under house arrest because funds were so low.

Such were the burdens beyond a prison sentence. I failed to consider this condition when I decided to deal drugs. The shame and anguish. The ruined plans. The maddening logistics of liquidating or storing my possessions. Suicide loomed as a possibility to end the pain. Oh, to return to more carefree days when I continued pissing away my life.

Even at age forty I didn't buy that hard work and dedication were keys to a happy life. I made an unfocused attempt at internet video broadcasting. I also chauffeured a town car for a year, hauling the likes of a hungover Rosie O'Donnell, and a testy, humorless Billy Crystal. The job paid poorly, though, so I returned to courier work and dicked around waiting for another break.

Courier driving was my default occupation for over fifteen years, in theory for the freedom to take time off to perform at comedy gigs. Instead, I used the freedom of an independent contractor and good pay to golf, vacation, and follow Phish around. I lived paycheck-to-paycheck, with no plan for the future besides the next party. I rarely engaged in sober reflection as I aged into my forties. Life was to be enjoyed.

But deep down I knew I was wasting away. Living irresponsibly robbed me of any real serenity or contentment. Fewer women seemed to be available to date as I grew older. I was miserable. And then the heavy shit came down.

Lung cancer took my dear mother, a mere four months after her diagnosis. A month earlier a dear friend of mine died suddenly at age thirty-seven. My ache from being a failure at life tripled. Enter the painkillers.

While I helped attend to her, Mom was prescribed copious amounts of Oxycontin pills, fentanyl patches, and morphine drops, most of which she didn't want. I used them with impunity and ended up with a habit. As with my addiction to party chemicals, my bout with pills was more insidious than acute. I never overdosed, but stayed in a haze instead. I tapered down my use several times, only to resume levels in the wake of some trigger, real or imagined. Facing days was easier when numb.

Soon Mom's surplus drug supply ran out, around the same time my income from courier work tail-spinned. To make up the difference, I utilized excellent connections from the jam band community and began deliveries of high-grade cannabis in addition to blueprints and other legitimate cargo. I set a monetary goal for when I'd quit. Once I saved enough money, I'd start a limo company that specialized in tours of Atlanta. I planned to only sell weed, to keep my legal jeopardy low.

I secured a solid wholesaler in California while on a Phish concert festival trip, and I assembled a mostly upscale Atlanta clientele. Wholesale pot prices out west were plummeting, yet retail prices in Atlanta remained high. I'd found the perfect side gig. My arrest record was clean, and I looked like a middle-aged golfer, beyond police suspicion while driving a modest Mazda.

My supplier mailed up to three pounds at a time to a post office box I rented for a "custom knitting" business. The vacuum-sealed nuggets arrived without fail for nearly a year. For payment I shipped $100 bills, stashed in a hollowed-out hardcover book, which we sent back and forth. I chose *Atlas Shrugged*, since the words removed were probably superfluous, anyway.

Dealing weed proved tiresome and annoying. Weighing out the product and running around town to distribute it was a lot like work. Unsavory associates incapable of being on time or keeping promises were headaches. The logistics of dealing with all the cash were most tedious of all.

Unless moving serious weight – high in the food chain of dealers – one can't dictate the denominations of incoming cash. Retailing drugs means lots of small bills to deal with. Counting all this paper sucked, and not much of it could fit into the stealth compartment to be shipped. I paid my supplier only with hundreds to win brownie points. I believe she offered better credit terms and more generous product samples thanks to this.

My solution for changing small bills to hundreds was polite society's mega-banks. My respectable air allowed me to roll up to a bank with a ton of small bills and leave with a tidy stack of hundreds. My laminated courier company ID and their magnetic signs on my low-key car shouted legitimacy. My bank featured dozens of Atlanta branches, so I hit up drive-thrus all over town to squelch suspicion.

"Good morning!" I'd say cheerfully into the camera above the cool tube-shooting thingy, after I'd pulled up.

"Good Morning, and welcome to MegaBank, sir! How may I help you today?"

"Welp, I just sold my old motorcycle/boat/dairy goat, but the buyer paid with small bills. May I change these for hundreds please?"

"Do you have an account with us, sir?"

"Yes. Yes, I do. And when I opened it, I never thought your monstrous size would make managing drug money easier. Thanks!"

I had pot dealing figured out, but carelessness plagued me – almost like I wanted to get caught. I drove around with bags of pot barely concealed. Customers who took short rides with me said my car reeked of weed, but I didn't particularly care. Then, all at once, my greed and sloppiness merged.

Had I been content with dealing weed an arrest would have been a nuisance, even back in 2011. But I chose to walk the high wire of selling MDMA too. Molly was easier to sell on Phish concert tours, i.e. my "business" trips. Demand for the love drug far exceeded that of weed and concealing the powder was much easier. And while I usually doubled my money selling pot, I tripled it with molly.

The high-quality product I supplied more or less sold itself. Instead of walking around drumming up sales of pot I filled most orders by word of mouth. And I enjoyed an unlimited supply for myself. Life was good, except it wasn't.

Huge chunks of the credit card debt I'd amassed over years began falling away. I bought the good turkey breast slices at Costco instead of the cheapest. Vacations came often. But I was miserable. Typical joys no longer interested me. The thought of dating bored me. No decent woman gets involved with a drug dealer, anyway. My shortcut to success brought no pride with it, but did bring a chance of getting busted. The respectable would never respect me.

Living this life is how a major arrest can make a person feel relieved. And how a rigorous rehab stint is worth all the pain it brings.

CHAPTER TWO

Commencing Corrections

Ten weeks after my arrest I entered the thirty-day in-patient program at Caron (pronounced Karen) Treatment Center near Reading, Pennsylvania. A friend referred me there, promising top-notch therapy. I figured an expensive, highly regarded rehab facility might help my case more than something like Bill's Recovery Center (enter around back). My counsel insisted that my best strategy was to impress the Asheville DA.

None of this was on my mind as I drove up to the quaint hilltop campus in June 2011. I sincerely hoped thirty days cold turkey from painkillers would lead to long-term sobriety. I couldn't picture my shattered life without the pills, but life with them was unsustainable.

A plush reception area greeted my arrival, like a small VIP airport waiting area, minus the bar. My stomach, knotted with anxiety, wanted nothing to do with a fully stocked snack nook. It seemed to mock me. "Bet you wish you'd like a fresh muffin right now, don't you, loser?"

After paperwork, a friendly intake counselor led me to the medical clinic wing. New patients were monitored there the first night in case of violent withdrawal symptoms. I met my first Counselor Assistant (CA), a staff member that made sure residents followed the rules and schedules. He happened to be a dwarf.

"Welcome, Garrett! My name is Bill, and I'll help you get settled today."

He extended his hand skyward. I reached to shake it until I saw my hand looked like a catcher's mitt compared to his. Fist bumps relieve awkwardness, just put it that way. Bill led me to what looked like a nice hotel room except for two single beds instead of queens. I placed my suitcase on one of them, and he hopped up next to it and started digging.

"Just looking for contraband. Don't worry," he explained, anticipating the question, "it's in the contract."

Given the day's weirdness, he seemed to be standing *in* my suitcase as he sifted through items that surrounded him. I stared into a dresser mirror and saw both confusion and amusement. He held up a tie-dye shirt commemorating Albert Hoffman's discovery of LSD.

"Can't wear this!" he declared, a bit too happily. "It glorifies drug use and may tempt your fellow clients."

Soon Bill left and my roommate entered. He was a pale, spindly guy in his twenties who sported a large DJ-related tattoo on his arm. I assumed the tatt was in lieu of actual skills on the decks.

"Yeah, I'm in here for alcohol treatment. I detoxed from the opiates in the hospital the past few days."

Hours later the same guy woke me as he convulsed on the hallway floor and screamed "Don't let me die!"

Many newcomers were in similarly bad shape. Most were at least hungover from a "last hurrah" bender, if not hardcore addicted. Over the next month I heard comparisons of blood alcohol levels upon arrival. The highest I heard was .42, with many others in the thirties.

In a lounge area my first night, three guys compared arm veins or the lack thereof. They asked to see mine, which have never been punctured for recreational purposes. I sheepishly turned my elbows to the floor.

"Damn!" a guy exclaimed. "Those are goddamn garden hoses! I'm seriously jealous."

These fellows shared a credo: "Why snort it and waste it when you can shoot it and taste it!"

Caron's exorbitant cost seemed like money well spent, especially since my broke ass qualified for half-off (15K). Creature comforts included a dining hall that resembled a buffet at a four-star hotel. Dudes wearing chef hats manned cooked-to-order stations: "What may I prepare for you today, sir?" Patients had access to spiritual advisers, personal shrinks, and yoga sessions. Massage and acupuncture were available for an additional fee. Most importantly, the counseling staff proved warm, caring, and professional.

The twelve steps of Alcoholics Anonymous were at the core of the treatment curriculum. Daily workshops in a large, comfortable lecture hall focused on the physiological nature of addiction. The three-hundred seat room also hosted AA speaker meetings, which is when addicts tell their stories about abuse and recovery.

Often former Caron patients took to the lectern. Most notable of these was an eighty-six year-old lifelong Philadelphia tough guy who looked like George Carlin. He had been sober for thirty-seven years, but shared "war stories" – basically boasting about his using days, which is normally frowned upon in twelve-step circles. He also blew past the meeting's ending time by twenty-five minutes, mostly telling tales of drunken fights. Dude could spin a yarn, so no one complained.

The lecture hall really bounced on Sunday mornings, when it became a worship and communal celebration that family members and locals could join in. These high-energy assemblies included many current residents displaying musical talents, several which seemed near professional-level.

One minister was a counterculture type and a dead-ringer for actor/comedian Andy Dick, only gayer. He sported bright trousers, busy scarves, and waved his hands in the air while spouting non-traditional spiritual ideas. To the crowd's delight, the minister often added comic relief, including the contradictory notion of "sober reggae."

The stage also produced tear-jerking displays of gratitude from patients nearing graduation. Family members often joined in, describing their depths of anxiety and depression before they found Caron, and expressed thanks for newly found hope. This initially sounded like parroted testimonials from the brainwashed, but they seemed more heartfelt as the weeks passed. The message to recently arrived patients facing recovery was pure: It works if you work it.

In addition to lecture hall rehab gatherings, smaller counseling and treatment sessions filled the schedules of patients. Large Groups of about twenty focused on AA and broader program goals. Small Group required the most intense personal examination and produced the most drama. These consisted of only five residents and one counselor, and mostly analyzed feelings in the aftermath of substance abuse. I often felt like someone had dropped me into the middle of a movie scene.

At one point my Small Group included a self-pitying Jesus freak, a no-nonsense senator who was ex-army, an ex-con Philly hustler, and a genuine Pennsylvania Amish farmer. One day the Amish guy – committed to Caron against his will by his wife – finally stopped denying his alcoholism and broke down in tears. The Philly guy, a Hispanic former gang member, consoled and embraced him. Seeing these two fish-out-of-water bond brought tears to everyone's eyes.

The Amish guy in my group was named Ames. He sported the classic Puritan look of beard, pageboy haircut, boots, and suspenders. He came from a semi-modern sect in nearby Lancaster, home to the largest Amish population in the world. They consent to certain modern societal norms, like electricity. Catching a booze buzz every night is not among these.

Ames usually spoke only to bitch about Caron banning his tobacco pipe while everyone else smoked cigarettes like sailors. He loosened up over time, however, and his offbeat stories – delivered in a heavy accent and peculiar cadence – made him a fan favorite. Sample punchline: "What, are you crazy? That's not how you fix a wagon wheel!"

He basked in the sunshine while wearing both his shirt and undershirt, black trousers raised over his knees, and long socks pushed down to ankle-high boots. I witnessed the first time Ames had ever done laundry himself, at age sixty-five. I felt lucky to be there to help. He looked at the washer like it was Stewie Griffin's time machine, wondering what buttons to push.

Contrary to Amish Ames, "Jesus Jack" was a guy no one liked. Bloated and rosy-cheeked, JJ could easily play the part of an adult baby wearing a diaper and bib. He frequently babbled scripture-filled sob stories and reeked of phoniness. He interrupted lecture hall speakers as if they were solo counselors for him, invoking Jesus every two sentences in the process.

The no-nonsense senator showed the least amount of patience for JJ and his trust fund kid entitlement. Our group counselor didn't realize this and sat them face to face for a counseling exercise. The senator was working through grief from his son's death, and the counselor chose JJ to sit in as the dearly departed.

"Okay, pretend Jack is your son," she instructed. "What would you say to him right now?"

The senator squirmed and mumbled through a very pregnant pause.

"I can't do it," the senator finally barked.

"Of course you can, you simply need to channel your feelings and embrace the pain," replied the counselor.

Knees almost touching JJ's, a sweating senator took a deep breath and focused directly across from him. He barely began, then stopped short.

"Nope. I can't fucking do this!" he snapped. "I mean, I can *do* the exercise, just not with this ... this *cartoon character* as a prop. I can't stand looking at him, and I'm sure as hell not spilling my guts to him! I can't do it."

Several beats passed before the counselor spoke, annoyed with snickers from the peanut gallery. "Okay, I'm hearing you. How about you speak to an empty chair instead?"

The senator agreed and did so. JJ sulked back to his original chair. The counselor kept the two behind after the session to iron out their differences, like two feuding classmates in the principal's office. They agreed only to ignore each other from then on.

Caron welcomed patients from all walks of life, but mostly professionals and the well-to-do. Among these was Richey, nephew of a famous fashion designer. He was an Upper East Side man of leisure and narcissistic phony who couldn't laugh at himself to save his polo horses. He constantly tried to bullshit bullshitters, and his lack of self-awareness made him the butt of many jokes.

One day in a Large Group counseling session, Richey asked: "I'm supposed to list how my substance abuse affected me both externally and internally. I know 'externally' means my career, my family, and so forth, but what does 'internally' mean?"

Amazed group members looked at each other for a few beats. Finally, the Philly street hustler all but shouted: "It means *feelings*, dude. You're exempt, though, because you need a *soul* to have them." A fistfight might have broken out if Richey were tougher.

These group meetings and closely examining my past mistakes in a sober light every day ground my emotions raw. I usually slept poorly. Comfortable beds didn't stop my mind from spinning at night and wanting my mommy. Sleep meds were forbidden. Fellow residents suffered the same challenges, and we shared thoughts and suggestions to cope. What felt like lifelong friendships were forged in mere days.

Despite our heavy tasks, or perhaps because of them, the community mood during free time mostly stayed light. So much so that I dubbed the place *Camp Wiseacres*. We liked to joke, and also test how far Caron rules could be bent.

The most odious rule concerned caffeinated coffee, which was tightly controlled in the CA office next to a kitchenette. They limited residents to one small cup of the drug each morning. Motivation to roll out of bed early ran high, to be served before the ration ran out.

Several guys not addicted to coffee bartered their cups for cigarettes, because smoke supplies moved fast. The main social circle during free time, at the smoker's cabana, set records for chain smoking. Even "non-smokers" bummed them.

Anyway, a mere one cup of coffee was unacceptable to many "caffiends." Someone slipped into the CA office and swiped a whole case of the black gold, undetected.

"Hey Garrett," a buddy whispered one afternoon at the coffee counter, "the decaf pot of coffee is actually real right now. Help yourself."

As this juiced java flowed, afternoon nap time suddenly became game time in the lounge area. A game of living room handball broke out at one point.

CAs began observing us closely, with furrowed brows. Soon they found an empty regular coffee packet on top of the trash, in the afternoon. *Busted.* We all felt lucky to receive only a warning for the crime, and the new tradition skidded to a halt. Risking a sanction of an entire week of no coffee at all was out of the question.

Speaking of addictions, romance with patients from the adjacent women's unit was strictly forbidden. Flings kept people from focusing on recovery. The women didn't need to be newly addicted to dick, and men were in rehab to penetrate enlightenment, if anything.

The genders crossed paths often though, walking around the campus and especially in the dining hall. Ladies often cast sexy eyes through a large window that separated the two designated areas. Deprived males stayed on high alert for this, needless to say. Guys agreed that a special hunger emerges when a girl eats an ice cream cone a certain way.

Non-verbal, non-physical "flings" with a few ladies lifted my spirits, but I consummated none of them. Others sampled the forbidden fruit after hours, occasionally ending up with expulsions from the program.

I welcomed the distraction of rehab's social life. The shame of my arrest and being broke left me lonely and isolated in the real world. At Caron, I practically became an extrovert. I even resuscitated my stand-up comedy act one evening, enjoying a captive audience starved for entertainment beyond shitty DVDs like *Clean and Sober*.

The crowd loved it, at least until delivery of ten pizzas arrived five minutes in. After that I told jokes for a bunch of sober drunks watching their comfort food get cold on a table behind me. If I could make it there, I could make it anywhere. No one complained when I cut the set short. My "pay" for the set was being closest to the pizza when I ended the show.

Farewell rituals, which seemed to take place every other evening, provided another chance for laughs. Everyone assembled to pay tribute to the guys going home, who sat at the front of the room. Each man took a turn saying goodbye, often sharing heartfelt tidbits about those soon to depart. Others roasted the fuck out of them. After a couple of weeks of becoming familiar, I took part in good-natured cracks with those who knew the victim well.

My favorite was at the expense of Larry, an overweight and profoundly average-looking guy whose gorgeous spouse visited for family week.

"I learned a lot from Larry," I began. "Most importantly, a beautiful wife may stick with you even if she repeated her vows at gunpoint." The packed room exploded, and Larry took the joke with grace.

My social stimulation ratcheted up during the back half of my stay, when evening lecture topics repeated from two weeks earlier. When this happened they permitted "veteran" patients to road trip to twelve-step meetings in neighboring towns instead. These slices of Americana were a welcome change of scenery, and a glimpse of AA in the real world.

Caron passenger vans unloaded into these blue-collar church basement meetings, like a cruise ship docking at a small village. I sensed a reality TV camera effect, and few locals seemed to speak freely amid the transient audience. Or perhaps the meetings simply sucked all the time. The tedium left me staring at the worn linoleum floor as minutes limped by, wondering if prison felt like that. Something had to give.

One day at the dining hall I heard a couple gay residents rave about the local LGBT meetings they attended. They described a fun and lively vibe that included gourmet coffee and tasty confections. Jealous, I made a plea to my Caron counselor for permission to join their meetings.

"But you're not gay!" she insisted.

"You're right, but I've heard it's not that complicated and I'm willing to learn."

My officially gay roommate Matt and my overwhelmingly gay pal Russ took up my cause. "Please let him come, we can make fun of him!"

The next group that headed to the gay meeting included me. A man named Henry seemed to light up as I boarded the "gay van". He invited me to sit with him, so I did. I felt like a pretty girl – a hot commodity.

Henry was in his sixties, slight, and known around campus as interesting. He'd taken up residence at Caron's neighboring ninety-day rehab unit, so I'd seen him around but we had yet to meet. The collars on his pastel-colored polo shirts stayed popped, and he defied world history by somehow wearing a toupee with aplomb. As the van hit the road Henry explained that rehab tours were basically a hobby for him.

"I'd rather call my out demons than let them lurk," he claimed. "And rehab joints are great for that."

He was on his second stint at Caron, and had also "located" his "compass" at high-end places like Betty Ford, Hazelden, and Promises in Malibu. He liked Caron the best, praising its alternative spirituality angle, and a relatively laid-back approach to recovery.

I found these rehab notes useful, but considered Henry's life story downright fascinating. An heir to a Philadelphia industrial fortune, he occupied himself with philanthropy and sat on the board of multiple charities and museums. Never have I been so enchanted by a blatant name-dropper and braggart.

Mentioning a Park Avenue brownstone or a booze bender with Liza Minnelli was merely Henry's life, not necessarily boastfulness. He even offered dirt about the aforementioned Richey, with whom he crossed paths among the beautiful people in New York. (They considered Richey to be a douche, too.)

Henry's charm carried over to the LGBT AA meeting, too. He regaled the lively gathering with a share that lasted fifteen minutes, but no one seemed to mind. The guy coined phrases and told stories like a seasoned novelist. We addicts learned that even when one "has it all," he struggles like all of us. And while Henry's life was hardly a breeze, sitting on a nine-figure fortune probably softens the bite from a hangover.

Henry inquired about my sexuality on the ride back to Caron, which meant we talked about me for two minutes and him for the other twenty-three of the trip.

"I didn't realize we were teammates," he said with a wink. I wished not to disappoint him, so I played coy.

"Well, my mother always claimed no one is entirely hetero or homosexual," I began. For a precious moment Henry was all ears. "People land somewhere on a 1-10 scale that runs from totally straight to completely flaming," I explained.

"So where are you on this scale," he purred.

"Depends. I get really bored watching lesbian porn. After a few minutes of that I *really* want to see a hard penis involved."

Henry laughed loudly, which drew someone else into the conversation and changed it. Sadly, that was the last time I saw him.

The arduous personal treatment portion of Caron's program proved to be the easy part. Each patient's thirty-day stay culminated with Family Week, about which stories of emotional horror circulated. Parents, siblings, and significant others came to town, first to spend two days in classes to learn about the physiology of addiction and the best ways to live with it. My Dad attended, but was probably far more interested in the dining hall buffet, free for visiting family members.

Following the educational portion of Family Week, patients joined their visitors for growth exercises. These gut-wrenching, tear-inducing interactions addressed deep-seated issues between relatives to help smooth out relationships. This prospect evidently moved Dad deeply, because he broke into tears during basic opening introductions to the full group. Knowing him it was probably an act. I half-expected him to peek over at me to see if his waterworks were working.

The first day of family therapy included lighthearted listening exercises. One of these required two strangers to pair up, and I quickly chose the lovely girlfriend of Richey. My satisfied smile from this coup made him glare at me from across the room.

The program called for her to talk to me for three straight minutes, followed by me summarizing what I heard her say. I fought laughter as she spent the time bitching about traffic en route and how she didn't want to be there, anyway. Richey's endless boasts about their wonderful relationship suddenly seemed pathetic.

Next our roles flipped, and I ranted to her. I complained about beautiful NYC women choosing rich douchebags as boyfriends instead of underachieving yet witty men like me. I also suggested women should try to "fix" broken men as a path to true happiness. Or something like that. Frankly, I just enjoyed an excuse to stare at her beauty again for three minutes.

The final, widely dreaded exercise of the week facilitated face-to-face reconciliation between family members. Four patients and family, typically the two parents, formed a small group and took turns addressing specific gripes between them. Lists of "I'm sorry for," and "What I need from you going forward," helped to clear the air. Family members detailed broken promises to each other as their group watched. This explained the multiple boxes of Kleenex nearby.

I squared off with Dad, seated facing him with our knees nearly touching as a counselor and ten others looked on.

"I'm sorry," he managed between sobs at one point. "So sorry for my apathy towards you. I promise to try harder."

I'd heard versions of this from him before, but this time he sounded sincere. When my turn came, my recent painstaking self-examination came pouring out amid tears. I babbled a lot, but probably covered only one sentiment.

"I'm sorry to be an embarrassment. That I'm such a loser."

Crying and heaving like this in front of strangers was as fun as it sounds. Watching others suffer the same way felt like attending multiple funerals in one day, five minutes at a time. Raw emotions spilled freely, as did tales of tragedy and regret from those tormented by addiction for far too long.

When family week closed, Dad took off immediately. He had nowhere to be, that's just him. Participants that thought they'd bonded with him approached me as everyone hugged and exchanged numbers.

"Has your dad left already? I really wanted to say goodbye. He was so great!"

Given the lack of improvement in our relationship from that point on, he might as well not have even come. Full of shit, as usual.

Emotionally spent from the past thirty days, I welcomed my own farewell roast. I paid the Karma Gods for the cracks I'd made at the expense of others. My gangly height and goofiness invited comparisons to Big Bird on *Sesame Street*. My slow cadence reminded people of the muppet Snuffleupagus. Thank god for the jokes, otherwise I might have cried the whole time. I hate even standard goodbyes more than most, let alone those for special people I really like.

Leaving Caron was hard both emotionally and physically. Like me, one of my car's tires arrived at rehab noticeably deflated. I got better. The tire didn't. Complications with the spare and the repair expense welcomed me back to the real world. I wondered when the next curveball would come my way.

I drove straight to Atlanta. I was under a deadline to report to a "supervised recovery residence" for the next step in salvaging my life. This halfway house encouraged continued sober living and potentially bolstered my case to the Asheville DA. He could pursue prosecution that didn't include a mandatory minimum prison sentence if he saw reason to.

A solid recommendation from a halfway house would help this cause, so perfect behavior for the boss woman was crucial. I would have to impress Denise, a thin and stylish middle-aged SoCal native with a New Jersey gruffness. She had some twenty years sober, and all the leather she wore gave me the feeling she substituted drugs and drinking with really aggressive sex. She called the shots and accepted no bullshit.

Denise was director and drill sergeant of the halfway house which consisted of several clean, functional apartments in the same complex in a nice part of town. Each housed four men trying to get their shit back together after rehab or jail, for $600 a month. Denise administered drug tests, checked for curfew busters, and kept tabs on AA meeting attendance – requiring ninety meetings in ninety days. The strict schedule sheltered me from temptations as I continued working as a courier throughout Atlanta.

Denise and I got along well, but only after I earned her trust and she figured out my dry, offbeat sense of humor. People who don't "get" me dismiss me sometimes, thinking I'm a dork from outer space. Anyway, Denise held those who truly wanted to stay sober in high regard. Those caught in a lie quickly found their belongings piled into the parking lot, per the recovery residence contract. Few guys I met here dared test her authority.

The brilliance of the twelve-step recovery method revealed itself over my months of intense study. The "new me" came to realize it's an excellent blueprint for a fulfilling life. I wish I'd adopted it back in high school, when I knew it all. Soon my fog began to lift, and I focused on the future instead of dwelling on regrets.

While attending AA meetings for ninety straight days, an old roommate joined me for one. Jason was a raging yet functional alcoholic in his forties. He came along ostensibly to support me. I suspected, however, that he considered adopting the AA lifestyle for his own health and sanity.

We found an Atlanta meeting downtown one afternoon, but I felt a bad vibe as the start time neared. Not like a pending explosion or crime, but I sensed a boring waste of time. Jason and I slipped out at the last minute to find a better option.

Thirty minutes later we landed at a black church near the house we once shared. I welcomed new perspectives from those found in the overwhelmingly white AA meetings I normally attended. We bumbled through corridors trying to find the correct room before learning a shack next door with the same address hosted the meeting. A nearly empty parking lot there had me thinking twice, but Jason and I forged ahead. We'd searched long enough and besides, how bad could this one be?

I opened a squeaking door to reveal eight middle-aged or old black guys sitting in what resembled a tire shop waiting room, without the old tube TV. A noisy pedestal fan moved thick air around. Even more uncomfortable were the stares coming from our "hosts." I felt like a white kid from Faber going to see Otis Day and the Knights in the *Animal House* bar scene. One could say the music stopped when Jason and I walked in.

We stood for a few beats, not greeted by anyone. A circle of chairs showed no vacancy, and not much space was available to add a pair should anyone bother. "Um, is there an AA meeting here?" I asked, sheepishly.

"Yeah," a guy mumbled, as if I'd interrupted a game of checkers he was losing. "It's about to start."

No "Welcome!" or "Thanks for coming, let's find you some chairs" about it. Our greeting grew colder thanks to another guy, who muttered: "There's a fungus among us."

This reference might have slipped past me, but I knew the lingo. I'd heard it in a '90s-era AOL chat room when they called me out for posing as a black person discussing Whitney Houston. The disrespect prompted Jason and I to leave our second meeting in an hour before it even began. No sense in making this meeting uncomfortable for everyone.

"Whatever happened to AA Fellowship?" I said to Jason, in the parking lot.

"I sensed it, dude," Jason joked. "I heard a guy say 'how about you and that fellow ship the fuck out of here?"

I laughed. "Did you just make that up?"

Jason answered only with, "Okay, fuck this. Time for me to start drinking!"

"One more try, dude. No way it could be any worse," I promised.

We arrived at our third venue early enough to enjoy a cigarette among other attendees before going in. A steady stream of attractive young women passed into the meeting. I struggled to keep from ogling. Females outnumbered males two-to-one once we got inside. This is nearly impossible in AA — a Christmas miracle in August.

"Dude, here you go," I said to Jason. "Get sober with a bunch of hotties!"

"Nah. I'm just here supporting you, guy," he replied.

"Bullshit. We ditched two other meetings to end up here. It's fucking destiny!"

Besides the women, the urban-hipster meeting was lively and interesting. These were my people. I had found a new "home group," which is where one finds a "sponsor." Afterward I tried to reel Jason in, too.

"None of that was encouraging?" I asked. "Everyone saying how glad they were to be sober and in AA?"

Jason shook his head. "Wanna join me at the pub?"

CHAPTER THREE

Recovery and Downfall

I stayed focused on AA study for a couple months, barely even flirting with the women even as temptations taunted me. I adhered to an unwritten rule in twelve-step programs – the "thirteenth step" is to not date other addicts. It's like throwing sparks around a fireworks factory. Dating is a self-esteem landmine even with "normal" people.

On the other hand, North Carolina was about to force celibacy on me. And where else could I find women okay with a guy being bankrupt and living in a halfway house? The only chance for a loser like me to break a six-month slump was with an equally desperate woman. My final rationalization to find a hookup from a meeting was Laura Randall's beauty.

Think actress Kirsten Dunst, but prettier, taller, and with a flat ass. Following weeks of internal debate and longing for her from afar, I talked to Laura.

She locked her baby-blue soul windows on me after a meeting wrapped up and left me no choice. We stumbled into the thirteenth step. We met for coffee.

"I gotta tell you right up front, I'm an inmate walking. I'm probably going to prison in a couple of months."

"Oh well," Laura said, unfazed. "We all have our baggage. I'm fucking bipolar."

My girl!

Conveniently for me, laid-back and not fancy described Laura perfectly. She demanded little materially; she made mucho dinero on her own writing computer code. Her smooth porcelain skin needed no makeup, and her self-deprecating sense of humor melted me. She was like hanging out with a guy friend. The flip side was Laura wasn't exactly *warm*. In fact, if not for her answering my calls and letting me insert my penis into her vagina, I wouldn't know she dug me romantically.

A few days after we became an item, I learned that Laura was an AA sponsor to a girl named Emily. I referred to her as "the sidekick." When you saw one, there was the other. Emily battled heroin addiction, going in and out of jail and general torment. When I met her, she professed to be staying clean. She beamed sweetness and intelligence, seemed to really "get it." Two days later I got a call from Laura, in tears.

"My psychic is dead."

Laura spoke rapidly and failed to enunciate, so I misunderstood. My stupid sense of humor tempted me to say, "It's okay, your psychic knew she would die today. She was prepared."

Instead I said, "What do you mean your psychic is dead?"

"No, my *sidekick!* Emily. She's dead."

The suburban heroin epidemic had claimed another victim. Laura and I grew closer immediately. I longed to comfort and care for someone, and Laura needed a decent guy to hold her hand through a tragedy. We propped each other up and bonded. It was nice.

(The loss of Emily marked the grim beginning of a list of people I met post-arrest who died, confirming yet again the deadly nature of addiction. This included two guys from prison and at least three of the small group I met at Caron, including my lovely roommate Matt. I also lost one of my dearest friends to a boating accident while locked up. I was braced for my elderly father possibly dying during this period, but a friend passing on never even occurred to me. Furloughs to attend funerals applied to direct family only, so absorbing this loss without the comfort of our circle of friends cut deeply.)

Morbid start aside, I delighted in my time spent with Laura. I tried to ignore that our future together was finite, to think dabbling with love was a bad idea. I probably didn't even love her; I only craved the feeling of it. Wondering about her kept me awake at night. But at least I stayed sober.

Laura and I did our best to enjoy Christmas time and pretend our doom didn't linger. Instead of typical dates that involved catching a buzz we sampled different AA meetings around town. We revelled in caffeine-fueled discussions about authors and philosophy. Then, while I performed courier duties about town one day, I received a text.

Laura: [Hey. Interested in some hotel sex?]

Me: [Does the Pope shit in the woods?]

Laura: [I'm at the Westin. Come make me not lonely.]

I dipped out of work and grabbed a power nap in anticipation of a long, dirty night. I awoke to a text that sank my heart.

Laura: [I need to be honest and tell you: I've been drinking all day. I understand if you don't want to see me this way, but I wanted to warn you.]

Cue that gut feeling telling me not to do something. I've come to believe this is my higher power communicating with me. Alas, I can mute the message as if it's a loud TV commercial. So I did.

I understand if you don't want to see me this way rolled around in my head. Seeing her trash her sobriety would be sad, yet I wanted to meet the "happy drunk" she claimed to be. And I wanted to see her having snookered monkey sex with me. If not *me*, some random guy from her hotel bar would join her for the night. And I'd spend the evening at home picturing it.

Heading to the liquor store en route to the hotel, I told another gut feeling to fuck off. I'd soon endure mandatory sober time, so breaking my sobriety suddenly seemed reasonable. My legal goose was all but cooked by then, anyway.

I drove up to a pricey part of town, sad about trashing the six months of sobriety I'd compiled. A prison send-off party for me loomed anyway, so fuck it. I needed to get my kicks where available.

Notes from a grand piano intermingled with the smell of money in the bustling hotel bar. The stylish crowd might as well have been cardboard cut-outs as I sought to find Laura.

Sure enough, an attractive middle-aged businessman sat next to her, trying to pick up my ravishing date for the night.

The proverbial needle scratched across the record; his dance was over. For once *I* wasn't the guy whose lucky night was snatched away by some douchebag. Laura lit up upon seeing me and hugged me like she meant it.

She looked amazing, and indeed proved a buoyant, happy drunk. We shared several toasts and ignored the elephant in the room – our blown sobriety.

We soon found ourselves in her posh room, stocked with room service champagne and chocolate strawberries. I insisted we share a shower straight away, both for the foreplay and hygienic benefits. We got clean to get dirty.

Upon exiting the shower, Laura knocked over a champagne flute, which shattered on the bathroom counter. The stem-cum-spike fell directly on top of her foot, puncturing a vein. A pool of dark blood immediately began forming on the floor.

"Buzz kill. That's gonna need stitches," I declared.

Laura pretended the gusher was a mere surface cut. She clumsily wrapped her foot with a towel, tied it with a bathrobe belt, and dragged me out to the bed.

Following a clumsy fornication attempt, Laura rolled over, revealing impressive gore. The white towel had turned a dark maroon. Blood had tracked up her leg, and the sheets looked like a Halloween prop. The jig was up, unlike my penis.

Laura casually weaved back into the bathroom, plopped into the bathtub and elevated her foot. She re-wrapped her improvised bandage.

"This sucks, but that thing needs stitches," I reiterated.

"I'm a Randall!" she nearly screamed. "We're *tough*. We don't give up over shit like this!"

She'd changed from happy to mean drunk. This argument took forever. Nervous energy from anger kept me cleaning up blood from the bathroom floor. Finally, Laura dropped the tough girl act. I called for an ambulance.

Since she still had a buzz to maintain, Laura asked me to bring her a bottle of champagne. I gladly fetched it from the other room. I exhaled with relief that our bickering had ceased.

While I grabbed the bottle Laura called out, "And if you happen to see my dignity will you bring that in too, please?"

The paramedics arrived with a stretcher to remove Laura before we located her driver's license, which the hospital would require. "I'll be there as soon as I find it," I promised. They rolled her out while I stayed behind to look for her ID. This allowed me time to simmer down after battling her for the past hour. I'd hold her hand later.

I took a few minutes to watch the end of a good football game and enjoy a cigarette, since Laura had blown the fine for smoking in the room, anyway. Two hotel security guys soon arrived to take photos of the Dexter-worthy bloodbath.

"What relationship are you to the guest?"

"We're dating," I replied, not looking away from the TV.

"You're dating, but you're sitting here watching the game while she's going to the hospital?"

"Listen Detective," I cracked. "If you'd spent the last hour listening to her bitch, you'd be doing the exact same thing."

I think he got my point, not that I gave two shits. Fate had ruined my night of debauchery; my last tango had been foiled. That's what you get for breaking your sobriety. I threw back another gulp from my drink.

I soon scooted over to the nearby hospital waiting room, finding Laura in a wheelchair, foot elevated and sporting a silly grin. My girl was back to happy drunk. Or she was a complete lunatic.

She looked at me all earnestly and blurted "I love you!" followed by "Did I just say that?"

Before I could respond, she said, "No – yeah. I love you!"

I paused and then assured her. "No problem."

Laura grimaced and punched my shoulder. "No problem?! What the fuck?"

"Babe, I really like hanging out with you, but love isn't a word I throw around lightly. I've only said it to three girls, like, *ever*."

"Yeah, I don't tell people often, either," she contended.

"Tell you what. If you still feel this way in the morning we'll talk about it then, okay?'

"Okay!" We kissed.

Irresistible and cute Laura again transformed into stubborn drunk Laura once we made it to a treatment room. She wrestled with her IV and snapped at hospital personnel. At one point she casually proclaimed: "I should've just gone ahead and killed myself."

"Wait, what?!"

"I brought a knife and a bunch of psych meds with me to the hotel. I was really going to do it until I texted you." (That's me: Lifesaver!)

I tried to remain casual. "Please don't do that. You have a ton going for you, and I'd miss you terribly."

She cast me a stern look. "If you tell *anyone* about this, I'll *kill* you! They'll put me back in the psyche ward! No. Fucking. Way."

"I won't tell anyone," I assured her. "And please, for god's sake, don't kill yourself."

"I won't. At least until you go to prison, anyway." I greeted this with a sideways frown which drew a grin from her.

"Thanks. I needed more bad shit on my mind once I go in!"

Eventually we returned to the hotel room, Laura's wound stitched. It looked like a murder scene. Brownish dried blood settled into towels, tiles, sheets, and carpet. We downed a couple shots and failed at rekindling our lust. The drama had drained us. Laura ended up crying herself to sleep as I imagined what prison would be like for the ten thousandth time.

I spent the next day with a melancholy Laura, helping her out until she was more mobile on her bad foot. The air felt like change, and it wasn't just our hangovers talking.

"Do you even want me here right now?" I wondered aloud. A long pause.

"Yeah, if you want to be."

Laura pulled me tight when I left a few minutes later, my coat soaking up her tears. "I have to end this now," she managed. "You are fucking with my sobriety. The sooner we end this, the better."

I could only hope my long, hard hug back spoke for me. Words couldn't escape given the shape I found myself. My time with Laura gave my soul a port during an emotional hurricane – she buoyed my confidence at its lowest point.

The soundtrack for my dazed drive home came from an iPod shuffle. Remarkably appropriate songs surfaced, like Yo La Tengo's *Daphnia*, which is the perfect background for gloomy reverie. It seemed made for that exact moment in time. The drive's last song: *When the Whip Comes Down* by the Stones, fit my circumstances perfectly. My mood brightened from rocking it out. Might as well try to lighten up.

I used music to cheer me up the following day, too, when a prison term of thirty-five months became confirmed.

For all the Asheville DA cared I could have gone on a Vegas bender instead of investing in Caron and everything else. He showed zero interest in my preemptive recovery efforts. His anti-drug crusade of punishing people seemed to be his only concern. I ended up charged with possession and trafficking of MDMA, marijuana possession with intent to distribute, and six other felonies.

At least my lawyer managed a plea deal that merged eight charges into one, which saved me multiple additional years behind bars. The burden of post-release probation got waived, too. These victories aside, shit was about to get real.

This sentence seems ridiculous for a first-time drug offense, but I deserved to do time just for being a shithead. I filed chapter seven bankruptcy at the last minute, so I headed to debtor's prison, one could say. I lived a selfish life. I pulled irresponsible stunts like driving on acid. Three years locked up would be my just desserts.

Officially becoming a prison-bound felon shocked me back into a permanent daze. Not obsessing over this prospect proved impossible. Storing my possessions was a major hassle, and the goodbye process began. My aforementioned friend Jamal threw a going away party for me at his bar, which helped soothe the sting. Casual friends were relatively easy to bid farewell to as drinks flowed, but the agony of deeper goodbyes added up.

My final days following the party left only my closest friends and family to say goodbye to. Much fewer words were necessary — or available — upon our final embraces. Last among these were with those that came to Asheville the day before my intake. Their efforts at not appearing devastated touched me.

My friends Tim and Brad were there, the rare dudes willing to discuss emotional issues. My only sibling, Dena, came along with our maternal uncle and de facto father, Tom. I hardly felt worthy of all this love. I felt like a piece of shit, imposing on everyone.

Rehab taught me to face crisis head-on, but fuck that. I gulped Xanax and Lortab as I tumbled into the worst day of my life — intake. Before entering the court building I enjoyed a last cigarette with my great friend Tim, who drove me up from Atlanta the day before. I cherished that smoke and longed for its comfort often over the following weeks. My whole *life* called for soothing from nicotine.

An ornate, historic courtroom was half full, which still meant roughly eighty people were there. My knees almost buckled for nerves, even though I was high as the thirty-foot, intricately carved ceiling. My support group sat in the front row with me. I wanted to sit close to hear the cases before mine, which might be entertaining. I do the same at traffic court.

Sure enough, a high profile murder case was on the docket before mine. The defendant tried for a respectable vibe by wearing a suit and tie, but a huge neck tattoo killed that. His persistent sneer made it easy to believe he dunnit, too. Alas, the jury merely received brief instruction from the judge and cleared out. My dance with Lady Justice soon began, except not really.

The mandatory minimum law made my outcome a *fait accompli*; the only question was whether I wished to address the court. A younger Garrett would have relished taking such a stage to rant about the absurdity of the war on drugs. About the idiocy of North Carolina locking me up a first-time offender that doesn't even live there. I might've even taken a crack at the DA for his bowl haircut.

Instead, I skipped the drama. The months of dreading this day had beaten down my smartass tendencies. The powers on hand probably knew sending me away was silly, but they didn't care. The judge read my sentence terms and made a face that said *don't make me use this gavel.* "Do you wish to address the court?"

I shook my head, defeated.

My loved ones and I shared a final embrace. "Thank you" and "I love you" fell from my mouth through sobs. My sister broke down as a bailiff handcuffed me. I exited stage left into an alternate plane of existence, kicked out of the world.

From the opulent, oak-paneled courtroom I dipped into a dingy backstage elevator. In it, I met the murder defendant wearing the suit. Only one of us wore handcuffs, and it wasn't the accused killer. They treated him like a Wall Street banker – with kid gloves. The distraction took my mind off my living nightmare for a while.

I spent about an hour in a holding cell with Murderer Guy, who proved glib and entertaining. He relished in his celebrity status while holding court, so to speak, with other jailbirds. They knew many details about the notorious local case and debated it.

"I ain't did it, shore as shit stinks," he insisted in a Carolina Piedmont accent that reminded me of my paternal grandmother.

Soon I re-visited the freezing holding cell from my arrest night, before being processed into the jail population. This involved my first cavity search, and luckily my starfish was numb from the cold. My chattering teeth also kept me from scolding the Correctional Officer (CO) for not at least buying me a drink first.

I followed orders and took a quick ice-cold shower and stepped into an ill-fitting jumpsuit. *Maybe I should've stayed in college after all.*

An inmate worker tossed sheets, a blanket, a large hand towel, and a few toiletries in my direction. Next stop: my cell. Sure enough, *shit was real.*

I felt totally alone and alien. Stone-faced guards directed me through a series of hydraulic doors that slammed shut after I passed through.

Hiiissss ... Boom!

Deeper into the abyss I plunged; into a gloom with walls painted an ironic bright white. The maze ended at my cellblock. A scowling guard pointed down a line of cell doors. "Twenty-nine." A dizzying walk of shame began.

The new neighbors peered out their cell door windows to assess the *fresh meat*. They couldn't spit on me like in the movies – they shot daggers with their eyes instead. I tried to be cool and look forward as I trudged to my cell, a lump in my throat. Towards the first of many unseemly bedrooms I'd occupy in captivity. I assumed a fight with an evil cellmate loomed. The Xanax hardly quelled this fear.

Cell twenty-nine. My long walk proved too short. I glimpsed a hulking skinhead through the window. A menacing *hiiissss* as the cell door unlocked. *Please let him have kind eyes.* Welcome to the jungle.

My new roommate stood six-foot two and easily weighed a solid two-fifty. He wore a long goatee, crudely drawn tattoos, and a scowl. He looked like he may have killed a man with his bare hands and was about to again. The door hissed and shut behind me. I edged into this lion's lair and introduced myself with a wavering voice. He looked at me like I'd shot his dog.

"Great!" my first cellmate thundered. "Another goddamned cho-mo!"

My back to the door, I wondered how to ask what he meant without provoking him further.

"I just got these motherfuckers to move one of you out yesterday. I was about to kill the fucking guy!"

Words somehow tumbled out of my mouth.

"Um, I don't know what a cho-mo is, but I've never been called that before."

His narrowed eyes probed me. He shouted, "What are you in for?!"

"MDMA trafficking," I replied, almost proudly.

"Really? You look like a fucking child molester to me. A cho-mo."

I shook my head and summarized my story, using the lingo of a drug dealer and longtime party lover. This came naturally.

Knowing this language is like a secret handshake between inmates. We were soon chatting like old friends, and I breathed again. At least until Nick ripped a rosy fart for the first of five thousand times. I didn't breathe so well then.

Nick proved to be unrefined, but not mean or stupid. His quick wit showed he was a thinking man's brute. No stranger to incarceration, Nick was down this time for gunplay over an OxyContin deal gone bad. Past raps included larceny, pummeling a pedophile, and other violent acts short of murder. Substance abuse plagued Nick, like most inmates. He claimed he snorted Oxy 80s "for breakfast."

"So, why do I look like a pedophile?" I asked once we became friendly.

"You're goofy, your haircut ain't tight, and those glasses," he explained. "Cho-mos always seem to have wire frames."

Nick offered to help. I planned to get a buzz cut to reduce grooming time, anyway. The less time spent in a prison bathroom, the better. Seeing how weird I looked with a sheared dome excited me, and I longed for a bushy beard to go with it.

I assumed jail was Homophobia Central, but dudes fussing with each other's hair is a big part of life on the inside. They often sat for it whether or not they needed a cut. Many black guys maintained short dreadlocks by endlessly twisting them, or they weaved braids for each other. Seemingly half the population fine-tuned their buzz cuts, intricately engraved hair lines, and shaped whiskers. Backstage at a UFC fight couldn't be much different.

Needing a haircut seemed beside the point; as with their obsession with brand new sneakers, intense barber maintenance shows prosperity among the working class. In lockup, the habit may be more about human contact – tender loving care – than taming hair cut only days earlier. This hands-on attention despite jail's despair proved touching and inspiring. Not everyone lives as cold and hard as the walls that enclose them.

Nick grabbed the community clippers in the common area and tended to my scalp during "free time" that evening. He clipped to a half inch on top and even tighter on the sides, for a "fade." "This makes you look like you know what's going on," my makeshift barber professed. "Eighty percent less cho-mo."

I enjoyed both the human touch and looking more like an ax murderer. The more menacing my look for when someone confronted me physically. Not if. When.

I considered myself an embedded reporter during my lockup odyssey. I socialized a lot during my first week in county jail. I ate at whichever table I happened to land, especially at four-thirty breakfast time. Seating concerns at that hour require too much brain power. I liked experiencing new people, too, unlike nearly everyone else. They sat according to race, or age, in the same place every day.

One morning I plopped down at a table of six or seven black dudes. No foul vibes came my way, as usual, until a smallish diner called "Flow" mumbled something unintelligible. He and I had been cordial previously, so I assumed his comment was chill and nodded along. Plus, too early. Flow repeated himself: "You and me gonna have trouble. Why you eyeballin' my tray."

I was, in fact, transfixed by the "food" on his tray. More specifically, how he mixed the slop together, supposedly to make it more palatable.

"No need for trouble here, man. I didn't mean anything by it."

"Nah, we got trouble," replied Flow.

What we actually had was Flow sending a message to

Whitey. He didn't give two shits about me looking at his tray. I didn't mind sitting with black people, but never considered they might not want to sit with me. They had street cred to worry about.

I shook my head in response to Flow's second comment, hoping his posturing would pass. The breakfast finished with no further incident. Later in the day, however, I caught Flow glaring at me as he spoke with a buddy.

My stomach dropped with dread. In truth I'm a giant six foot-six pussy. My last fight was in fourth grade, when Annette Volzer broke my glasses and made me cry. I did not want to "go" with Flow, even though he stood only a slender five foot-nine.

My primary goal was to survive prison with all teeth intact and no new scars. Scrapping with Flow could earn me a shanked artery as far as I knew. Or a transfer to a more dangerous cell block upon release from the infirmary. I sought the counsel of my cellie, and class was soon in session.

"It's all about head games," my jailhouse mentor declared. "Your glasses and buzz cut already make you look half-nuts. Act totally insane and motherfuckers will want nothing to do with you."

I peered into the slab of polished stainless steel on the wall that served as a mirror. I tilted my head with a demented grin like in *The Shining*: "Heeeere's Johnny!"

Nick burst into laughter, then managed: "Do you know *Dirty Harry*? Do the psycho from that!"

"Scorpio? Oh hell, yeah!" I bugged out my eyes like that character and copied his maniacal laugh.

"That's it," Nick said, laughing. "You front like you'll bite a motherfucker's nose off. No one wants nothin' to do with that shit."

"Scorpio Eyes" it would be.

"See food, eat food, or be food," Nick continued. This meant an inmate either recognizes weak inmates and takes advantage of them or becomes exploited himself. Passing this test early made all the difference.

"If someone tries you, get all drama-like and take your

glasses off," Nick instructed. "Then bug out and yell: 'If you think I'm food, you better start eatin'!"

The thought of controlling a confrontation excited me. Bonding with my cellmate felt good, too. Nick chuckled as I spent ten minutes looking in the mirror like a lunatic. I felt ready to make "Flow" look like "Flo," the chick from the insurance ads. Bring it on.

Free time arrived. I walked the perimeter of the common area for exercise, as usual. Flow sat in his typical spot, playing cards with his homies. He glanced at me, but nothing beyond that. Perhaps he had second thoughts about the "trouble." Maybe I sent off a new don't fuck with me vibe. About ten minutes later, however, Flow and two of his buddies started walking the circle, counter to my direction. We started about sixty feet apart, closing fast.

Fifty feet. Forty feet. Thirty. My stomach felt like I'd lost my phone (back when I could have one). I felt my heart pump. When we passed, I feigned indifference while still alert for a sudden move. Our sleeves brushed because neither of us gave an inch. Flow offered a sarcastic "excuse you." We both kept walking. The next pass would be the real test. Fortunately, it would be near where Nick was playing chess in case I needed backup.

When Flow and I headed towards each other again, I made eye contact and kept it, trying to read him. He seemed to notice this and looked away. He looked again when we were about ten paces apart. I suddenly ditched the Scorpio Eyes plan, instead using a Clint Squint, like Eastwood's movie characters. A look somewhere between neutral and insane.

Flow shrank, looking away. He never messed with me again. My first triumph in this strange new world was in the bag. Or Flow decided I wasn't worth it. Whatever the case, I'd lived to bluff another day.

Back in the cell I celebrated, probably looking like a pro golfer trying to dance. Later, Nick loved hearing the showdown details. He laughed, then confessed, "I knew the dude wasn't gonna do shit. Blacks are usually all talk. If they're talking about it, they ain't doin' shit," he explained. "If they're quiet and look at you sideways? Then you gotta worry."

"Why didn't you tell me this earlier, asshole?"

"Fuck that," Nick replied. "It was too funny watching you get all bent out of shape about it!"

I deflated for a few beats and then launched my Scorpio Eyes at him. "Well, I'm glad I amuse you. Make a move, motherfucker!"

After my run-in with Flow I stopped dicking around with my seating choice for meals. I sat at the middle table with Nick and the white guys no one messed with. Prime symbolic real estate in the overwhelmingly white cellblock. The surrounding tables divided mostly by race, followed by the fringes: pedophiles, weirdos, and those in deathly shape from withdrawal symptoms.

Sad indeed were the addicts plunging cold turkey from dope or alcohol while locked up. Nick described being in the delirium of opiate withdrawal while in jail and once failed to display his ID bracelet in the window at count time. The guards on duty removed all of his bedding for twenty-four hours for the infraction. He detoxed on a bare stainless steel platform in a cold cell.

Nick as a cellmate was a best-case scenario for this greenhorn. He advised me; we laughed constantly and made county fucking jail almost fun. I told tales of the big city life and following jam bands around, and he regaled me with stories of crazy meth binges and violence in the trailer park. We were a tag team worthy of broadcasting.

In fact, our next-door neighbors – two black kids, no less – said they listened through the air ducts to enjoy hearing our bullshit sessions. They joined our pact: no talking about how jail sucked or how bad we missed pussy. Doing so only made our deprivation worse.

I took two showers a day, strong and warm, mostly to warm up my toes for a while. Water flow required pushing a button every fifteen seconds, and keeping the stream steady was a skill to be mastered. Anything to stay entertained. I once dropped the soap in there, just to see what happened. Besides a small dent on the corner of my Dove bar (1/4 moisturizing cream) I detected no further incident.

CHAPTER FOUR

Transitions, Transitions

Nick served as my jail coach, so I appointed myself his life coach and psychologist. Introspection wasn't his game. He didn't realize he was worthy of more than hanging out with low-lifes. His smarts and charm could take him places, where he'd be angry less often and perhaps end his cycle of drug abuse.

"You should try NA (Narcotics Anonymous) meetings," I suggested. "Hang out with sober people and hot women that have been to college and stuff." I described a beautiful woman I met at a local meeting when in Asheville for a court date, as a lure for him. In his desperate case, the thirteenth-step could mean a major life advancement.

Nick seemed to approve of this plan, but knew saying so in jail was easy. Temptations there are nil. He feared he'd never be able to quit opiates. I saw sad cases like this over and over on the inside; good people hamstrung by addiction. A huge percentage of inmates are there, either directly or indirectly, because they can't use intoxicants responsibly. Changing life paths would be a challenge for Nick, especially since he owed his girlfriend.

"She's out there stripping and selling pills right now to make my bail money," he explained. "And she forgave me for banging her daughter before we hooked up. I really didn't know they were kin."

Nick needed to stop living real-life Tarantino movie scenes, one of which landed him in our cell. Dope Sick Nick ventured solo to meet a noted Local Hustler in a Home Depot parking lot, suspending an old grudge against him. LH sold Nick's lifeline, OxyContin pills.

LH's driver to this meeting was Pill Whore. LH paid for this service with pills, since they suspended his license. Nick hopped into the car to make the transaction. Once Nick realized the pill count was short, he put a gun to PW's head. He didn't exit the car until he had its keys, all the pills, and his money back.

LH followed an order to get out of the car, but refused to lie on the ground as instructed. Nick pistol-whipped him as an encouragement to do so. The gun discharged, and the bullet grazed LH's head. Nick dashed to his car and raced from the scene, but not before PW jumped in the car with him. Nick had the pills, and the cops were coming. All of a sudden she loved him.

A local hospital treated LH's head wound, and the cops corralled him there on an outstanding warrant. LH ratted out Nick's gunplay adventure. Hello, assault with a deadly weapon charge. Nick's next ten years depended on whether PW sided with his story or LH's. The Wild and Wonderful Whites of West Virginia have nothing on Nick's world.

After a week of laughter and learning with Nick, they moved me to my own cell, just across the way in the same block. This allowed me to breathe easier. Literally, because Nick farted constantly. I swear the guy breathed in through his nose and out through his ass. My new privacy simplified going number two instead of waiting until the bunkie was in the common area during free time, too. I welcomed the timing of the move. I'd learned the ropes and now had more peace in which to read and write.

My new place proved quite the upgrade besides alone time. Sunlight and warmth poured in through a small, frosted window and lifted my spirit. I could hear a nearby bell tower toll on the hour and the halves, so I limited myself to masturbating only every four hours.

At noon the bells sounded off either *God Bless America* or *My Country 'Tis of Thee*. As a drug war casualty, the second one taunted me. Sweet land of liberty? Let freedom ring? Are you fucking kidding me? They imprisoned me for distributing MDMA (the love drug), which helped people "let freedom ring." In fact, most enjoyed the best moods of their lives while on it. Liberty? How about tyranny? I felt blessed to be jailed in America instead of a third world country, at least.

Without Nick around to mirthfully pass the time, my thoughts bounced between fearing my future and dwelling on my checkered past. I thought about where it all began.

My Ohio childhood provided little excuse for being a failure at forty-six. At first blush, anyway. Mom loved me unconditionally and stayed supportive and helpful. Dad was a fine provider materially. My sister and I attended excellent public schools, with no worries about life's necessities. Neither parent drank heavily or was physically abusive beyond spankings typical in the '70s.

Emotional and verbal reprimands were another story, however. I later figured out that my sister and I withstood a father plagued by Paranoid Personality Disorder. Its main characteristic is assuming everyone has ulterior motives and is always plotting to screw you over. A PPD parent is not suited to deal with the main role of a child, which is to challenge boundaries and fuck shit up.

I drew Dad's wrath even when I did my best. For example, as a ten-year-old, I whitewashed a fence, and the result was fine. Instead of encouraging me and showing faith in my potential, Dad dwelled on a few mistakes. He thought I had played him for a sucker and half-assed the job. I ended up confused and grew resentful. I suspect my lack of drive in life was rooted in defying my dad, the perfectionist lunatic. You want perfect? How about underachievement instead, asshole?

Despite Dad serving as my opponent instead of a mentor, my childhood was not a constant nightmare. He could be fun, and those who knew him socially loved him. They couldn't see his PPD from afar.

Besides Dad's destructive influence, I served as my own worst enemy in the fifth grade. On a standardized test for middle school placement, I decided to be the first to finish instead of doing my best. I randomly filled-in circles on my answer sheet, winning a contest that existed only in my head. My reward for this was stunted academic development because it placed me in classes with the slower kids for the next six years — a nice preview of prison. The lower expectations were fine with me. I saw school as a social gathering rather than a learning opportunity. Classes required a work ethic I lacked.

I considered how I learned about skirting the rules from my miserly father, who was so cheap he'd cross state lines with several full five-gallon gasoline containers in the back of his SUV to save a few bucks on the price. Although not an archetypical thief, scruples weren't always his thing. He swiped hotel towels and items from work and used "creative" accounting on his taxes. Dad later urged me to plead poverty on college financial aid forms even though he was well off. Rarely introspective, he probably still wonders how I ever conceived to cut corners in life and ended up in jail.

Other times I obsessed about my prison future as I stared blankly at the cell walls, my fear ratcheting up. I projected worst-case scenarios. My attention span for reading and writing waned and sleeping became a challenge until I adjusted. I felt more alone than ever. The walls surrounding me matched my outlook: stark and empty.

At least I was finally cutting into my sentence. In my excitement, after eleven days I announced I'd done over one percent of my time. This invited Nick's derision. "Dude, if you're counting days already, you're gonna have a long ride!"

Laura lasted about a week into my incarceration before she ceased contact. To her credit, however, she sent me a copy of *Infinite Jest* before she blew me off. Her dumping me proved to be a favor. Pining for a loved one while locked up makes a dismal experience worse. Compared to guys with significant others or young children haunting them, I was on vacation.

My introversion reawakened in the solo cell. I abandoned walks and bullshitting sessions in the common area for the relative peace of my bunk. My habit of staying cell bound produced my first jailhouse nickname: "Lock Back," the punishment of your cell door not opening during free time. I explained that time to read and write doesn't punish me. Most seemed baffled by this.

Jail is nothing if not a boredom test. Many go to extremes to avoid idle time. Some county jail inmates worked janitorial jobs for free, just for something to do. Others worked twelve-hour shifts in the kitchen, starting at four in the morning, seven days a week. Not for pay or reduced time, but for freedom from the cell and slightly better food options.

My "job" became blocking out distractions – a vital skill for avid readers doing time. Jailbirds that fluttered by my door during their free time strolls posed the greatest challenges. Most shouted in conversation to each other, disrupting me with context-free bits of conversation difficult to ignore.

Typical snippets included: "They can't do that! Listen, my lawyer told me …" and "So I told the bitch, 'Bitch, get the fuck out …'" I sometimes felt like chasing down the storytellers for elaboration.

Occasionally guys stopped walking as they emphasized a point, within earshot. Blacks did this more often. They act out conversations as if on a stage.

"I'm tellin' you, da bitch is true! No matter what, she there for me."

"No 'ho would put up with mo'!"

And a line in a rap song was born.

Once I heard a black dude explain: "It's not snitching if they're white!"

Immersed in a book, I didn't bother to go see who dropped this bomb. This story outraged Nick and other pale faces when I shared it.

"Now just how in the fuck do you hear that and not find out who said it?" my ex-cellie asked. "Lock Back, you're lazy as hell!"

Also disappointed by my failure was an affable fellow called Montgomery, who spoke in a thick Appalachian twang. He admitted he'd prefer a year in jail, exempt from child support payments, than pay money to his "bitch of an old lady." Besides, Montgomery enjoyed hanging out with jailbirds, many of whom he knew from the street. His bail when I met him was $163, but he'd rather do two months than pay it. "Sad, isn't it?" he admitted.

County jail prepared me for living among sex offenders, and some of that which passed for comedy on the inside. One "joke" covered both ...

The joker gestures towards a random guy nearby.

"That guy's in for a drug offense."

"Oh, yeah? What he get popped for?"

"He drug a kid out of a sandbox."

Such was the level of "humor" I suffered through for three years.

COs alerted select inmates about incoming cho-mos, and word spread. The guards despised them too. Two molesters in my block fit the profile Nick described: dorky, middle-aged, and wearing wire-frame glasses. They both carried a Bible at all times, probably as last ditch protection against harm. As if god-fearing assailants would reconsider.

I felt a duty to interview at least one cho-mo, but I was torn. My impulse is to consider pederasts despicable, yet I sympathize with them. Sexual arousal via children must be horrific, and a cho-mo's self-loathing must be unbearable. Many of these offenders realize they're demented, but still can't stop themselves. Does this make them evil, or victims?

I never sought answers from those two in county jail. I didn't want anyone to see me talking to them. I already had a rep to maintain, even at the expense of journalistic duty. The cho-mos probably would've talked about Jesus the whole time, anyway.

Seeing myself as a one-timer in the system, just passing through, allowed me to laugh at the power drunk correctional officers. Most of them acted professionally, but a few were sadists-with-badges, unworthy of authority.

One CO occupied a common area desk for twelve-hour shifts while others monitored cell block video feeds nearby. Six rotated through each week. Four accepted their jobs as babysitters and concierges and appeared to be decent people. Two of them belittled inmates and punished us by enforcing all rules, no matter how silly.

For instance, a rule stated that a hot water fountain could be accessed only during the last five minutes of free time. This meant many guys ended up with none, so nice guards let it slide.

Physical abuse of Buncombe inmates practically never happened, so mean COs chipped away psychologically instead. One of these – a fat, middle-aged fuck I'll call Donald – bore the rosy, bloated face of an alcoholic. He constantly appeared ready to vomit. Instead of standing at the desk and chilling like most guards he roamed the second-tier catwalk. He paced back and forth, barking commands like a conqueror addressing his subjects.

"They'll be no talkin' during mealtime!" Donald boomed, referring to an oft-ignored rule. His voice echoed through the cavernous block, over the clicking of plastic sporks on metal trays as inmates chowed. "You'll take no longer than ten minutes to eat, and head back to your cells," he declared, even though we had fifteen minutes and everyone already knew the drill. When Donald's gaze wavered guys would yelp or hoot, just to fuck with him. This raised both his temper and the entertainment quotient. I felt like I did in elementary school.

"Okay, who's the wise guy?" he'd shout. "If you keep it up, breakfast will be over right now!"

Free time seemed to piss Donald off. He hated seeing captives enjoying themselves instead of wallowing in their punishment. "Let's keep it down at those card tables!" he'd thunder. Or, a minute later, "Walk slower. This isn't an Olympic event!"

Donald put me on lock back three times. Once for placing too many books and papers on my stainless steel shelf/desk, once for failure to make my bed before breakfast, and the third for using the windowsill as a bookshelf. No other CO cared about such violations.

Thankfully Asheville's jail provided a counterbalance to asshole guards. AA meetings and church gatherings brightened days, and GED studies and criminal behavior rehab provided inmate betterment options. Local civilian volunteers administered several of these, a high privilege compared to typical jails. I attended many of them, including a Relaxation Gathering.

An actual photo from inside the jail, but obviously of a different cellblock.
(Photo courtesy of Buncombe County Detention Center.)

A forty-something ponytailed Trustafarian named Bernie led the group. His soft-spoken manner reminded me of Mr. Mackey, the teacher in Southpark. 'M-kay?'

Bernie sported a rabbi-like beard, with beads carefully woven into the long whiskers. Designer hippie glasses matched his stylish New Age outfit and a leather choker that held a polished stone. He probably purchased his moccasins from a relaxation instruction magazine.

He claimed to be from New Jersey, but didn't sound like

it. I asked where specifically, and he grudgingly copped to affluent Saddle River.

"I've been in Asheville since 1991, though," he sniffed. "Which is before everyone else got here."

My sense of Bernie's phoniness was stronger than the stench in the under-ventilated room. I pictured him at a hookah bar later that evening, casually mentioning his altruistic jail visit to seduce some holistic chick. Or perhaps his lifestyle was revenge towards his absentee father, a hedge fund manager.

No good reason existed for my one-way feud with Bernie. I should have been thankful he was helping downtrodden guys like me. Perhaps lockup had made me a dick, just over a week into the game. What was next, calling the volunteer that ran the AA meeting a dry drunk? Picking a fight with the jail chaplain? This relaxation gathering may have saved me from time being added to my sentence.

"Stamp your place in the realm of relaxation," Bernie advised. "Breathe in slow, slowly, slowly and ... out again."

During a closed-eye exercise I busted him peeking over at me, like a little kid pretending to sleep. Perhaps he sensed I was onto him. Or he wondered why I kept looking at him.

At one point Bernie instructed: "Now, tighten your anus."

I could easily picture him saying this to starry-eyed hippie chicks during one-on-one sessions. For inmates, the notion brought widespread laughter. Lightness promotes relaxation. Maybe Bernie was a pro after all.

"Use a finger to close one nostril, and breathe deeply through the other," said Bernie.

"I done this one a lot, except I got a rolled up dollar in the other side!" an inmate exclaimed.

Bernie emphasized stretching during another exercise, delivering instructions just above a whisper: "Now I need you to face your palms forward. Now slowly reach your arms above your head, like so ..."

"Yo, I think we've all done this pose before!" another inmate cracked.

While not exactly Zen-like relaxation, demoralized souls

laughed and forgot their problems for a while. Thank god for people like Bernie.

Jail days seemed to repeat themselves and always felt rainy. All windows were frosted and the dark concrete floor looked like wet pavement. Walls were stark white, and all furniture gray stainless steel. I once carried a bottle of bright green shampoo to the shower, and guys ogled as if it were an Oscar statuette. Anything colorful stuck out. I resolved to never take thoughtful interior design for granted again.

Radio, newspapers, and news broadcasts on the one tiny TV in the block were unavailable. They never allowed inmates outdoors. I could feel my spirit slowly dying in there. How people do years in county jail amazes me – and plenty to do, in far worse conditions. At least Buncombe allowed six hours of free time outside cells and the recently built facility stayed in good repair.

Many people rotted there for weeks until their trial date, some for lack of $75 bail, or a competent lawyer to get the bail waived. Innocent defendants or those held on trumped-up charges fought the state, which repeatedly delayed trials. They know how county jail can break a man's will. Eventually many agree to unfair plea deals solely for the relief of moving on to the comfort of prison.

After ten days or so, the gloom and physical grind wore on me. I found little comfort on a steel platform, cushioned with a blue slab of foam normally used for floating in pools. My limbs fell asleep more often than I did. I longed for prison beds I'd heard about, which consisted of real mattresses suspended on springs.

Still, I dreaded my impending move. Discomfort and gloom of jail aside, at least I was used to it and felt safe. Prison was the unknown. Additional freedom and comfort only meant I'd be more vulnerable to attack.

Nick told me to expect no warning when moving day arrived, possibly weeks away. My next stop would be "processing," an evaluation facility for all convicts besides murderers and other highly violent cases. I'd join a jeopardous mix of offenders, with no divisions based on crime or length of their sentences. Real danger — and interesting case studies — loomed.

My "pack it up" order came at 3:30 a.m. after serving only sixteen jail days, far fewer than most inmates headed to prison. I arranged a goodie pile for Nick before leaving the cell, per his instructions. I placed the items not allowed to go with me near my cell door: thermal clothing, socks, and snacks. Nick could drag them out later, when the guard wasn't looking. I also wrote him a note, through tears, thanking him for the memories and my instructional class. I'll never forget him, the kindly fart machine.

First stop, more comfort. I traded my jumpsuit for my sorely missed street clothes. Since I dressed decently for court — in corduroy slacks and a button-down shirt — I looked like an alien compared to the other guys. And a target. This is part of the reason most defendants dress like bums in courtrooms: in case they get taken in and end up on a prison bus.

Next came a holding cell to wait for the bus. A dozen others joined me for this festive occasion with everyone thrilled to be leaving jail behind. They celebrated for three hours by shouting in conversation with dudes right next to them. A few of them never settled down, nor did they care who they disturbed. The cinder block room felt like a dog kennel, the way the sound bounced around. Each series of barks made my stomach burn.

On the way to boarding the bus, I saw the sky for the first time in over two weeks. Even though my world had crashed down, the sky remained. I gazed up to a bright moon and infinity beyond, thankful to finally be on my way. I nearly wept.

Not so soul-affirming was riding on a school bus, basically, except with metal mesh on the windows and a wall separating the driver from the passengers.

Hours later, the ride ended at the prison processing facility,

Transitions, Transitions

a grim compound that appeared suited for the Soviet Union in the mid-'60s. It looked like a bunch of school buildings and one twelve-story stack of cells resembling a public housing project. New inmates herded into a chilly check-in area. Inspection of my meager belongings came next.

A sadistic CO declared my half-read copy of *Infinite Jest* as unauthorized. It joined my clothes and personal effects in a box to be shipped to my dad's place. The only approved reading material in processing was the Bible, the Koran, and AA literature.

This force-feeding of religion didn't work on me. I found the Bible to be a plodding and unrealistic story, especially for a bestseller. I later learned that prison libraries overflow with spare Bibles. Guys going home forget about God again, leaving hundreds of them behind. I guess throwing away a "prayer book," as they're called in the American South, is a ticket to hell.

The real fun came next: a strip search. A hapless guard, who I assume drew the short straw, needed to look for signs of lube around the balloon knot, which suggests "suitcased" contraband.

"Bend over. Cough. Spread your cheeks," he ordered. I came up clean.

This backside diddling aside, the novelty of the intake procedure kept me in an upbeat mood. And it sure beat sitting in a cell. For my official inmate photo I clowned around, looking like an ax murderer on speed. I figured potential assailants would hesitate if the picture on my ID made me look nuts. Later I realized this file photo is more important for getting prison officials to sympathize with me. Oops.

Next came clothes and bedding. They gave everyone brown pants and coats made of a stiff cotton/polyester blend, and white t-shirts. The place looked like a UPS Guy boot camp. An inmate stood at a counter in front of a big room full of shelves and folded clothes. He asked for my coat size.

"Forty-six long," I replied without thinking.

Clothes Guy seemed to not hear me. Either that or he just stopped and glared at everyone. Finally, I got it.

"Um, extra-large, I guess?" I said.

He tossed a tent-like jacket my way and handed me small stacks of other clothing staples. Next came hard plastic shower shoes and a pair of sneakers. Both were made in China and somehow offered less cushioning than going barefoot. The gummy soles on the sneakers made me think of the environmental waste caused by their production. When I walked on wet ground in them, water seeped through. At least the price was right.

I then accepted the burden of my linens: a canvas mattress cover stuffed with bedding and a towel. I threw my clothes in with them and moved on. A long, grim trudge to my bunk followed, with me tottering under the weight of my load like a drunken hobo. My heart began racing as I crossed the empty recreation yard to reach my new home.

A military-like sleeping barracks served as my new bedroom in a dreary building; basically an unadorned warehouse stocked with poorly tattooed humans. I circled the room of seventeen bunks twice before locating mine, feeling eyes on me from everywhere. I pretended to yawn to avoid looking like a rookie. I blew my cover anyway when I failed to ask for help to apply my mattress cover.

Taming a floppy canvas mattress is a two-man job. It's basically applying a pillowcase to a pillow that's six feet long and three feet wide. The correct, veteran move is to yell: "Yo, can I get a hand over here," no "excuse me" or "please" necessary. Instead, I took on the bedding solo, afraid to bother anyone. A full house watched me stagger, grunt, and sweat through the battle.

Once I'd made my bed, I noticed they had issued no pillow to me. I wandered to the common area up front to find a linen closet. There, I noticed a burly guy eyeing me at the gate to the barracks. His hands gripped bars of the gateway above him – a pose a body language expert would label as dominant. He reminded me of the bounty hunter in Raising Arizona, only without the charm. His dad probably gave him a carton of cigarettes for his thirteenth birthday. And several tattoos. My stomach plummeted.

Pretending to be unaffected, I asked: "Hey, where can I hook up a pillow?"

Steely-blue eyes lanced my façade before he replied, as if to a child: "You wait 'till someone ships out, then you take the one they left."

Instead of saying, "Cool, thanks," I pulled out my Ned Flanders impression: "Allll-righty then!"

Bounty Hunter Guy shook his head and scoffed.

This was not clutch on my part. My Flanders impression is never necessary and using it here probably advertised me as food to the most menacing guy in the block. I pictured Nick laughing at me, and heard his voice: "*See food, eat food, or be food.*"

I returned to my bunk and fashioned a pillow with folded-up shirts. I laid down on my bottom bunk looking up at a chain-link mattress suspension, scared but also exhausted. I was twelve anxiety-packed hours into the day. I soon faded into a nap despite constant PA announcements for various inmates to report here or there. My slumber soon ended with the sound of two large men in a fistfight, ten feet from my bunk. A line of blow wouldn't have made me more alert.

The fight even featured a referee, a huge guy who bunked right next to me. He kept the combatants from holding or using shady tactics as they pounded each other. An eerie silence descended over the room, except for deep thuds and slaps from each blow. Soon, a little white guy approached the battle.

"C'mon guys, knock it off! No one needs a trip to the hole in goddamn processing!"

This seemingly innocent action pulled the pin on Bounty Hunter Guy's emotional grenade. He leaped into the would-be peacemaker's face.

"Shut the fuck up," he explained. "That's why we have a lookout, dumbass!"

The fight continued for another minute or two until the slightly smaller guy limped off to the bathroom, holding his ribs. Turns out he ratted out the other over a drug deal in their hometown. The authorities assigned them to the same processing barracks, anyway.

Before calm settled in, Bounty Hunter Guy dashed up to the peacemaker's bunk. "Let's go, motherfucker! Get up!"

"I'm not gonna fight you, man."

"Fuck that, GET UP!" he yelled, voice cracking.

Peacemaker remained on his bunk. This further agitated the fired-up redneck. He skittered down rows of bunks, staring everyone down and shouting "I got nine years! I'll kick anyone's ass that wants to go!"

Everyone stared into the distance in silence. Bounty Hunter Guy neared my bunk, which probably shook from my fear. I figured he'd see me and think: *Oh, yeah – this new dork who looked for a goddamn pillow! Why not beat on him?*

Instead, his crazy eyes passed me without recognition, a Tasmanian Devilish pummeling avoided. Passions simmered down soon enough, and day one in a real prison passed without my ass being kicked. Small victories.

The next notable day included a prison orientation meeting, where I probably achieved my lifelong dream of being the smartest person in the room. About eighty cons filled rows of chairs in a standard meeting space, dressed uniformly and loudly speaking out of turn. At the lectern stood two fast-talking, foul-mouthed COs.

One of these reminded me of Denis Leary on coke, vigorously chomping gum and grinning as he drew cheap laughs from the captive audience. Like a white, uncensored Steve Harvey. Two or three curse words in a sentence guaranteed laughs, as if the audience was made up of ten-year-olds. Professional jealousy ate away at the standup comic in me.

"Don't Step on Your Dick" seemed the unofficial theme of the program. They repeated it often. It meant don't do stupid shit that might cause an ass-kicking or extend your sentence. "Mind your own business," was emphasized. And my favorite: "If you must smoke just don't do it where officers can see you." They had only recently forbidden smoking in prisons statewide.

The Bureau of Prisons was under new management: the Department of Public Safety. This meant we were officially referred to as "offenders" instead of "inmates." The gum-chomping CO chuckled at this and quipped: "You don't look very offensive, but I'm not gonna get close enough to smell ya!" This drew big laughs.

An ominous instructional DVD capped off the meeting: "How to avoid being raped in prison." Topping this list was: upon arriving, don't accept beverages from inmates simply to fit in. Evidently, offenders who fall for this trick could drink a Thorazine-laced potion and wake up later with a violated rectum. Alas, the video did not address the prison scourge of introverts: auditory rape.

Also not covered in the orientation meeting were camp assignments, which dominated conversation among inmates. Everyone needed to be as close to home as possible, but not at a strict or dismal facility. My ideal options were in the Western region – closest to Atlanta. I learned most everyone considered the Asheville facility the most coveted in the state. I wrote a letter to my case manager (guidance counselor for inmates), begging for an assignment there. She never replied, but my quest had begun.

My IQ test the next day placed me at one-fourteen, and I learned my long division math skills are gone. I aced the spelling and reading exams, however, and correctly pronounced "assuage" on the oral test. Several days later medical tests confirmed I was disease free and declared me fit for warehousing with the masses long-term. In the meantime, I got a feel for prison barracks life – the chaos of comings and goings and the PA blaring announcements all day long.

A gymnasium-sized chow hall served as a parade ground for me. Here hundreds of inmates crossed paths, including many doing life sentences at the adjacent medium security camp. Four COs patrolled the area, including an armed one on a platform. A sense of ominous fear greeted me upon each visit, but the oddities of my new brethren helped distract me.

Many offenders sported ghastly body ink and scars. Their eating habits were even more menacing. Most shoveled food into their mouths, two inches above their trays. I gawked too much at first, imagining their rap sheets and wondering how the scars came to be. I learned to keep my rookie head down while dining if only to keep my appetite.

I felt scrutinized too, although this was probably paranoia. People naturally look around, so naturally, I'd sometimes be the focus in a large room. Just because they may be killers doesn't necessarily mean they want to kill me. Or so I hoped.

CHAPTER FIVE

Big Boy Prison

Back in the barracks, I felt like a fly on the wall. I was suddenly privy to sordid conversations, shenanigans, and customs I'd never otherwise know. One eye-opener involved plans some had to make up for lost time once they re-entered society.

"I'ma put one in a bitch (impregnate a woman) right off the bat. That's what a *man* do!"

I learned filter cigarettes can cost five dollars each. More often they sold in portions, cut to size along the faint vertical lines on the paper. Cheaper hand-rolled versions − "roll-ups" − were more common, but still expensive. Many looked forward to leaving the processing camp to find more affordable tobacco at their next one, where inmate work crews smuggled more.

Prison's social life defied most conventional wisdom. I expected to find a bunch of irredeemable psychopaths who'd just as quickly stab me as say hello. I'd often wondered how Johnny Cash played Folsom State Prison and made it out alive. Instead, I found most inmates aren't evil or constantly violent; they made one fateful mistake, probably while intoxicated. Lockups house many "mean drunks" who are delightful when sober.

I discovered another unexpected charm of lockup in these early days, too. People rarely said, "God bless you," following a sneeze. This habit annoys me because I'm already peeved that I sneezed in the first place. Being on the hook for a "thank you" to a stupid platitude that follows only makes it worse.

Who knew the lack of empathy shown by most inmates could be a benefit?

My spirits rose once I became comfortable at the processing camp. Its relatively light, social vibe interrupted my typically negative thoughts. Compared to the mood of the county jail, laughter came easier to everyone. Inmates enjoyed a common area at all hours instead of only during free time. Outdoor activities were available several hours a day.

During evenings time got killed by reading, writing, playing cards, or watching TV. The more industrious drew portraits from snapshots or created crafts such as "flowers" fashioned from toilet paper, servicing a market of lovers sending sentiments to their significant others.

I became used to conversation circles in the barracks that at first seemed odd. Four guys typically sat in a group, two each on beds facing each other with knees nearly touching.

I soon dive-bombed into conversations like most others, careful to conceal my lofty self-image. This worked for about a minute.

"Yeah, I really shouldn't be here." I'd say. "First time offense, mandatory minimum."

"Did you fuck up your life, or not?" one guy asked.

"Well yeah, but —"

"Then I got news for you, genius, you deserve to be here!"

He was right. I was one of them, regardless of my education and relative privilege. Or probably *because* of my privilege. That advantage I squandered. Time to stop fronting like I wasn't a failure at life before I got my ass kicked.

All cons seemed to have an alias, so I needed one too. The fewer potential rats that know your real name the better. I regret not keeping my county jail moniker "Lock Back," which was both fun to say and sounded dangerous. Instead, I chose the "whitest" name I could think of, to make fun of myself. I settled on "Biff" for its silliness, and it carried a bold sound. Shouting it to greet me, or just for the hell of it turned into something of a thing.

Much like in high school, I hung out with multiple circles of friends. I joined the rednecks, talking about cars, heavy metal, and drugs. I kicked it with the black dudes, talking basketball, hip hop, and drugs. I spent time with the geeks, talking about books, movies, and drugs. And of course I chatted up the druggies – about drugs. Most free time felt like a big party, only without women and intoxicants.

The vibe wasn't all enjoyable, though. Some party attendees were unpleasant types who couldn't be kicked out, as in who invited him? Teenage behavior like pretend fighting was common. Arrested development in action, I figured. Everyone's least favorite ritual was count time. You drop everything, including sleeping at six a.m., to line up.

As an expert on MDMA and DMT, my fellow felons enjoyed talking to me. Guys proved eager to learn about DMT, which I used to extract myself. I shared stories about those mystical psychedelic trips. And tales of my more practical ones, like being pulled over in Memphis on acid. It goes a little something like this.

I partied for three straight weeks on a stand-up comedy trip out West and ran out of money. A fourteen-hour drive home stared me in the face, and I was exhausted to start with. I couldn't count on even gallons of coffee to keep me awake. Instead of sleeping in my car at rest stops I ate my last hit of LSD to serve as extra-strength NoDoz.

Not only could an acid trip keep me awake, I could put it to professional use. I could save any "profound" psychedelic ramblings on my voice recorder I used when I performed. Perhaps I'd figure out the meaning of life, or at least a good stand-up comedy bit for future use.

Driving on LSD is not an activity I recommend, but back then I didn't care. I figured driving is like walking to me because I drove as a courier in Atlanta for fifteen years. I'd also tripped over one hundred times over thirty years, so I knew my limitations under the influence. Contrary to popular belief acid hallucinations don't involve, say, a unicorn suddenly materializing in the road. Objects may morph oddly if stared at, but not enough to disrupt driving on a freeway that involves no oncoming traffic.

The amount of LSD I ingested wouldn't completely distort

reality, anyway. To me it was like a really amusing five cups of coffee. Soon, my psychedelic reverie made a mundane ride vivid and exciting.

I cruised through Arkansas. In the rearview I enjoyed a colorful sunset over the farmlands of the Mississippi Delta. The Talking Heads or Blind Melon on the stereo transported me further. I marveled at the heap of metal that carried me, careening along at seventy-five miles an hour while in air-conditioned comfort. The tech gadgets and their charger wires next to me: camera, phone, minidisc recorder, iPod, fascinated me. Traffic was light, and so was I.

All was good until I came upon a dizzying amount of freeway construction, like a sinister video game come to life. Shifting lanes and uneven pavement. Bright orange barrels and concrete barricades inches away. Bullying tractor trailers. Senior motorists panicking while going forty miles per hour. The commentary recorded during this interval was hardly philosophical or profound; I was cussing like a tattoo artist. "*What the fuuuuuck!!!*"

I soon surrendered to the flow and enjoyed myself again, however. The video game became fun. I efficiently navigated the construction zone, speaking play-by-play of my driving maneuvers into the microphone …

"A typical driver would be flipping out, but I'm possibly the best driver in the world. I am completely unfazed," I boasted. Thirty seconds later I exclaimed: "Whoa, blue lights! … Just kidding, they're in front of me."

About thirty seconds later blue lights appeared again, directly behind me. Words failed me as practical thoughts intruded. The next sounds on the recording besides traffic noise were roadside rumble strips moaning as I pulled over. The recorder kept rolling.

I remained cool, like Dock Ellis throwing an acid-fueled no-hitter. I scrambled to dig my license out of my shorts in the back seat and prepared to present it casually to the cop. "I got this," I said to myself. The weed sitting on the passenger seat said otherwise.

Yes, amid the aforementioned mass of wires and gadgets

next to me sat less than a gram of shitty marijuana, in plastic from a cigarette pack. A fan in New Mexico gave it to me during a drunken evening, but I'd forgotten. Decent-quality weed would have been stashed carefully. Instead, this weed sat in purgatory: not good enough to hide well, but not bad enough to throw away. Either way, in 2005 Tennessee it was illegal.

My license and proof of insurance were in hand as a cop approached on either side. At the last second I spotted the herb on the seat and threw a towel in its general area, luckily not covering the recorder microphone. I presented my ID to a strapping young cop built like a linebacker ...

Lead Cop (LC): "Sir, we've stopped you for speeding in a construction zone."

"I see."

"Where are you coming from, sir?"

"Memphis."

"You're in Memphis," he replied, seeming to chuckle.

"I mean, Albuquerque ... I'm a stand-up comic."

"A comic? Do you have a CD or anything?"

"No, but here's one of a lady I worked with this week."

I handed him a CD case. The cover photo featured comic Jessie Campbell shooting pool with a cigarette in her mouth. *A great character witness.* With a smile, the officer asked me to step to the rear of my car.

Meanwhile, the Second Cop (SC) grabbed the poorly-concealed weed through the passenger window, and handed it to the one asking the questions. They returned to their vehicle to run my plates and strategize. I succumbed to psychedelic thoughts such as the nature of freeways, too amused to worry much. The cops reemerged ten minutes later. Or fifty. Acid trips warp time.

LC dangled the paltry package of pot in front of me. "Now, I'm not going to arrest you for this, but you need to tell me right now if you have anything else in this car."

"I got nothing to hide, search it if you want," I said. It was true: Since I'd eaten my acid I didn't even possess an empty beer can of shady cargo.

"No guns, drugs, anything like that?" asked SC, suspiciously.

"No officer, go ahead and check."

I must've looked like I harbored more drugs, and possibly a lot. My twelve-year-old Lexus GS 300 had blacked-out windows and out-of-state tags. I presented my license with a shaky hand and didn't seem to know what city I was in. Sketchy as hell.

They escorted me to the back of a K-9 equipped 4-by-4 SUV. Clad in a golf shirt, sandals, and funky light blue swim trunks – hardly dressed for a treacherous Memphis jail should I go there. As they placed me in the vehicle, I asked the cops if they wanted my keys, but neither heard me. My minidisc recorder caught the following exchange for posterity before they moved to search my car.

LC: "Did you get his keys?"

"Uh, no. Don't have the keys."

"Get the keys from that motherfucker."

After retrieving the keys from this motherfucker, they left me alone to absorb a strange new world. I noticed how hard I was tripping, three hours after ingesting a relatively small dose of five-year-old LSD. Although I fully recognized reality, the visuals were delightfully vivid, enhanced by flashing blue lights in the dusk.

Just behind me loomed a cage containing a sizable dog. I turned and offered a little puppy talk and received two ear-splitting barks and a vicious snarl for my trouble. But for the thin bars of the doggie cage, my aorta would've been torn out. Tough crowd.

I don't advocate animal abuse, but I admit I heckled the canine cop in return for it being a dick. "Bet you wish you could bite me, don't you, pig?" After all, what was he going to do, arrest me?

The human cops dismantled my car interior and rummaged through my belongings as I amused myself. They looked under my trunk liner and behind door panels. "They are literally airing my dirty laundry!" I said to the K9 unit. He responded with another snarl.

Big Boy Prison

I didn't take the dog as a bad omen, however. LC had sent off good vibes, so I felt at peace. He didn't appear to know I was tripping, and I was confident my wits would keep me in the clear.

The pair of police trudged back to me and their vehicle twenty minutes later. Or an hour. They muttered to each other for a minute, then LC asked: "OK Mr. Phillips, are you a *famous* comic?"

"No, but after *this* story I might be!" I admitted. I then described my recording mission and how they pulled me over moments after I declared how great a driver I was. They found this amusing.

"Where did you get this pot?" LC asked.

"A girl I met in Albuquerque gave it to me. I was probably going to throw it anyway, because it sucks."

"Yeah, this looks like Mexican weed," LC professed. "I guess you call it 'dank?'"

I quickly corrected him: "No sir, that's schwag; the *good* stuff is dank." I realized I shared industry lingo with the enemy, and blurted: "Shit, I just spilled pot smoker inside info."

"Yeah, I think you did. Show me the handshake too."

We all laughed. Clearly no arrest was coming, so I turned *really* talkative. I told the cops how my schwag source was a hot chick in Albuquerque that got me high in her car after a show. I expected to hook-up with her, but some random guy warned me that she fucked every army guy in town. And she turned me down, anyway.

Following more small talk LC, a West Tennessee Judicial Violent Crime & Drug Task Force Special Agent, released me from my temporary cell on wheels. We moved in front of the vehicle, and he waved my weed as he spoke.

"Now I'm going to dump this out right here. Just do me a favor and tell your friends not all cops are dicks."

He handed me his card and added: "And give us a call next time you have a show in town."

"Oh, wow!" I blurted. "Thank you, officer and have a great night!"

"You're welcome. And slow it down."

His final remark reminded me why they pulled me over in the first place, seemingly a day earlier. I didn't even get a speeding ticket. Life was good.

I never returned to Memphis to perform stand-up and hang out with the benevolent Lead Cop. My recording of his pullover, however, opened the door to an on-air position on a top Atlanta morning radio show, *The Regular Guys*.

LC moved on to other ventures too. Specifically, he got prison time for taking part in a steroid distribution ring, which probably operated during the time he was recognized as Tennessee Narcotics Officer of the Year. I hope his replacement on the police force isn't a dick.

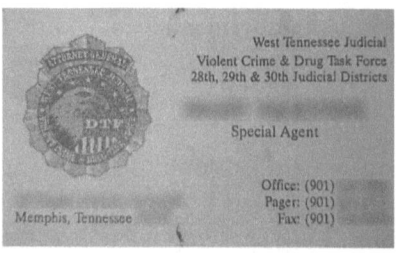

LC's business card.
Luckily, he wasn't DTF me!

If inmates love anything, it's tales about getting over on the buzz-kills in blue. By the third time I told this story in this place I went the opposite way. The story's antagonist – me – started to seem like a real asshole. A bunch of jailbirds laughing about me beating the cops suddenly felt idiotic and shameful given what it got me and where I sat.

A day at processing allowed four hours of yard rec time. This felt like hanging out in an inner-city crack park if the park offered weight training, horseshoes, basketball, volleyball, and a nice walking path. A hernia limited my activity, but horseshoes was sufficiently low-impact.

Except for the trash talk.

The old school cons hung out at the horseshoe pits, where sharp tongues cut deep. "Yo Mama" jokes may have originated there. Like: "Yo Mama hair so nappy her comb had to get dentures!"

The game within the game was to avoid cracking a smile when a great barb hit you. "You so lazy, you think a two-income family is when yo bitch has two jobs!"

"This ain't shot put – get the motherfucker (horseshoe) to the stake!"

"That throw so weak it should be seven days long!"

Gamesmanship included asking a shoe-tosser on a hot streak what his tattoo is supposed to say. Dudes hate having to explain their ink. "Pisses him off, then he can't throw for shit!" one old-timer explained.

One day I talked to a cool cat named Tim in the rec yard, who I knew from county jail. I recounted the fight, Bounty Hunter Guy's explosion, and spoke poorly of another guy in my barracks. Tim stopped me short.

"Yo, this kind of shit will get your ass beat in here," he explained. "You don't really know me, and I could be tight with who you're talking shit about."

I worked hard to stop gossiping from then on, grateful for the warning before arriving at my permanent camp. Loose lips fuck up your reputation faster than anything.

Also advising me about lockup was "New York," a huge, muscular black dude and the aforementioned fight referee. He sported bullet scars from heroin and coke deals gone bad and was currently down for shady check cashing. He did time on notorious Riker's Island and promised North Carolina was "daycare" by comparison. He mentioned he owed over thirty grand in child support, but besides this I found him to be a great guy.

My geeky look prompted New York to call me "Clark Kent." The first time he did so, I joked: "That's right, and you better hope there's not a phone booth nearby!" Luckily he found my trash talk amusing, as did most guys I interacted with. It's like a secret handshake.

New York advised to never disclose how much money was in my canteen account, "Cuz broke niggas be hearin' that shit and come after it." He might've added that "broke niggas" could be of any race. He opposed the Nick-endorsed "Scorpio Eyes" approach to bluff out of a fight. New York claimed dudes would sense bullshit and abuse me even harder for trying to front. He figured passive reasoning was my best option, to put it nicely.

"Say, 'Man, I'm forty-six years old. I'm just tryna' do my time and get home.' And if that don't work, hit the motherfucker first. Quick, and hard!"

I laughed, despite myself.

"Of course you go to the hole for three or four weeks," New York continued.

"But everyone in the camp will respect you when you get out."

I treasured New York's advice, but my primary prison mentor in the early days proved to be a "shopper" (shoplifter) named Jason. He was attractive and well-spoken – attributes he applied to thieving from upscale Charlotte clothing stores. He'd been freed from custody for just three years total since 1989. Besides an appreciation for nice clothes, we shared a passion for quality books, bands, movies, and bullshitting about philosophy.

Everyone nearby became two-dimensional when Jason and I chatted, as if a budding love affair had overtaken us (no homo). He gave me something I missed more than sex: stimulating conversation.

Above all, Jason urged me to keep to myself. This would help avoid bums who never paid debts and dumbasses who talk too much. He'd been driven crazy by how stupid our fellow felons were. He devised a basic knowledge quiz to prove his point.

"Not one in fifty will know who Hunter S. Thompson is," Jason claimed. "In fact, you may not find one guy in the whole place."

"Dude, of course these people will know," I insisted. "He was all about drugs!"

"Yes," Jason replied, like a wise sage, "but he was also all about reading books!"

I spent a couple of days asking, under the guise I needed an argument settled. The first twenty men responded with blank stares and shrugged shoulders, and none with the right answer. I stopped asking about Hunter S. Thompson. I kept up with other questions though, amazed.

Too many thought the US contains fifty-two states since it recently added Hawaii and Puerto Rico. Roughly twenty percent could name America's vice president. Most had heard of Amsterdam – a pot-smoking mecca – yet practically no one knew its country. The country where Jerusalem is also proved a tough question, even among bible-thumpers.

Jason damn near relished prison life. He liked having decisions made for him and had been degraded by the system for so long he barely noticed anymore. Lining up for headcount six times a day was just part of life.

More remarkable, Jason preferred maximum security. He amassed demerit points to gain residence there and to serve the high-end of his sentence range. He enjoyed insulting guards with his acerbic wit to earn write-ups. He figured the reduced chaos of a private cell was worth missing out on minimum security privileges. Living among hardened criminals didn't faze Jason. He found them more respectful and mature and claimed the heavy, more competent security presence in maximum is actually safer.

By contrast, security at the processing camp appeared to be lacking. A good deal of COs would be pushovers in the face of violence. They were often middle-aged, out of shape, or sometimes petite females. The guard desk offered only partial views of the sleeping areas, and video surveillance covered only the corridors. Over one-hundred-forty men were "policed" by two guards most of the time.

Luckily most inmates avoid trouble while in processing, for multiple reasons. Most guys wanted work-release jobs and home furloughs later in their sentences, rewards for excellent behavior. Inmates stayed in line in hopes of better camp assignments. Some camps were more lenient than others, and physical features and conditions varied. Problematic people were usually sent to lousy places.

My neighbor New York moved out to his home camp after about a week, revealing prison at its worst for me. He was the enforcer, the referee, and when he said shut up, niggas shut the fuck up. He was like a teacher with authority over a classroom. When he left, it shattered a peace. As with when a substitute teacher comes into class, the wilding began.

One posse in particular – most likely the same fuckheads who break into cars or swipe purses on the street – made noise long after lights out. They even climbed on top of lockers while roughhousing. This crew mocked the "no pants on the ground" prison rule in the evening. They'd wear two pairs of boxers, the outer layer slung low enough to fall over their knees as they swaggered around the barracks.

I could do little about the new mayhem around me. Anyone that dared try invited payback of a beat-down or being framed to be busted by COs performing random searches. Most guys kept their heads down and quietly endured to stay out of trouble. New York's strength became even more clear in his absence. I swallowed the pain of the chaos begrudgingly, keeping my prison goals in mind: no maimings and doing my time in Asheville, closest to home.

Inmates in processing trudged to an early morning line twice a week to exchange dirty clothing for clean, teeth chattering from February wind-chills. This process also interrupted post-breakfast sleep time, which left me both cranky and groggy.

One morning I'd advanced to the exchange window and handed in three pairs of boxers, among other items. I failed to notice my replacement stack of clothing did not include boxers. I explained this to the CO on duty, who laughed at my error: "Tough shit, get back in line."

Ten minutes later I headed the line again, desperate to get my fucking underwear and return to my warm bed. Suddenly, the same dickhead CO halted the operation for no clear reason and started reading the paper. After a couple minutes, I quietly asked the clothes-dispensing inmate in front of me what was up.

"He stopped the line because it's too loud," the guy whispered.

Trying to be helpful, I turned back and yelled to no one in particular, "Yo, quiet down or the line won't move!"

This only increased the volume, particularly among a few African-Americans, who thought I singled them out. I suppose this was true since they were the ones running their mouths. At the time I didn't care who was talking. I wanted to get my fucking clothes and escape the frigid dawn.

The CO remained smirking, not letting the line move. He relished fucking with the inmates. A couple more minutes passed, but the chatter didn't cease. So I turned again, this time yelling directly at the offending crew: "Yo, if you don't shut up the line isn't going to move!"

The disruptors started screaming at me as if I were the problem. They called me the "*powe*-leece" and "white motherfucker." Far from defending me, my fellow pale faces stood slack-jawed, like I'd punched the CO or something. The CO stepped up and pointed out the shit-talkers.

"You, you, you, you, and you. Get the fuck out. Better luck next week," he barked with a grin.

This made them slightly perturbed. They threatened to see me "in the yard" later and wandered off to wear dirty clothes for a few days. Meanwhile, the line started again, and I finally scored clean boxers. I might as well have asked for a shirt with a bullseye on the back, too.

I returned to my barracks, greeted by a glare from a guy who I got kicked out of the line. "Yo, man. I'ma need some of yo clothes. *Powe*-leece pulled me out, and I ain't even do nothin'!"

Rattled, I apologized and threw him a few items. When I reached my bunk, my mentor Jason materialized. His presence steadied me. Then he laughed in my face.

"Man!" he managed. "You don't fucking do that!"

"I didn't mean to do anything. I thought I was helping!"

"No, man. All you did was tell black dudes to shut up! They knew why the line stopped, they just didn't care. That shit is part of prison, don't try to fight it."

"Great! So now I'm getting shanked?" My stomach sank.

"Maybe, maybe not," Jason said. "Watch your back for a couple of days, for sure. Do you have any friends bigger and younger than me?" This was his idea of a joke.

Right about then a heavily tattooed offender stormed in, long dreadlocks flailing. You'd think I doomed him to wear dirty clothes for a few days. I recognized him as the main troublemaker from the line, and he was pissed. I moved to stand up from my bunk since etiquette demands one not remain seated when greeting visitors.

"Don't stand up like you gonna do somethin'!" he shouted.

I settled back down and listened to him rant about disrespect and how I did the *powe*-leece's job for them. Like I was a snitch.

I wanted no trouble with Dreadlock. I'd get a write-up for fighting and go to the hole, followed by medium security to start my bid. Also, I like my teeth. I didn't take the offensive by using Scorpio Eyes, too, because I'm a pussy. Besides, even if I got through Dreadlock five others were after me, anyway. Diplomacy was my best option.

"I didn't want to 'dis anyone or get you kicked out of line. I thought I was helping."

Dreadlock circled in a huff. "Man, this some bullshit."

"This is my first time down," I pleaded, sounding as street as possible. "I don't know what's up."

As Dreadlock considered this, an African-American neighbor of mine called Trip chimed in. "Yo, he straight. He don't know shit, but he a'ight."

This hardy endorsement nearly made me blush. Another buddy, Kaz, who shared a barracks with Dreadlock, offered a similar testimony: "Yeah, he's just a dumbass. He doesn't know any better, but he don't mean no harm." I resisted an urge to defend my intellect. Diffusing the tension seemed more important.

Dreadlock calmed, presenting his demands to make things right. He wanted some of my clean clothes and a honey bun or equivalent snack from the canteen to be named later. This was fine with me. Dreadlock and I didn't exactly bump fists as he left, but we seemed good.

Trip later explained that Dreadlock's visit actually displayed respect, not a menace. Otherwise, I would have suffered a pop-up shanking or beat down, no discussion involved. Perhaps Dreadlock remembered me from spectating at the basketball court.

Other inmates, however, weren't sure my peril had passed. The whole barracks soon knew of the drama, and two veterans pulled me aside and laid out my new reality. Despite Dreadlock making peace they now perceived me as a potential snitch. They suggested I watch my back on the yard, avoid hanging out solo, and to shut the fuck up. And also: Shut the fuck up. I was more out of my element than Donald Trump at a Chris Brown concert.

My first move outside the barracks involved the long lunch walk to the chow hall. I needed a security phalanx, so I placed myself in the middle of a group of white guys for the trek. This did not go unnoticed. "You're hot, bro. Stay the fuck away from me!" I assumed they were kidding, and thankful they didn't avoid me.

Besides a few leers – possibly imagined – this first trip proved uneventful. My next hurdle was the afternoon yard session, towards which time flew. I could have waited out the danger on my bunk, but that would make me look like a pussy. I cared about my prison rep, much to my surprise. I thought such concerns were beneath me. And I hadn't even graduated to my permanent camp yet.

More importantly, I craved a resolution so I could relax again. I'm a big fan of relaxation.

CHAPTER SIX

Hello, Home Camp!

I strolled out to the basketball court to shoot baskets as usual, with my head held high. The court occupied the center of the yard, so I'd see trouble coming. A guard shack stood about thirty yards away, but the CO working it faces away from the court. I started shooting before anyone else arrived and hoisted mostly air balls because of nerves. Soon Dreadlock showed up, along with his sizable sidekick and two others from the clothes debacle.

At first, they pretended I wasn't there. This included not returning the ball to me after I made a shot, a sign of major disrespect on a court. Then the situation literally came to a head. A ball drilled me square in the back of my noggin as I waited for a rebound under the basket. I staggered away dazed but stayed on my feet. I expected a barrage of balls or fists, so I covered my head. Instead, I heard laughter and jeers. "Yo, don't hit the *powe*-leece!"

Once my bearings returned a little, I wobbled up to Dreadlock's sidekick to talk it out. "Yo, my bad this morning. I didn't mean to get anybody kicked out of line."

Sidekick looked towards his boys as if he didn't hear, but stayed put.

"This is my first time down. I didn't know what was up. I didn't mean disrespect," I said, head throbbing.

"Maaan, dat's some of dat bullshit! You tryin' tell a nigga to 'shut up?' What the fuck you call it?"

"I thought I was helping get the line moving. That's all."

Hello, Home Camp!

This comment invited two more dudes to yell at me. I wouldn't recommend this, but it beat the hell out of them swinging at and kicking me.

"It ain't your job to fuck with the line, that's the *powe*-leece, snitch-bitch!" one suggested.

"And who you to tell a man to shut up!"

Another guy made an offer of physical harm, which I ignored.

I felt hopeful amid this humiliation. However crudely, the air was clearing and sharing a peace pipe seemed near. Further physical pain seemed doubtful. "Let it all out!" I felt like saying. "This is productive. I'm sensing some real growth here!"

The bitching and insults gradually subsided, and Dreadlock again spoke of reparations.

"Whatchoo gonna buy us, *powe*-leece?"

Resuming my "I'm not the police" argument seemed silly, so I ignored the 'dis. I'd be shipping out soon and leaving this new nickname behind, anyway. I offered to get each of my tormentors a honey bun as soon as funds hit my canteen account.

"You mean a hun-bun and a drank?" Sidekick suggested.

"Yeah, that's fine. Like I said, I didn't mean to fuck anything up." I replied. "Are we straight now?"

"I ain't eating no hun-bun yet, so fuck no we ain't straight!" someone said. I joined the laughter despite my headache. The cloud that followed me around dissipated. I headed back to my bunk, looking for some aspirin and a well-earned nap.

My clothes line terrorists never got their canteen items from me. I got shipped out before money to buy them anything posted to my account. I finally feel safe enough to say: Suck it, bitches!

Following fifteen days in processing – blessedly shorter than a typical stay – I packed up to head to my home camp. Before leaving, I spent one night in an eight-story high-rise building comprising both minimum-security sleeping areas and maximum-security cells. I'll never forget looking out a window at "dog runs" there – eerie fenced-in areas where the most dangerous inmates underwent outdoor exercise time.

These souls took their "walks" in full shackles, with a guard right next to them. To think some of them made one poorly considered choice; committed a crime that made these dismal shuffles the highlight of each day for the rest of their lives. *Oh, the humanity.* I tried to keep this in mind throughout my prison odyssey. No matter how bad my situation became, at least I wasn't one of these guys. I had a chance to enjoy life at least a little and ultimately redeem myself.

Jason happened to move to the high-rise with me that last day, and I bid farewell to him with a lump in my throat when the time came. I felt we shared a special bond, a real appreciation for each other. Instead, he said, "Okay, see ya!" as if we'd chatted for five minutes over the whole two weeks. I'd learn such nonchalance is typical for the emotionally dead in the transient nature of the big house.

Before enduring another bus ride, our crew of fifteen stopped in a small holding room. Excited inmates shouted in conversation and ignored multiple CO requests to quiet down. The door slammed closed as a reprimand, causing me to miss hearing my camp assignment. This added more uncertainty to an already nerve-wracking process. A CO stuck his head in the door.

"I know you're wearing extra clothes. Throw it in a pile on the floor," he instructed. "Anyone caught trying me gets a write-up!"

Suddenly, dudes shed their clothes like they'd deplaned a winter's flight from Alaska to Hawaii.

Cursing filled the air as discarded clothing formed a small mountain. Practically everyone but me wore multiple layers of nearly new apparel, in case the clothes issued to them later were in bad shape. The same cats that don't dress decently for courtrooms go to great lengths to look good in prison. Especially at the bus transfer depot, where we were heading, and

Hello, Home Camp!

where many would run into friends. Inmates dress for each other, just like women.

Prison bus rides reminded me of urban construction crews, only less classy. Freeway travel provided a steady stream of cars passing below, often carrying North Carolina hotties. Guys overloaded the left side of the bus to better hoot and catcall. Those towards the back shouted alerts for those farther up to leer out the window as beauties, or even skanks, passed. Standards weren't exactly high. Young women in pickup trucks or piece-of-shit cars drew the most attention. The odds were better for them to hike up skirts or flash titties.

Two CO drivers took breaks at rest stops or retail areas. Pity the unsuspecting women that came within earshot of the bus. Hoots and propositions fired through the steel mesh over windows. One time a young mother not paying attention bent over as she tended to her toddler, exposing her tramp stamp and thong. After finally noticing her audience, she blushed and pulled up her britches without shaking her lovely booty for the gallery. Boos rained down on her.

A spirited young lady on a smoke break behind a fast-food joint once decided to play along. Attractive in a skinny porn chick kind of way, she sat in a storage shed doorway when our ship of fools rumbled up. Instead of scattering, like most women, this sex kitten remained, despite the unsavory comments and propositions that cascaded from the cage.

"Shit, you ain't man enough for that, and you know it!" she sassed. The bus erupted.

"Why don't you show me what you're working with instead of talkin' about it?" she answered to another.

Moments later she stuck her cigarette between her lips, rubbed her crotch, and moaned, provoking ear-splitting whoops. She then crushed out her smoke and sashayed past the bus. The weight shift from dudes scrambling to the other side nearly tipped us over as they angled for a better look.

"Call me!" she shouted over the din as she passed. Back to work at Wendy's.

Episodes like these made bus rides bearable, as did scenery different from prison. Amusement from eavesdropping on apocryphal street tales and boasting also helped pass the time and serve as advanced-placement anthropological study.

One gentleman claimed to own a "straight pimp" (Chevrolet) Caprice outfitted with twenty-two-inch rims. "My bitches ride high!" he boasted, referring to the car's added height from the after-market wheels.

My new peers delivered a torrent of street modifiers and transitions, particularly: "Shiiit, Goddamn, Motherfucking," and the phrase, "You feel me?" "Goddamn" was spoken as an adjective or adverb – often multiple times in one sentence – which I found hurtful toward religious guys within earshot. Worse was the disrespect shown by two dipshits shouting in conversation across two or three rows of dudes minding their own business instead of just sitting next to each other. This happened all the time.

"The Bullpen" is the prison term for the bus transfer depot, but it could be called the "Convict Convention and Fashion Show." Old friends crossed paths here, and sure enough, many wore crisp, fresh clothing, including spotless new shoes. Hair and whiskers had been shaped to perfection. "They just frontin' like they got somethin'," as one con described it.

The facility featured ominous guard towers, peeling paint, and baying bloodhounds. The dogs prompted inmate discussion. One guy claimed his dog could detect if a "bitch be burnin'."

"I don't get herpes," another guy assured us, staying on topic. "Because I hygiene myself."

The bus entered through a double gate, eased past a long commercial-style chicken coop and parked. My brethren and I disembarked and shuffled up to — the chicken coop, which was actually the waiting area for inmates. I found this fitting because inmates squawk and crow too much.

Our bus arrived last, so the huge shack was already packed. When a guard opened a back door for our group to enter, two guys stumbled out. They re-entered, followed by twenty of

Hello, Home Camp!

us from the bus. The CO pushed the last guy in like cops in a Tokyo train station at rush hour and forcibly closed the door to the powder keg from the outside.

A fit of cotton mouth hit me. I feared a stampede or violence. A water cooler stood about eight feet from me, but might as well have been eight miles. Anxiety kept me from asking the criminals to pass a cup of water to me, a tall order in shoulder-to-shoulder conditions. I tried to keep my eyes down lest an innocent glance be misconstrued. The masses did not include protective COs.

After about an hour the bus departure announcements began. Guys exited the shed, a busload at a time, like steam being released from a pressure cooker. New sightlines emerged, revealing remnants of brown bag lunches issued when we arrived. I finally found space to eat mine. Narrow benches along walls of corrugated steel led to a few soiled toilets with no stalls around them.

In misery, with nothing to read for distraction, I had an epiphany: I belonged there – a dismal place for the dregs of society, eating next to dirty shit bowls. I lost in the game of seeing how far I could get in life with minimal effort. I can't imagine a lower low.

Whatever you do, don't break down and cry here!

Many of my fellow losers, lost in conversation, shouted loudly even while names were called out over the PA. They kept me from hearing my destination. You could say they victimized me in this way coming and going.

Finally, a CO with a bullhorn emerged: "GARRETT PHILLIPS. GARRETT PHILLIPS. MOVE IT OUT, NOW!"

As the last poor bastard to board the bus, I ended up in a bulkhead seat, which means practically no legroom. My presence ruined the ride for a menacing con who thought he had the seat to himself.

"Sorry man, this is the only seat." He responded only with a fart.

Four different prison camps – two honor grade and two medium security – would receive human cargo from our bus. I learned this while waiting to use the bus pisser, from a couple of dudes seated nearby. A dreaded medical camp, home to sick and infirm inmates, was on the list.

"That's probably where you're headed if you got a hernia," one suggested. "We're going back there now."

"So, what's it like?" I asked.

"Brother," the second one said, "it's probably the last place you wanna be stuck in the whole state!" The first guy laughed.

"You're kidding, right?"

"No, man. Ask around. Everyone knows it's the worst."

"Well, I'll make the place more fun if that's where I'm going!" I replied, fearing more detail. I'll never understand where this optimism came from in that scenario. The two guys I spoke to exchanged a look of confusion.

The bus traveled the freeway for an hour, and then rumbled down secondary roads until a double-fenced, multi-story prison came into view. Guard towers added to its sinister appearance. I gulped.

"There's that women's max joint," someone said.

Thank god.

The bus stopped a minute later in a small parking lot. Through an eight-foot fence common in playgrounds stood a "prison" worthy of the old TV show *Mayberry RFD*. If not for a little razor wire I'd swear I was looking at a schoolyard. Flowers and well-kept shrubbery flourished in the late-winter southern sun. I imagined my joy if this were my stop and squirmed thinking my dismal bus ride could last into the dusk.

"Phillips!" a CO barked through the rear door. My face beamed like it does when the house lights go down to start a Phish concert.

I skipped down the aisle past the gloomy passengers that remained. As I exited, one dude from the medical camp said: "You dodged a bullet!"

"Good luck, bro!" I replied, sincerely.

I hopped out into a mild afternoon, relatively thrilled to be alive and at my home camp, the Southern Correctional Institution, the original building circa 1932.

Hello, Home Camp!

Southern street view. Warden's office, clothes house & canteen, chow hall, original building. (Imagery © 2019 Google, Maxar Technologies)

Six of us walked to a small classroom, led by a skinny, energetic CO named Portis. I'd learn he's an oblivious redneck that calls other people rednecks. He looked sixty, with gray hair combed straight back, and he looked like an old NASCAR driver. Soon a second CO helped Portis inspect our belongings, and we signed paperwork. A scattershot orientation speech began.

"All smokin' and dippin' is illegal on North Carolina state property," Portis advised. "All we ask is that you not smoke in the barracks and keep it down by the weight pile. You respect us, we'll respect you." We chuckled, but Portis seemed unamused.

After our briefing we headed to the clothes house and traded our brown apparel for the hunter green reserved for honor grade inmates. "God *damn* I've waited eight years for this!" one dude exclaimed. This showed me why a demotion to medium security was known as being "browned-down."

The clothes house loaded me up with a mattress cover full of apparel and bedding. I slung it over my shoulder and began another "fresh meat" walk. Chest out and head high, I aimed to pretend my testicles were large. Soon I felt like a Caucasian walking through Manila – a custy.

"Hey, buddy. Need some roll-ups?" asked a guy sitting on a bench.

"I got a radio for sale cheap if you need one!" offered another dude from under a tree.

"If you need a lock, let me know," someone else called.

Ah, the sounds of the free market at a laid-back honor grade joint. I needed all three items, but recalled advice from Jason. "Hustlers run game on new guys," he'd warned. "You'll pay too much if you're not careful."

Those who hit me up seemed shady, even for convicts. I needed intel about how lax rules were. Buying anything from an inmate was technically a write-up.

"No, I'm good," I told each solicitor, trying to sound confident.

I soon reached barracks nearly identical to those at processing — a bunk bed warehouse equipped with a big bathroom and showers. As I settled in, I noticed words etched on my bed frame: **fuck you**! My laughter helped calm my nerves.

"Fuck you" also could've described my new bunk position. A wall-mounted industrial-strength fan blasted a wind shear directly at my bed from six feet away. I tried to swivel it away, but no dice. An older con standing nearby explained the fan was wired in place and added, "Your new bunkie is bad news. You should go ask the sergeant for a bunk switch right now."

"What's wrong with my bunkie?"

"He's worse than that fan, just trust me. And go to the sarge's office now, before the yard closes. The cool one is on duty."

I trusted the dude. He seemed too old and downtrodden to be a prankster. I shuffled up to the sergeant's office, near the camp entrance gate. He motioned me in while laughing, probably at his conversation with a couple lingering COs.

"Good afternoon, Sarge."

He nodded and seemed friendly. "Um, my assigned bunk is right in the path of a fan. Any chance I could get a different spot?"

He raised an eyebrow and turned to assess a whiteboard on the wall showing a list of bunk assignments. "What bunk are you in now?"

Hello, Home Camp!

I answered, to which he quipped: "G. Phillips ... afraid of a little breeze!"

Before I replied, he raised a hand to stop me. "Never mind, never mind," he said, grinning. "There's an open bunk across the room you can have."

I liked this camp already.

My new bed position proved an excellent upgrade, as did my bunkie, despite his poor judgment in body ink. Jack was a huge white guy who sported a ghastly tattoo: a thick chain necklace suspending a large, poorly drawn swastika medallion. I asked him about it. He mumbled something about falling in with the wrong crowd back in the day. I let the topic die.

Jack proved nice and courteous. I'd let his offensive tatt and learning that he killed someone fool me. It was only manslaughter, after all. He chipped away at a five-year bid, which, although long, beat our neighbor Billy's sentence: life for a double murder.

Billy, a skinny guy in his forties, was soft-spoken and polite. This made sense since guys doing life can't make it to minimum security unless they play well with others and boast clean disciplinary records. I slept a mere four feet away from him, yet felt comfortable. Even though Billy wasn't physically threatening the guy talked way too much, which in confinement may be worse than homicide in my book. In his defense, he had years in solitary to make up for.

Billy helped me with prison lingo. I joined him on a bench and asked what's up. "Just nigging," he replied.

This was a new one on me, even though I'm from Atlanta. I called him out. "Dude, it's not okay to say you're 'nigging' simply because you're sitting on a park bench doing nothing."

"No!" he shouted, laughing. "Not 'nigging,' nicking. Like, craving nicotine!"

Billy needed a smoke or a dip but lacked the funds to buy any. I bought a roll-up to share with him, and we headed down to the weights area to enjoy life for a minute. I hadn't smoked since my court date. Clearly, I'd picked the wrong time for quitting.

I quickly gained a camp reputation as an amiable, self-deprecating greenhorn — an easy mark for practical jokes. I took most anything fed to me at face value. For instance, one day I responded to a PA call to report to the case manager's office. A sign reading "Inmates Must Knock Before Entering" hung on the door.

I approached the door, prepared to knock. Instead, a bystander helped me out. "Man, that sign is old. No one pays attention to it. Just go on in!"

I dipped into the office with a stupid grin on my face and endured a withering glare from the head case manager. It asked me: *What are you, stupid?* I backed out without a word and knocked.

On day four of my stay, a busybody female CO pulled me aside. "It's come to my attention that you haven't showered since you got here."

In fact, I'd showered for the second time an hour earlier. I explained this, but she gave me a personal hygiene lecture anyway. "Someone has reported that you are afraid to take a shower," she added. The fact was, "someone" had toyed with both of us. I returned to my bunk and told Jack about it.

"You're gonna get fucked with like this for a while," he explained. You're too nice and proper." I was a square peg, soon to receive a lot of rounding.

I found the (not so) underground prison yard economy both confusing and fascinating. A guy selling a lock asked me to make an offer. Given locks from the canteen cost around nine dollars, I said twenty stamps ($6).

"Tell you what, I'll take ten stamps," he said with a grin. What a nice guy!

Soon I learned that second-hand locks routinely sold for $2, and only rubes bought them from the canteen. Guys going home sold locks all the time, along with used radios, dictionaries, and even used New Balance sneakers that the system allowed inmates to special order. iPod-like personal radios retailed for $20 but new ones went for $3 on the yard, and as low as $1.20 used.

This seemed impossible, but several factors skewed prices, including broke inmates. "Indigent packages" (toiletries, stamps, etc.) came their way once a month, and they included new radios once a year. They then sold many of these items far below retail value, flooding the market with underpriced goods. Indigent guys needed stamps for tobacco more than anyone.

U.S. postage stamps served as currency to buy black-market items and unofficial inmate services like shoe cleaning, or laundry service. The canteen sold stamps, but only suckers and those desperate during stamp droughts bought them there. Despite the retail stamp price rising to forty-nine cents during my stint, their yard value remained at only thirty cents.

Stamp prices stayed under face value because tobacco and drug dealers preferred them as payment. They collected hundreds of them, and sold them only for cash, easily smuggled in following weekly visitation, or other ways. Dealers gladly accepted twenty dollars in cash for one hundred stamps, ten cents below the market rate. Indigent inmates received ten free stamps a month and sold them for thirty cents each.

Sometimes stamp droughts hit when not enough guys smuggled in cash. Dealers then hoarded their stamps until greenbacks circulated again. Even when stamps were scarce because of hoarding, the price among inmates rarely rose. Sellers trying to charge thirty-five cents did so quietly, embarrassed to break an inmate code to not price gouge. Full price often got paid at the canteen instead of encouraging the gougers, based on principle. As a result, stamps hit the yard economy under retail value. Additionally, many desperate nicotine fiends bought stamps at retail during droughts, to buy tobacco. This kept stamp value on the yard depressed.

Visitors slipped me cash a couple of times. Holding one hundred stamps at once feels like hitting a jackpot. Or being tax refund rich. I'd splurge like a Vegas boss to have my sneakers cleaned, or tip my clothes house connection to upgrade my sheets or buy out a sweet bunk position from somebody.

I rarely ran out of stamps anyway because my locker stayed full of good reading trade bait. My primary lures were magazines, specifically *Us Weekly*, to which I subscribed. Cons loved them for the pics of hot chicks and the salacious, simple stories. One of the biggest tobacco dealers loved to read, and I traded him a steady supply of good books, sent to me by family and friends. They kept me connected. Bless them all, forever.

Southern Correctional Institution is nestled in verdant, rolling terrain, which included a pond frequented by Canada geese that offenders loved to feed. A pleasant walking path followed the perimeter fence line, and comfortable spots to chill out filled the yard. Even the visitation area sat under trees in a park-like area, a stark contrast to concrete patios at most other N.C prisons.

Southern's no-frills interior stayed clean and in good repair. Bunks were positioned an ample distance apart, and six-foot-high lockers between them provided a partition at head level – a semblance of privacy not found in every joint.

Four different TV-equipped day rooms graced the main barracks building. The BET network stayed on one TV since blacks comprised seventy percent of the camp population and watched TV a lot. I enjoyed hanging out in there, often the only white guy. I found the "black people at the movies" phenomenon entertaining. They yelled at the screen all the time.

Eventually, I tired of TV in general, but I still hit up the BET room for *106 and Park*'s "Freestyle Friday" rap show. Both the show and my inmate brethren's reactions to it were hilarious. Other favorite memories from BET included commercials directed at women who wished to gain weight. The reason for this became clear whenever chunky cheerleaders came on the screen in sports TV rooms. The black dudes burst into jubilance, often alerting pals to come to look.

Watching TV could be fun, but the "playground" was even better. Picture detention at a downscale all-boys school, except the kids are allowed to play. Having playmates available all the time reminded me of childhood, except these new ones offered to connect me with quality street drugs at good prices when my sentence expired.

Sporting my luxury sneakers, with my best friend Toby playing visitor

Volleyball was the game of choice among those too slow physically to play basketball. In other words, white guys. I loved watching a bunch of brutes playing this game of finesse well. Basketball was the top spectator sport, however, and played at a dizzying pace. I'd always imagined prison basketball involved players leaving on stretchers. Turns out the only difference from street games "in the world" was more arguing and fewer fouls called.

Occasionally tournaments were staged, and the inmate referees talked more trash than did the players. One of these officials absorbed a barb: "I might trust that call if you wasn't a goddamn felon!"

I learned prison is a decent lifestyle choice for many. Downscale life out in the world is hard. Most folks trudge to dead-end manual labor jobs and never come near financial security. Many of them fight addiction issues that make life even harder. Prison gave guys a break from that pressure, and also from bitching baby mamas and needy kids.

Some inmates seemed to think babies just happen. I once asked a buddy why he continued to sire kids, considering he didn't really want them and couldn't afford them. He shrugged and pointed to his crotch. "It do what it do!"

I noticed that inmates – usually low on society's economic ladder – share lifestyle traits with those on the top rung. They don't sweat the small stuff. Someone else cooks, cleans, and does the laundry and landscaping. Leisure time abounds, assuming you're not a workaholic. Inmates even have a driver and security whenever they travel. Many even enjoy being locked up with their buddies from the outside. They might as well be country club types hanging out and playing cards to their heart's delight. Some didn't mind the lifestyle at all.

Unlike the top one percent, though, this inmate population at Southern was a melting pot. This continually delighted me. Young brothers from the 'hood chatted and made trades with old white country fellows. Guys looked out for each other,

Hello, Home Camp!

and even for me, the rookie. For instance, I once unknowingly splashed beans and rice on my brand new sneakers, and a black guy brought it to my attention.

"Yo, get that! They're too new for that shit!" He even provided a napkin to wipe it off. "Here, use this – I ain't done nothin' to it."

This community vibe made me an extrovert for a while and probably kept a severe depression at bay. What's more, to mope on my bunk and not join in the fun would be to hand victory to The Man. Fuck that. Besides, I still hadn't learned to block out distractions enough to read a lot, anyway. Movement around the barracks in my peripheral vision and abrupt noise were a constant. I figured I might as well mingle and let the good times roll until I adapted.

All along, though, I felt the ache of longing, remorse, and regret. My sense of dread and loss tempered most laughs or other pleasures. I faced a long time of living in discomfort and loneliness, and this hurt. Starting every new day knowing I'd see the same people, eat the same tasteless food, and constantly endure the same people sucked. I lived with nothing to look forward to other than reading and a decent radio show once in a while.

Perhaps worst of all, my life in limbo meant a delay to make up for my past mistakes. This made wallowing in regret inevitable. Moments, when reading was impractical, were the worst – particularly at a urinal, with my eyes fixed on a dingy corner of the floor so I didn't accidentally look at someone wrong. Many months passed before optimism emerged, perhaps thanks to writing at least two hours a day. Any sense of accomplishment helped.

Visits and phone calls helped my mood, but they could be a bummer, too. Contact with friends and family felt like freedom, but after the time flew by I was back in the slammer, worse off for the taste of real life. As if I'd walked out of the courtroom and into custody all over again, every time.

Six hours of driving in a day separated me from most of my people, so I rarely asked for or received a visit. I placed phone calls frequently early on, but only once every couple of months towards the end. Long-distance calls were expensive, and standing at a payphone for twenty minutes sucked given the typical background noise. Inmates rarely keep their voices down out of courtesy.

Overhearing others on the phone could amuse, however. Some guys called their "old lady" multiple times a day, incurring enormous fees. Most dudes were more independent. The conventional wisdom seemed to be if a woman waits out your sentence be pleasantly surprised. Some openly argued on the phone, making eavesdroppers out of anyone nearby.

"Listen here, you bitch! Just 'cuz I'm in here now doesn't mean I can't smack you when I get out!" Minutes later, the same couple would be making menu arrangements for an upcoming visit. Ah, true love.

I preferred to raise my spirits with letters. I exchanged hundreds of them over my time, mostly to roughly a dozen regulars. These old friends and relatives were a link to intelligent life – a good conversation with people who got me – which was so rare in the joint. Some letters inspired quality journal entries, as I ranted about prison life or explored other tangents. Upon my release, several people apologized for never writing, afraid that a happy description of real life would only bum me out. I get this, but I dealt with deprivation and longing anyway, all the time. Any letter was a joy to read.

Besides direct letters, I kept my people abreast of my exploits with satirical Q&A's with myself and faux "news" stories. Friends scanned them and posted them to an email group, saving me from writing the same letters a dozen times. My pen pals reciprocated with printouts of interest, photos, and a ton of books.

I read books until I was cross-eyed, finding comfort in stories about people in worse situations than mine – anything to diminish my predicament. *The Naked and The Dead, Cold Mountain, Escape from Davao,* and *Nothing to Envy* (about North Korea). I also enjoyed books that took me away, like *Lonesome Dove,* and the whimsical *Goose Music,* which I luckily found in a box of shitty books in county jail. All Kurt Vonnegut were

Hello, Home Camp!

welcome escapes, and *Where'd You Go, Bernadette* is probably the funniest book I've ever read.

Another boost for my morale was seeing multiple inmates go home every week. Minimum security was the final stop in the system for many and hearing whoops of joy and seeing joyous embraces outside the gate – some after doing twenty years or more – was awesome. Knowing I'd be that guy someday helped me stay positive. Until then, however, I'd step on my dick multiple times, piss people off, and make more enemies.

CHAPTER SEVEN

Stepping on my Dick

A half-crazy guy named Melvin, who arrived on the bus from the bullpen with me, was among those I hung out with early on. One day I joined him and two other black dudes in a discussion of hometowns, which prompted me to joke. I said the rap star T.I. and I "Set the standard in Atlanta how to *git, git, git it!*"

This drew snickers, and Melvin correctly observed that I didn't set a very *high* standard, given where I ended up. Then he asked: "Whatchoo know about rap, anyway?"

Feeling the rush of fun conversation, I reminded him that my hometown is the hub of the "Dirty South," and even white dorks like me enjoy rap there because the ATL dominates the game. I then plunged overboard with my trash talking, loudly adding: "Like Goodie Mob says: 'What you niggas know about the Dirty South?"

This line — which I merely quoted — went over about as well as Joan Benoit Ramsey joke at a child beauty pageant. The guys I stood with grew cold.

Melvin warned, "Yo man, you need to watch what you say. People heard that shit and looked back."

Melvin and company seemed to know I didn't "mean anything" by my comment, but claimed not everyone would realize this when passersby repeated what they heard.

"Well, do me a favor and get my back if you hear anything," I said. As far as I could tell they agreed.

This taught me how delicate race relations can be in the

joint. Our small group soon parted ways with the problem minimized. Or so I thought.

The next morning I sat alone in the chow hall, since my dining partners had inhaled their food as usual and already left. I noticed Melvin seated not far away, glaring as if he hates me. I quickly looked away, with my stomach dropping. The next time I looked up, two others at Melvin's table – one who looked like Charles Manson – also stared, as if to say: "Oh, that guy?" Evidently I was a marked man for the second time in a week.

I spent the rest of the meal with my eyes down and slipped out of the room without incident. Melvin had turned on me, and my first test to forge my reputation at my home camp had arrived. I ran my tongue across my front teeth as I returned to my barracks, doubtful I'd survive three years with my originals intact.

For the next couple of days I felt like a descendant of a Grand Wizard. I occasionally came across Melvin and his boys, only to have them glower at me. Everyone seemed to whisper or point at me. I prepared for a confrontation. I tried to make friends like it was my job, figuring the more allies I had when shit went down, the better.

No matter how many dudes I befriended, however, loneliness nearly broke me. I was too green to assess the seriousness of my predicament or know who were trustworthy advisors. Any "fun" in this place was long gone. I even pondered applying for an emergency transfer to a dreaded medical camp so I could relax. But time ran out.

The following evening one of Melvin's buddies, Chang, appeared at my bunk and invited me to hang out with the crew. He seemed too excited. I sensed a set-up.

"Um, sure. Where you guys at?" I answered in the improper English I'd recently adopted.

"Back by the Red Door in A block," Chang replied.

I nearly gasped. The Red Door is both an object – an emergency exit, painted red – and a figurative expression. "Going to the Red Door" meant to fight.

I'd already heard many stories referring to the Red Door. At some prisons, inmates drew numbers out of a hat and fought there just for sport. The doors stand at the back of each barracks, far from the guard desk and in low-traffic areas, so it's the best place for shit to go down. Now it was my turn to go there. Time to grow up — at age forty-six.

A knot formed in my throat. Adrenaline rushed through me as I locked my locker. I took a deep breath and embarked for the Door in an adjacent barracks. I felt glad for the warning instead of getting jumped. I wandered into the foreign territory. Guys I'd yet to meet seemed to stop and stare at me as if word had gotten out.

Melvin was of average size, and I expected to at least hold my own against him. He would at least feel some sharp elbows. Not so if Chang or others jumped in. I suddenly noticed the hard plastic shower sandals I had on would make keeping my footing difficult to throw a solid punch. A rookie error, too late to correct.

Melvin greeted me with a smile as I approached and invited me to sit down. I did so, but on the edge of a chair, coiled and ready. Evidently he *did* only want to talk and make peace. But suddenly Chang took an interest in my relatively fancy glasses and reached for them. I drew back and unleashed Scorpio Eyes on the motherfucker.

I bugged out my eyes, cocked my head, just like I practiced back in county jail with Nick. Chang backed off immediately and stammered an apology, his eyes nearly as wide as mine. I then cast The Eyes towards Melvin. He also took me seriously and extended open hands forward, as if to say: *easy, fella!* Too bad Nick couldn't be there to laugh his ass off.

Turned out Melvin merely wished to introduce me — the strange dude with the quick mouth — to his neighbors. His coldness and aggression towards me over the past couple of days was mostly in my head. I learned that foul moods descend often in prison, which has little to do with me.

Considering this, my Scorpio Eyes stunt embarrassed me, but I played it off as a joke. Soon enough I relaxed and joined six or eight chaps in telling crude jokes and drug stories. As I sat socializing, they repeated an important prison lesson for me.

Chang walked away briefly, revealing a tattoo on the back of his neck that said "LAOS." I asked Melvin about it, and he explained, "He's half Thai and half whatever that shit on his neck says."

Upon Chang's return I asked, "So, you're half Thai and half Laotian?"

"Who told you that?"

I immediately pointed at Melvin, who laughed and then protested. "Damn, why you wanna rat me out?"

I had snitched. That's how sensitive the topic is in prison, even over seemingly insignificant detail. "Yo man," Chang emphasized, "real men don't squeal about nothin', no matter how small."

"If a nigga chirps about little shit, he'll also tell tales about *big* shit." Melvin added.

Being discreet is of utmost importance on the inside. It creates trust among the honorable, although that term is relative in the joint. The correct response to prying questions is always: "I got my ways," or "Don't worry about that." Chang's lesson would prove highly ironic down the road.

Upon returning to my bunk, I felt exhausted and emotionally beaten. Despite my successful encounter, I was tired of being on edge and alone. Given my lack of serenity, I might as well have been dealing drugs again. I longed for comfort and diversion – like music provides. Fortunately, that very evening a local blues singer/guitarist was playing in the chow hall, so I sauntered over to check it out.

The chow hall – basically a large shotgun shack – served functions besides a place to plop down lousy food for inmates. Religious gatherings, AA meetings, and offender visitation during bad weather were held there. Linoleum flooring and fluorescent lights lent the feel of a church basement, along with cheap curtains adorning small windows. Inmates could thank God for these, the camp's sole decorating touch. Or the chaplain, at least, who ordered them.

I scored one of the few remaining chairs before the festivities began. As one of the few white people in attendance, I sensed a few disapproving glances coming from black guys. Probably just my paranoia though. I misread a lot of situations early in my sentence.

The chow hall tables filled a back corner to allow for inmate seating, facing a miked-up podium and a Casio keyboard. Three neatly arranged rows of chairs faced the stage, at a ninety-degree angle from the audience. Apparently a mobile Church of God had set up shop. A dozen smartly dressed civilians of both sexes sat there, avoiding eye contact with the convicts like an uncomfortable jury in a courtroom.

These visitors, in their thirties and forties seemed too full of vigor, like a movie director had just yelled "action!" A portly, middle-aged dude took the microphone, praised the Lord for the beautiful evening, and led an opening prayer. I half expected to hear a time-share sales pitch next. I thought this was a concert.

After the opening prayer, however, the preacher strapped on a guitar and played *Since I Found Jesus, I Lost the Blues*. The guitarist lost a lot of blues licks, too, if he ever had them. Next, a different chubby brother took the stage and passionately belted out a song. He also preached how the Lord had "filled me up tonight!" The endangered seams of his shirt agreed. He'd definitely filled up with something.

But I soon delighted in the occasion's spirit, the bait and switch that got me in the door notwithstanding. Someday visiting a gospel-singing church had always intrigued me. The boring Methodist ceremonies of my youth without clapping, hollering, or head-bopping were boring. This full-blown African-American church experience in the chow hall crossed off an essential bucket list item for me while being locked up. Can I get an Amen?

A steady stream of inmates grabbed the mic. "God is now in charge of my life," one of them professed. "It's time for me to get my shit together!"

They greeted this and similar platitudes with "Amen" and "Tell it!" Preachers laid hands on worshipers. One of the prison barbers, called "Tip," stood up and raised the passion in the room even higher.

"I love Jesus Christ now more than ever!"

He burst into a popular hymn with soul and skill that raised eyebrows and energy all around. Several worshippers rose and moved behind him to provide backup vocals. The usually sterile chow hall suddenly hosted a joyous, boisterous celebration. The sky through the windows in the background burst with the colors of a lovely sunset. Even the most dour inmates grinned and let loose the occasional "Hallelujah."

Tip sat and dabbed the sweat from his forehead following his vocal turn, but the choir remained front and center. They ripped through another hymnal standard while professing love for the Lord . A rotund visitor pounded on the keyboard, and a dreadlocked gentleman slapped bongos. They thrust dozens of hands in the air like they *did* care.

This mobile congregation cared about our poor locked-up souls. The beauty of it, paired with my pent-up emotions caused me to weep a bit. But not find Jesus. That will never happen.

Impure thoughts about one singer descended on me. A beautiful and shapely twenty-something woman I'll call Vision. She wore a revealing blouse and tight pants that demanded every sex-starved inmate's attention. God bless her impertinence. The Lord had bestowed upon Vision a booty to be proud of and hiding it was a fool's errand, anyway. She appeared to conceal two cantaloupe halves in the seat of her pants.

She showed the most enthusiasm among her group; frequently thrust her arms aloft in praise, which emphasized her blessedly full bosom. She drew sinful lust from many, and some failed to hide shameful gestures like adjusting their crotch area to look cool to other inmates. Most just stared, mesmerized. They craved Vision more than a tipsy trophy wife yearns for a crab cake at a Hamptons divorce celebration. And she knew it. But her eyes stayed focused straight ahead the whole time.

Eventually the music portion of the program gave way to redundant fire and brimstone preaching, punctuated by occasional keyboard notes. A tag team of preachers got on holy oratory rolls, although few of them cited scriptures or made coherent arguments for conversion. Each loudly proclaimed the greatness of God and the infernal fate of non-believers while pouring sweat and dabbing it away. A textbook move for evangelists that holler, I thought. Or a stall tactic to come up with a line that didn't sound like the previous three.

Seemingly hours into this, The Bishop – the headliner – took the mic. His words carried extra weight because he once did a six-year sentence, the last part of it right there at Southern Correctional. The spirit in the room reached ear-splitting heights, making me glad to be sitting toward the back. The Bishop exchanged high-fives with worshipers.

The preaching often veered into stand-up comedy territory, although the jokes were stock and unfunny. The congregation laughed and whooped it up despite the lack of humor, just like any Oprah audience. The Bishop's Bernie Mac impression was funny, though, but not funnier than the big dollar sign on his hankie.

The service climaxed with an endless prayer, punctuated by The Bishop hollering for offenders to come up and become saved. The choir belted out inspiration while preachers laid hands upon the sinners. I felt like a jackass for ridiculing bible-thumpers in the past. Who was I to say? These downtrodden folks seemed delivered, at least for a while. And speaking of deliveries, a true miracle then descended.

Three civilians emerged with boxes of genuine Krispy Kreme donuts stacked to their chins. Inmates scooted into three lines to receive six heaven-sent "sweets from the street" each. No wonder the room was full, and no one left early. I devoured three of the sugary blessings on the spot and placed the other three in a paper towel to smuggle out and enjoy later. Praise the Lord indeed.

"Whatchoo want for a donut?"

I heard three variations of this question before I even reached my bunk. Turns out lots of guys knew donuts would hit the trade market, so they blew off the church service. My canteen account was still empty, so I traded for six instant coffee servings and a pack of Ramen noodles. Wheeling and dealing violated official policy, but the rush of getting away with something came over me. Only as time stretched on did I learn the guards never cared about the trading.

By sheer luck I'd sold my donuts before the market became saturated. Soon people tried to sell donuts to me. Next time I'd act early again. I was catching on to penitentiary life, but I still had a ton to learn.

The most popular reading option for typical inmates, besides pop fiction and muscle magazines, was *Mugshots*, a bizarre social registry for the downscale. It kept people abreast of the exploits of local jailbirds and usual suspects – their peers – on the outside. The latest editions were highly sought-after, and sparked top-notch gossip and stories about the lawbreakers. I marveled at the attractiveness of some of the women who landed in those pages, usually for DUI or larceny. I tried to keep my guilty pleasure of reading *Mugshots* to a minimum, though, so as to devote time to my own reading material.

I've always loved magazines. Prison revealed how much I took for granted the artsy aspect of mags like *Vanity Fair, Esquire,* and *GQ*. The colorful and creative nature of the ads and fashion spreads offset the gloominess of lockup. The wit of *New Yorker* cartoons provided a respite from endless locker room humor.

Friends and family made sure I received many subscriptions, but they didn't start until later into my sentence. Once they did, I noted that each monthly magazine seemed to arrive every two weeks, just like on the street. The speed at which time passes was cause for celebration for a change. Before my reading stash started piling up, however, seeking others almost cost me dearly.

I found a sizable stack of magazines on a dayroom table while wandering around the barracks building. A dayroom is a "common" area, so I assumed issues of *Rolling Stone, National*

Geographic, and *Road and Track*, etc., were fair game. I hauled about ten of them to my bunk, giddy at my good fortune.

Soon my neighbor Billy came by and noticed my booty, so to speak. "Wow, where did those come from?"

"I found them in a dayroom. I'm pretty psyched."

"You didn't 'find' anything. Those belong to Ice," Billy said. He was not referring to the federal agency.

Turned out Ice was a huge, crazy-looking guy who "ran the block" over there. The magazines sat unsullied on his table because no one else was dumb enough to touch them.

"Yeah, you might wanna find him and confess what you did," Billy suggested. "He might be cool about it. Sometimes he's a nice guy."

So I grabbed Ice's reading material, gulped, and set off to find him. Soon I stood at his bunk. Although I stood on thin ice, this sure didn't describe him. He was about six-foot one, weighed at least two-forty, and sported a pony-tail that was menacing, like his steely blue eyes. I later learned this was why he'd been dubbed Ice. Insides trembling, I held onto his bed frame as I introduced myself, touching a towel hanging on it.

"First of all, take your hand off my towel," Ice growled.

I yanked my hand down. I swallowed hard and explained my predicament in an octave higher than usual. He paused a few beats before speaking.

"So let me get this straight," he drawled, through a frown. "You wanted to apologize for touching my shit while you were touching my shit?"

My next words are a mystery, perhaps because I stammered them.

Steely blue eyes studied me carefully and lowered his head as he grimaced. I prepared to run. "You're new at this shit, aren't you?" He laughed.

And with this, another thinking man's bruiser adopted me as a project. We began hanging out. Also, Ice offered full access to his magazines, "As long as you don't bend them or pass them around."

Ice was an oddity. He was both a brute (avid weightlifter), and an artist (a fine guitar player). His hometown was San

Diego, 2,500 miles away. He possessed a college degree in a population where fewer than ten percent had even stepped foot inside a college. Ice said he was on track for a good life, but a prosecutor didn't buy a self-defense excuse and gave him thirty years for second-degree murder instead. Ice seemed to have made peace with this, though, and remained upbeat despite twenty years down.

Soon after I met Ice, a prime bunk location opened in his barracks. The big guy turned into a real estate agent.

"You should move in here," Ice told me. "It's a good school district."

By this, he meant the bunk occupied a good space in which to read and write. Low traffic, relatively quiet. Peacefulness in a prison barracks is elusive and precious, and once achieved, Ice aimed to keep it that way. He needed a chill guy to replace a departing loud one to help keep his barracks low-key. The process was like removing dead underbrush to prevent forest fires, or a teacher separating disruptive pals in a classroom. I felt flattered that Ice chose me.

A prison barracks is highly susceptible to a "cricket effect." Multiple loud and inconsiderate guys in a sleeping area draw nearby similar asswipes into a symphony of chaos. The more of them around, the louder it gets. Especially in minimum security, where most want to stay out of trouble to keep their work-release privileges.

In medium security joints, most inmates faced long sentences. Many didn't hesitate to intimidate disruptive neighbors or beat them down. Would-be "crickets" shut the fuck up.

Anyway, I seized the opportunity to move. This involved pleading with the sergeant on duty, which wasn't hard to do at Southern. My new neighbors seemed happy to have me, but I was ten times happier than them. Enhanced serenity was nearly as important as breathing to me.

Soon after settling into my new living area I took a job as a janitor. My height allowed me to wipe down locker tops without a stepladder. My reach made mopping the floor easier. I was the right tool for the job. This humbling drudgery usually lasted only thirty minutes and allowed for lots of free time and hot lunches on weekdays. This beat off-camp workers settled for lousy sack lunches while working all day. I welcomed the sense of accomplishment and the workout of a job. Before that, taking three showers a week qualified as my most strenuous daily activity.

Pride and exercise aside, I soon became an "executive janitor." I hired an inmate subcontractor to do my job for a stamp per day. I still profited seventy cents a week and earned the gain time, which allows inmates release at the low end of their sentence range.

Many janitors in lockup showed criminal thought patterns on the job. Instead of doing good work and taking care of their fellow felons, they did the bare minimum to avoid a reprimand. For instance, one guy failed to keep paper towels stocked. He figured he was screwing over our overlords instead of his buddies who needed to dry their hands. I decided wasting hot water was a much better way to stick it to the state than shoddy janitor work.

Push buttons controlled the shower stream at Southern instead of hot and cold knobs. In theory, this allowed the bosses to set the water temperature. In reality, however, inmates controlled it.

When the water was too hot – almost always – dudes showering turned the bathroom's large industrial sink faucets wide open. Scalding, propane-heated water blasted out at five gallons a minute, which cooled off the shower stream. These faucets stayed open for three straight hours during busy times, in four separate shower areas. At least one hundred and fifty thousand gallons of hot water literally went down the drain every month.

I hated this waste for the sake of the environment, but North Carolina should have provided real shower knobs. Instead, their effort to save a few bucks at the expense of civility toward inmates backfired and cost them dearly. Serves them right, but I digress.

My Executive Janitor title may sound glamorous, but it

came with headaches. I still had to deal with the janitorial stockroom Nazi, "Chilly Willy." He was a middle-aged, dentally challenged career inmate who showed a zest for life just the same. He owned a catchphrase: "Wiiiind me up!" and often danced a little jig while moseying through the yard. I once heard him ask: "Why is everyone here so sad?" Chilly's positivity was rare for aging inmates but had its limits

Chilly's job brought out his surly side. He worked as the stockroom clerk and distributor of cleaning solutions, paper towels, and other janitorial supplies. The dude defended the always ample inventory as if he paid for the shit personally. He'd react to a request for an extra pack of paper towels like I was trying to sell them in the yard or like I'd asked for his last front tooth. Prison life was stressful enough without Chilly's bullshit.

At first I suspected his disdain for my janitorial needs was race-based; that he relished sticking it to Whitey. But he tormented black guys like my associate janitor too. I investigated Chilly's motives further. I asked the CO in charge.

"Hey, do y'all keep inventory on the stockroom stuff?"

"Hell, no. They don't pay me enough for that," Officer Bellinger replied. "No one cares."

Chilly Willie was drunk with power.

This led to a cat-and-mouse game between Chilly and me. I sensed when he was nowhere near the storage closet and got a CO to open it. I'd load a large trash bag so full of supplies I had to drag it back to my work area. The risk of Chilly spotting me made me sweat with adrenaline.

Dealing with Chilly was serious business for me, but others found his act highly entertaining. I learned this one evening when I attempted a supply raid. I asked a CO for storage access, but instead of unlocking it he called Chilly to the closet on the intercom. The CO knew a rant from Chill was imminent, which meant big laughs. The personable Sergeant Dellwood didn't miss the chance either. He showed up just in time.

"Biff, you know you 'sposed to get this shit in the mornin', not now!" Chilly bellowed. "I gotta come all the way down here! They prolly fuckin' up my checkers game this minute, goddammit!"

The two officers remained stone-faced, as if they took Chilly's complaints seriously.

"Well, if you'd give me enough stuff in the morning, we wouldn't be here right now." I countered. "No one cares how many paper towels we use, you know."

Despite my logic, Dellwood turned on me and deadpanned: "Why do you have to make Chilly's job harder?"

I stifled a laugh and played along: "This is an outrage! *He* makes *my* job harder! Who's running this place anyway, Chilly Willy?!"

Chilly spat a string of curses, but still surrendered the supplies.

"You need to follow the rules, goddammit!" he shouted as he pimp-rolled away. "And you need to pay my losses on the checkerboard!"

I headed back to my barracks, pleased to be well-stocked but reeling from the verbal abuse of a convict that does his job by-the-book. I laughed. This is exactly what I expected to be doing with my life at age forty-seven.

CHAPTER EIGHT

The Day-to-Day

Prison meant three things to me before I experienced it: violence, limitless sleeping, and reading all you want. In minimum security I learned only the last of these is really true. Rules at different prison camps varied, but weekday mornings at Southern sucked for sleeping. Inmates that didn't leave the camp for work were cast into the yard from 7:30 to 11:00 to loiter like homeless people.

This was ostensibly to make way for the janitors to clean the barracks, even though they typically finished cleaning by eight-thirty. I suspected the real reason inmates were forbidden to lounge on bunks all morning was so outside jobs remained filled. Guys were more willing to work picking up roadside litter, for instance, if they had to get out of bed anyway. A surprising number of dudes wanted even the lowliest jobs, mostly to change their scenery and add purpose to a day.

Keeping a journal covered this just fine for me, and took top priority. But getting kicked outside every morning made writing more difficult. Instead of reclining on my bed with a clipboard, I became a perverse "free-lance writer" roaming the camp to find a suitable place to set up shop. Sitting at a picnic table, often in chilly temperatures, didn't cut it.

Writing at a table in the tiny library could work, but being in close quarters with often smelly inmates made concentrating difficult. So did the typical commotion.

"Hey, Biff! You want in?" The inmate librarian asked me

this often. He used his check-out counter to deal cards, usually blackjack or casino.

"Not today," I said once. I'm looking for a thesaurus."

"A what?" The librarian wasn't kidding.

Usually, I'd drop in to one of two barracks, technically open only to those who had beds there. One was for the kitchen guys, the other for the highest level work-release inmates. I could steal an hour or two in these places before being run out by a patrolling CO and threatened with a write-up. When they came through I'd appear to be deep in thought, and sometimes they'd let me stay put. Other times a cool guard would wink and just let me slide.

Besides the morning eviction hassle, weekdays on the camp were pleasant. The vast majority of my neighbors slogged to off-camp jobs, so tranquility was easier to find. I came to love weekdays, but dread weekends, holidays, and snow days. The two-week Christmas vacation that most guys enjoyed drove me batty because the place stayed full. Thank god I never did time in medium security, where few inmates *ever* left the camp for work.

Donning my finest outfit for the 2012 Christmas photo

Some of my inmate brethren worked on various county Department of Transportation crews. They answered questions I've long had about road construction projects. Such as the stop sign and walkie-talkie people directing traffic when one lane is closed on a two-lane road workers. I wondered if those are coveted positions, to which workers advance. Or are they new hires, placed there because they may get run over? Turns out it's the latter, or the flaggers may be up there as punishment. Also, one reason six workers stand around watching as one works a shovel is they're often inmates earning a dollar a day, so who cares?

COs at minimum security didn't patrol these crews – inmates were supervised by civilian DOT workers instead. They were known to park for naps or simply drive around if they didn't feel like working. Inmates with generous bosses were sometimes treated to fast food or smoked without fear of a write-up. Some cons even got to steal away for quickies with significant others or pick up contraband hidden for them to smuggle into the camp.

Even guys who labored on guard-monitored litter crews enjoyed side benefits, and rightly so. Each day they walked upwards of eight miles of uneven roadside, in heat and cold, bending over to pick shit up. On the plus side, they often found discarded porn, cigarettes, weed and other odds and ends, easily slipped past casual inspections from COs upon their return.

I liked to imagine the story behind some of these findings, playing out a movie scene in my head. For example:

:: A couple riding on a freeway in a Chevy Camaro. The woman waves an old issue of *Barely Legal* in the air::

Woman: "You bastard! Another porno mag? In the *car,* where junior can find it?! What the hell is wrong with you?"

:: The man tries to grab the magazine from the woman. The car swerves. ::

Woman: "I'll show you, you sick fuck!"

:: She throws the magazine out the window. ::

———

On-camp jobs allowed fringe benefits for inmates, too. Clothes house workers profited by providing personal laundry service, for instance. Dozens of inmates paid five stamps a week to have laundry picked up, washed, folded, and returned the same day. The clothes house staff profited, and less dirty laundry was trucked away for cleaning, which saved money for the prison system. No wonder authorities looked the other way as clothes workers criss-crossed the camp all day with mesh laundry bags slung over their shoulders.

This laundry hustle saved guys like me from the official exchange process. Hiring a clothes house dude kept us from suffering early morning lines for clothes, outdoors. More importantly, we kept the same personal wardrobe. This sure beat rotating boxers and socks with everyone else and sometimes ending up with clothes in poor condition. Keeping my own laundry allowed for my greatest prison comfort: a plush, full-sized bath towel, inherited from a pal who transferred. State-issued towels were small and coarse – basically a defoliator. Burying my face in a real towel after a shower always felt like a win.

———

Clothes house workers enjoyed healthy incomes on the side, but crooked kitchen workers made the most. They enjoyed a storeroom full of food and ingredients to swipe and resell to hungry inmates. Powdered milk – protein for weightlifters – drew tons of customers. Sugar was also a big revenue generator.

The kitchen theft level fluctuated based on CO crackdowns. If the heat was on, chow hall entrees had plenty of meat in them. If kitchen guards were being lax, the main ingredient in dishes became scarce. An extra serving station in the chow line to make up for this would've been nice.

The Day-to-Day

"Get the chicken that's supposed to be in your pot pie right here — one stamp per clump!"

Somehow kitchen meat thieves weren't camp pariahs, since they basically stole straight from everybody's stomach. Instead, since dinner was over by five o'clock, "home cooking" picked up the slack. Kitchen guys supplied the best ingredients, so they were heroes. COs never cared what got eaten in the evenings, let alone sniffed out stolen food.

The dayrooms came alive in the evenings, with food as the centerpiece of the social life. Convicts donned latex gloves and got busy prepping. A typical concoction included chopped up onions, pickles, and multiple meat products. Chili sauces, squeeze-cheese, crushed chips, and Ramen noodles often filled out the ingredient list.

This stew would be dumped into trash bags, mixed, and then served on tortillas or spread on round flat bread, making a "pizza." A couple packets of mayonnaise would often be added to the final, microwaved product for good measure. The fat and sodium in these dishes could clog the arteries of people merely walking by.

Most aspects of North Carolina's prisons are perfectly humane. For instance, the bedding and clothing were in good shape. Most chow hall options, however, qualified as gastronomical abuse. Healthful eating was practically impossible. The best way to describe the prison menu is starch, fat, sugar, fat, starch, sugar, with a hard boiled egg, apple, or banana available now and then. Only guys lucky enough to qualify for a low-fat, low-sodium diet for medical reasons ate decently.

The most common main dish was a processed patty of beef, chicken, or fish. The pinnacle of these was the onion beef, which is worse than the worst burger you'll ever eat. Beef patty variations spiraled down in quality from there, past the Salisbury steak and meatloaf, to the aptly-nicknamed "dead wrong." Technically this was a beef patty, but smelled like road kill. It tastes like when you tongue too deep while eating ass, with a cleaning spray finish. Even the stray cats refused to eat it.

Shit on a Shingle was the other dish deserving of a nickname. This is a margarine-saturated biscuit, covered in "beef" tips and gravy that looked like sheep diarrhea and smelled like dog food. Other breakfast meats included a sausage that resembled an uncooked jumbo hot dog or giant stick of pink chalk. Sausage also came in patties, the sight of which renewed my despair for being locked up. The common saying is "no one wants to see how the sausage is made." In prison, you don't want to see the sausage, *period*.

Beverages were limited to tap water, iced tea, or a Kool-Aid knockoff drink that was served with rumors of stomach-damaging additives. A half pint of real milk came with every breakfast, and when their expiration dates showed a new month it always felt like a small victory. When stale bran flakes weren't on the menu I gave the milk away for future considerations. Take care of someone, they'll take care of you. I called this the "favor bank."

Prison dining options weren't entirely hostile, however. Decent breakfast options came about twice a week, including real bacon. Once every few weeks we enjoyed "chicken-on-the-bone," meaning unprocessed and as it's sold at restaurants. This "real" food on the menu ignited frenzied trading among inmates, sometimes two days before it was served. "Yo, I'll give you five smokes for your chicken," was a common offer.

The brightest aspect of prison dining were baked desserts, usually served daily. It's hard to feel abused by the system when enjoying an excellent confection. Eating cake three or four times a week seemed strange. On the outside I ate cake perhaps four times a *year*, usually at some celebration. Now I'm chowing down on fluffy, iced goodness practically all the time.

Occasionally these desserts ceased, because baking is a tough skill to master. The camp baker at Southern was sent to solitary once, and during his month-long absence we endured white bread and canned fruit instead of biscuits, cookies, and cakes. Prison can be hardcore like that.

The staple of my diet was oatmeal, but not the overly-sweetened chow hall version. I scored brown bags full of it from crooked kitchen help. I ate it plain, or sometimes with a banana or chopped apple, every evening. For some reason this bothered people. "You, like, don't even put sugar in it, or *anything*?" I didn't need a sugar buzz, I needed to fill my stomach during the thirteen-hour gap between dinner and breakfast.

I welcomed the plain flavor of oatmeal, the opposite of the state-inflicted diet of sodium and sugar. Oats cost less than ten cents a serving at Southern, a price far below any canteen items. This price soared when I was assigned to other camps where the kitchen storerooms were closely-policed. I lost weight like a prisoner or something.

My oatmeal habit made me subject to a write-up if a CO wanted to be a dick. Once, mere hours after I received a delivery, they randomly searched my locker. The CO who did the honors was easygoing, yet operated mostly by-the-book. He dug deeper on his inspection than most guards did, eventually getting on his knees. I tried to distract him with sports conversation.

He eventually stood up, holding a bulging bag of black market oats. He paused and scratched his head, seemingly taking forever to speak. I gulped.

"This sure is a lot of oatmeal you have here."

Normally glib and quick on my feet, I said ... nothing. Not a damned thing because no plausible excuse existed. To speak would only insult the guy's intelligence. I was either busted or not. I made a mental note to make friends with more guards.

"Well," he eventually said. "A man's gotta eat, I guess."

He checked my name off his list and bid me goodnight. Amazingly, he didn't even make me throw the oats away. He didn't say this at the time, but I will now on his behalf: *Just tell your friends not all cops are dicks!*

Locker searches in honor grade were usually harmless, especially if the COs liked you. I followed early advice and made sure they did. I respectfully chatted with them, laughed at their jokes, and let them read my many magazines. I even sucked up to the one that bragged about having a high school diploma.

Guards and I shared common plights. The pain of being surrounded by unruly louts all day. Vaguely fearing for our safety. Counting the days until our release, or pension, from prison.

My favorite of the men in blue was Sergeant Dellwood, a short, stocky, and low-key man of about fifty. He was an exception to typically self-important prison administrators – like a cool teacher at a strict school. By contrast, most sergeants were unhelpful at best. For instance, many refused to facilitate an inmate bunk change. Dellwood, on the other hand, helped a man when possible and treated us with respect. He swapped my bunk multiple times, but not for nothing.

"Ahh, Phillips! Just came by to chat, I assume." Dellwood might say, from behind his desk. He knew I'd come for a bunk switch, but he always made me work for it. The deadpan sergeant put me through a mock interrogation to pry life stories and prison rants from me. This spiced up a mundane evening for both of us, so I happily obliged.

"I noticed MDMA trafficking on your record," Dellwood said. "What's so great about that stuff anyway?"

"Well, it's like pushing a button that puts you in the best mood you've ever been in."

"So clearly Chilly Willy is not currently using MDMA. Have you broken into his supply closet lately? Why can't you respect his authority?"

And so it went. We'd talk about politics, sports, and those locked up with me. Sometimes a CO who was hanging out (the office also served as their break room) joined in the act. These visits with Dellwood helped counter my persistent self-loathing in those days. The Sergeant got my jokes and appreciated my company.

My case manager once stumbled into one of these bullshitting sessions when she clocked out for the day. She ended up hanging out for half an hour, during which time I convinced her to grant me privilege level promotion. This was the prison equivalent of running into your boss at a cocktail party and leaving with a raise. *And* Dellwood granted me a critical bunk switch.

I floated back to the barracks through the dark, empty yard that evening in triumph, with arms aloft. For the moment I wasn't a hapless inmate and failure at life; I could still win friends and influence people.

The Day-to-Day

Some COs fit the stereotype of assholes. Leatherman, case in point, was a tall, thick-necked bully. Old-timers claimed he was once nice, but he must have undergone a charisma bypass at some point. He stalked the barracks wearing a smirk, randomly enforcing oft-ignored rules such as one pillow per inmate. I suspended my policy of sucking up to COs in his case. The guy was that big of a jerk.

Sleeping at five-thirty one morning I heard a crack that carried the jolt of a cattle prod. I shot awake to see a sergeant, who rarely ventured into the barracks, ready to hit my bed frame with his flashlight again. "Get up!" he barked. "Go to the dayroom, it's a shakedown." I'd somehow slept through thirty guys evacuating the room.

Mass searches – rare in honor grade – were usually in response to an outbreak of a cell phone or the dangerous synthetic drug K2 being found. Sometimes the warden just felt like it or they were instructed to do so by higher-ups. I endured only two full-scale shakedowns in thirty-five months.

For this one I strolled into a packed dayroom, reminded of the introvert motto: "Hell is other people in the morning." And not only were my tender sensibilities violated, the room was full of goddamn criminals. I somehow found a seat, and whatever song was in my head at the time changed to the Grateful Dead's *Shakedown Street*.

Fretful faces filled the room, worried about ruin coming from a locker search. Cunning cons crafted solutions to limit liability and cut deals with neighbors. "Turbo," my next door neighbor, hit me up.

"Get on in there before me," he explained. "After they're done with you, take all the shit from under my bed and put it in your locker. I'll make it worth your while."

Turbo harbored craft materials for making necklaces. The guards might confiscate it all, and possibly give Turbo a write-up. I agreed to save him, but for five stamps in exchange. Truth is I never liked the guy.

My locker contained contraband too. I possessed bananas and peanut butter from the chow hall that a guard would throw away, but his suspicion would go up. Of much greater concern were porn pics, a roll of packing tape I'd borrowed, and a few magnets. Book and magazine limit violations existed too, of course. I could be nailed for that any time since only ten were allowed, total.

If the guard that searched me went by the book, multiple write-ups could devastate me. The thought of getting browned-down or even backing up my release date left me short of breath. This freak-out woke me up better than the coffee I hadn't yet had a chance to make.

The dayroom had become host to a twisted speed-dating event. Offenders formed a line, and the man in front was paired with the next available CO. The happy new couple first moved to the bathroom for a strip search, followed by the locker and bed areas. Before I found my match, however, I nearly shit my pants.

Nervousness triggers my spastic colon. I had to *go*. I raced to the bathroom full of dudes suffering strip searches complete with ball sack lifting. Luckily I'd become comfortable with taking dumps in front of people by this point in my sentence, because no stalls provided privacy. Three COs endured this particular eruption of mine, including the aforementioned Leatherman. I felt awful for three nearby inmates that became collateral damage, but at least the guards were pained by my blasting.

"It's Mother Nature's fault," I mumbled, to no one in particular.

Soon my own CO blind date was close at hand. I tried to time my spot in line to draw an easygoing guard. Eight of them worked the rotation, so an eighty-seven percent chance I'd draw an inspector other than ... Leatherman! *Of course* I was paired with him. Hopefully he didn't take my bathroom performance personally a few minutes earlier. Practically no one liked Leatherman, so perhaps he didn't realize I hated him. Otherwise, sucking up to him could backfire.

"Hey, sorry you had to start your shift off like this," I

The Day-to-Day

bullshitted as we walked to my bunk area. Most COs disliked shakedowns as much as inmates, perhaps unless they were perverts and enjoyed "nuts and butts" exams. "How about this weather we're having?"

Leatherman stayed silent and maintained his smirk, but at least he didn't say anything mean. We arrived at my bunk, and the moment of truth.

I swung my locker open, which exposed a paperback of *Catch-22* (swear to god). It sat on the middle shelf, staring Leatherman in the face. I'd forgotten to worry about it. Two hardcore porn pics were hidden inside, laminated with the packing tape. Hours earlier I was too lazy to hide them deep in my paper piles instead of in my current read. I'd seen guys written up for porn possession before, and they suffered steep penalties.

The loaded *Catch-22* stared at me. It seemed to flash a beacon for the cop: *Look here!* Beads of sweat formed on my forehead as Leatherman picked up the book and waved it around. I scrambled to think of an excuse for when the porn fluttered out. Then, instead of opening it, he tossed it on my bed and moved to the next item.

"You're way over the book limit," he growled. "If I find this many next time, that's a write-up."

"Fair enough. Thanks for the leniency."

"I'm glad some of you actually read," he grunted. "Maybe you'll learn something." Never have I enjoyed such condescension.

The CO counted my stamp inventory (limit twenty-five), picked through other stuff, and threw away the fruit and peanut butter he found.

"What are you, running a produce stand?" he asked with a smirk. This was hardly Hedberg-level wit, but I laughed loudly anyway as I wiped the brown from my nose. My great relief made it easy to act like Leatherman was the most charming person on earth.

He finished his probe, ignoring the bottom level because searching it would mean real on-his-knees effort. The upshot? My buddy got his packing tape back.

Leatherman left my books alone, but he took a clipboard

that I used multiple times a day. I considered this a small price to pay. As soon as he sauntered away and I grabbed Turbo's craft supplies from under his bed and stuffed them in my locker. I felt like I'd stuck it to The Man.

Hardly anyone found serious trouble from this shakedown. Conventional wisdom said the raid was mostly theater for the higher-ups in prison administration. The captain who ran the place even let us lounge around the rest of the morning as if it were a weekend. I still felt uneasy though, like a stray cat kicked by one person and then pet by another. Such was life in the Big House.

A write-up for possession of porn could be a ticket to the hole, which is ironic. The "solitary" part of that confinement means inmates can masturbate with impunity. I once heard an old-timer call a guard's bluff to send him there. "The hole don't scare me," he declared. "I ain't afraid of a good time!"

The official ban of pornography went hand-in-hand with the prison masturbation ban. Both policies were to protect the sensibilities of female COs, but this is just as silly as pasties on a stripper's nipples. Inmates that are pent-up sexually are counterproductive to everyone's safety. Prison is tense enough already.

What's more, mailrooms censored nudity of any kind in magazines like *Esquire* and *Vanity Fair*. Once, they red-flagged a crudely-drawn couple in bed that illustrated a silly sex advice column. Even small pics of '60s Euro-babes sunbathing topless were forbidden. Worse, the mailroom staff wouldn't remove the "offending" pages and give the magazine to its owner; they banned the entire issue. Subscribers were required to either mail it elsewhere – for about five dollars – or have it "destroyed."

Still more ridiculous, magazine censors removed ads containing fragrance samples, lest an inmate enjoy a literal whiff of pleasure. At least the mail Nazis forwarded the magazines to its addressee afterward. Why they couldn't do the same

The Day-to-Day

with the ones that showed nudity remained a mystery. Also unclear was where the pornography line was drawn.

American Curves, a typo-riddled rag that made *Maxim* seem high-brow by comparison, was an inmate favorite. It was essentially old-school print porn, except the models concealed their areolas and wore microscopic thongs. These photo spreads were far more suggestive than a topless actress sunbathing in Cannes.

"Jack pics" were also officially approved. These are three-by-five prints of barely-clad, average-looking girls in slutty poses. Most of these pics were of random women, ordered from crude catalogs for fifty-cents each. They got traded like baseball cards. Locker doors in the barracks were often covered with them – right next to pics of an inmate's wife and kids.

Stopping to admire a guy's locker pic collection was common. One day I stopped dead, amazed at the beauty of a girl on the locker of a new resident. She was way hotter than the typical model. Then, mid-boner, came a voice: "Watch it, bro, *that's my wife!*"

"Oh, my bad!" I replied, and moved on.

In retrospect, I was not at fault. The dude knew passersby like to look. He also displayed no pics of the wife with his kids on his locker, or even shots of her reasonably-clothed. In that case I'd have been less of a horn dog voyeur. Pics of wives and girlfriends bring out rare manners in inmates, holding back on saying how they'd like to fuck the hot ones. I decided the guy likes to watch his wife get banged, or at least they swing. I made a mental note to slip her a note at the next visiting session.

I once saw a fight over a jack pic. One hustler had a pile of pics to sell or trade, and the other was checking them out.

"I need to keep this one," the buyer said.

"Cool. That'll be two stamps."

"No man, I ain't paying for it," pointing to the pic. "This is my old lady."

Sometimes guys sold pics of their exes into circulation following a breakup. And sometimes they reconciled with the lady and had work to do.

"I don't give a shit if that's your damn *mama*," the seller replied. "You're paying for it, or I'm keeping it."

The buyer ripped up the pic, and fisticuffs flared. The fight was broken up before a CO showed up. Not sure if the seller ever got his two stamps.

All of this talk about pornography and sordid snapshots begs the question: when do inmates "shake hands with the milkman?" Most do it in the shower, especially at camps where they're taken solo or using separate stalls. Many dudes headed to the shower carrying a jack pic or porn in a zip lock bag to keep it dry. Occasionally a porn page was slapped on the wet tile for the next guy to jerk off to. I found it touching how some looked out for others.

"Roughing up the suspect" in the shower wasn't my style. Spanking it there is a young man's game, or at least for those with keen eyesight. Glasses get foggy. Instead, I *beat the bishop*, in my bed late at night while neighbors slept heavily. I used my imagination, and quickly learned which were my favorite porn scenes, my most intense all-time lays, and which celebrity I was crushing on hardest.

Later in my sentence I found more access to porn mags. I learned to disguise covers with a conventional one in case the wrong person came along. Porn was best kept secret from inmates and guards alike. Fellow felons always wanted a free look-see and the fewer grubby fingers on the pages, the better.

CHAPTER NINE

Everybody's Crazy

"Everybody's crazy. The only questions are subject and severity."

— Garrett Phillips

Some inmates had issues with porn and masturbation. Library, a guy doing time for indecent liberties with a minor, was one of these. Like most sex offenders, he was haughty and condescending. He played fire and brimstone preaching on the radio while working as the librarian, because who doesn't want to be converted while they try to read?

One day Library and I discussed a mutually loathed inmate. We agreed the guy was a pain, and that bullying control of the TV in a prison dayroom would be his pinnacle achievement in life. Then Library got weird.

"Yeah, and he's always back there masturbating, even right after he got sex from his baby mama on his home pass weekend!"

If you talk to most sex offenders long enough, you get left field shit like this. They can seem normal, but eventually something gives. I took a step back and muttered "Yeah, not cool," as I wondered how someone notices another guy's jerking off schedule. And how twisted one must be to talk about it as if it's a guy who burps too much.

As I did my time, the close-up view I had of people's strange habits helped amuse me. For instance, some inmates moved to and from the shower wearing clothes instead of a towel and shower shoes like normal people. Others pulled their pants over their knees while they took a crap. In psychology, this is called "projecting." These dudes probably stole peeks at the junk of other guys which made them paranoid they were being checked out.

Most inmates were comfortable with states of undress in the joint, especially if they'd been locked up for a while. For me, getting dressed in a busy barracks felt strange early on, but soon became second nature. I noticed this one day while drying off at my locker, clad only in boxers and shower shoes. My buddy "Ride Around" appeared to deliver some oatmeal, and we chatted for a couple minutes before he pimp-rolled back out the door. Only then did I realize I'd stood there nearly nude, talking to a fully clothed guy, unfazed.

Getting comfortable while taking a dump took me longer. Others were fine with just rolling up and blasting no matter who else was there instead of waiting a couple minutes for solo time. Some of these scoundrels even started conversations, across a low partition, as if we were sitting on a park bench. I'd rather chat with a bible-thumper at a dry wedding reception.

Stunts like these were typical of career inmates; guys accustomed to people being around practically all the time. One time I saw two old buddies reunite after one of them transferred into the camp. They were smoking in the bathroom and enjoying a chat when one of them dropped his pants to do number two. Their conversation didn't miss a beat. I didn't stick around to see if they kept talking for the duration of the dump.

Other oddities included an affable guy who looked like Charles Manson, known as the "Stare Master". His main activity was staring at passersby while sitting by his bunk in a high-traffic area. This freaked me out when I first arrived, like he was out to get me. He proved to be friendly, though. He just liked to sit and stare.

Some dudes woke up, drank coffee, went to breakfast for fifteen minutes and then went right back to bed. This seemed like a waste, much like those that brushed their teeth before breakfast. I asked someone about this once, and he claimed breakfast didn't taste right without clean teeth. Another guy lent me money-saving maintenance advice: "Getting teeth filled by a dentist only puts off having them pulled." Prison proved that a full set of chompers are hardly a birthright.

Quirky chaps slept on top of their blankets with their clothes on to avoid having to make their bed. Some dirtballs used nasty old pillows – not cleaned after the last guy – without even applying pillow cases first. Several guys seemed unable to stand around without plunging a hand down their pants to hold their junk. One fellow mindlessly scratched his jewels for two straight minutes as he stood in front of a crowd waiting for a dinner call. Others permanently dispatched a hand to hold their pants up while they walked, as if suffering from a rare birth defect.

A cold virus phobia haunted our trusty barber, so he kept the window beside his bed open for fresh air, even in freezing temperatures. I explained that viruses threw damn parties all day at his job anyway, so the air around his bunk was probably not the problem. Many others employed an equally dubious way to avoid a cold: sleep with their blankets over their heads.

I developed a germ phobia of my own after a couple months at Southern, from smoking. I enjoyed sharing roll-ups with pals, at least once I realized getting caught was unlikely. Guards only half-cared and dodging them was easy and kind of fun. Enforcement was so slack that one squeaky-clean inmate once claimed, "I don't break the rules" as he exhaled a huge puff from his Newport.

I once saw an inmate blow out an enormous cloud of smoke while also spitting tobacco juice. If only he had a nicotine patch.

On the flip side, roll-ups got passed around like joints, so the tips grew soggy with saliva. Passersby bummed puffs, too – often the less savory among us. And despite Southern's lax enforcement, guys still got busted from time to time. If that were ever me I could kiss a transfer to the cool summers of Asheville goodbye. I cut back my smoking drastically, to maybe a couple a month.

Tobacco dealers could profit hundreds of dollars a month. Most of the product arrived inside the razor wire the notorious way: in the poop shoot. Inmate searches in minimum security rarely involved a close nuts and butts examination, especially at Southern.

My buddy "Gear," a major tobacco supplier on the camp, once laid it out bluntly. "People say their back door is 'exit only.' Fuck that. It's my moneymaker!"

When a camp tobacco drought peaked, Gear became a messiah, his disciples a dozen jittery guys that loitered near his bunk waiting for his return from work. Luckily most COs were too dense or disinterested to wonder why they were there. To Gear's credit, he never jacked up his price in those situations. He could afford benevolence, as his stamp count could number in the thousands before he managed to exchange them for smuggled in cash

He also had his people on the outside sell stamps to eBay sellers he knew that spent a lot of money at the post office. There, a pile of ratty stamps worked the same as cash.

For those lacking money, a tobacco recycling program flourished at Southern. When smokers finished, or when a guard came near, they tossed the roll-up onto the concrete floor under lockers between the bunks. Inmates that couldn't afford their own came by often and ran push brooms under lockers, like throwing out a fishing net. They would unroll their tobacco catches and combine them into a poor man's roll-up. Their rolling papers were usually the outer wrapping of toilet paper rolls or, in a pinch, bible pages.

As a janitor, I could estimate the camp's current tobacco supply as I swept the barracks floor each morning. If I found lots of fat roll-up remains, this meant even the scavengers had plenty. If no leftovers surfaced, guys got stingy with their smoke. The long Christmas breaks for off-camp workers made supplies plummet. Nicotine fiends found no holiday cheer in that. Prices skyrocketed.

I learned about a *lookout for shorts* at prisons more strict with tobacco use. There, dudes stood outside the bathroom and watched for approaching COs as smokers puffed away. Their pay for this service was the remains of the roll-up when the session finished. As the comedian Pat Dixon has pointed out, these gentlemen knew what smoking and cunnilingus have in common: the flavor gets stronger the closer you get to the butt.

I also profited from tobacco. Offenders usually hid contraband outside of their lockers, which is a legally "common" area. If discovered there, the authorities couldn't charge anyone specifically. A very popular hiding place was deep within unassigned mattresses, in crevices around their crude cushioning. The longer one's reach, the farther away from guards trying to find it. My long arms made me the perfect tool for the planting task. I looked like a horse breeder on TV's *Dirty Jobs*, artificially inseminating them. I earned many stamps for minimal risk and effort.

My profits from the dip (smokeless tobacco) industry left me with mixed emotions once the juice spitting of others became my pet peeve. I didn't think twice about it when I first entered prison but soon became disgusted by its prevalence. Nasty brown spit flew around seemingly everywhere I looked. Spent chaws that had been spat out littered the yard like dog dookie at a poorly maintained park. I eventually learned to avert my eyes from these tobacco balls and those who spit them, but this barely helped.

Worse, the bunk I occupied longest during my sentence doomed me to constant exposure. A large trash can stood near the foot of my bed and invited a steady procession of fetid mouthfuls going *splat* into it. Once a guy walked up and exhaled an enormous cloud of smoke *while spitting a load of tobacco juice*. I suspected he also wore a nicotine patch even thought those were contraband, too.

My only defense against seeing this parade of discharges was to place the trash can at the foot of my bunk. There, at least my view of it was blocked by my reading material as I reclined. Sadly, my neighbors had opposing agendas, even though the can got emptied often and never produced an odor. They wanted it away from their bunks, so the thing moved constantly.

This became a passive-aggressive shuffleboard game, as guys calmly pushed it a couple of feet when they walked by, hoping to go undetected. Then someone else would push it back, and I'd position the can in the middle. This literal push-and-pull lasted for months. I tried negotiating a compromise, but the peccadilloes of a dozen different guys in the area made this impossible. Life on the inside is harsh indeed.

Far more risky to mess with than tobacco was "K2," or "spice," which is a synthetic marijuana and undetectable on drug tests. K2 retailers enjoyed much higher profits than tobacco vendors. One told me he'd take a pay cut once he got out and held a real job. A smuggler's shoe could conceal hundreds of dollars worth – over ten times what it would cost on the street.

The administration correctly saw the synthetic as potentially lethal, so punishment for possession included forty-five days in the hole, a ticket to medium security, and criminal charges. Despite this, many guys stayed high constantly.

The chemical-riddled smoke gave users persistent coughs, and it smelled like burning hair. The drug also eroded values and goals. They caught an inmate with a pipe used for smoking the stuff, but he seemed unaffected: "Fuck it. I may be getting browned-down, but at least I got to be high for a whole year."

K2 has a crack-like effect. The initial rush is intense but brief, followed by a major craving for more. Heavy users become sluggish, smoked into zombies. The camp's best radio repair guy became a waste case, disinterested in working anymore. Fun people turned into slugs. Needless to say, I gave K2 a try.

One misty Sunday afternoon I found myself socializing in the camp's bad neighborhood: the unofficial "smoking area" down by the weightlifting pavilion. I stood with a couple buddies, enjoying a roll-up. Chang walked up wearing a smile and handed me an extremely thin roll-up: "Yo Biff, try this stick!"

K2 cigarettes are called sticks, but were more like toothpicks. Only a minuscule amount needed to be inhaled to achieve a serious high.

"Fuck it, why not?" I said.

I reached a dream-state high almost immediately, as with a DMT blast. Laughter came easily, followed by deep introspection. I'd become somewhat used to prison life before that moment. K2 took care of that. I suddenly saw my new buddies as the thugs, thieves, and drug fiends they were. The kind of people I'd cross the street to avoid. Worse, they were laughing at me. Or at least my sudden paranoia told me they were.

After maybe two minutes I had to get out of there, and fast.

Back towards my bunk I floated, convinced everyone I passed knew how high I was. I settled into its goonie-free confines to pull myself together. I applied my earbuds and rocked out to my radio for a long time. Songs that bored me sounded fresh again.

Music restored faith in my sanity and let me enjoy myself. I'll forever hear Adele's *Fire to the Rain* in a special way. It spoke to me. Soon, however, my heart spoke to me as well, much, much louder.

It started beating at triple time. I began hyperventilating, veering into a panic attack. I glimpsed a full psychotic episode that K2 was infamous for triggering. My experience with trippy drugs came in handy, though. I rode it out, lying on my back. Once I came down, I swore off "smoking them sticks" for good. I did *not* intend to die on a goddamn prison bunk.

In addition to peace of mind, this decision saved me a lot of money. A single stick sold for as high as twenty stamps ($6.00). The farther into my sentence I traveled, the better swearing off K2 looked.

I both heard of and witnessed spectacular freak-outs. One poor guy wandered around asking "How high am I?" over and over. Several of his friends got him to his bunk before he found further trouble. Unfortunately, the space cadet slipped away and stumbled to the guard desk and asked: "How high am I?"

The CO sitting there let him know: high enough to go to jail for intoxication. For the record, inmates referred to segregation cells as "jail." The notion of going to jail while already in prison always amused me.

K2 took out a good guy named Larry one night. "I've risen from my grave!" he shouted. "I need to get away from my grave!"

He figured this required climbing onto top bunks, even though they weren't his. After being dragged back to the floor for the third or fourth time he spontaneously disrobed. Turns out this is a great way to get dudes in prison to stop touching you.

Larry then ran straight into a wall and knocked himself out. By the time he woke up nurses and guards surrounded him. The good news is he was sentient enough to plead: "*Please* don't tell my Mama I been smokin' that K2!"

Watching people succumb to K2 saddened me, but it worked to the advantage of non-users. Guys dying to get high were easy to exploit in trades because they caved early in negotiations. Such profits were perhaps compensation to non-users for listening to coughing all day and suffering the horrid smell.

At least the scourge made for rare comedy in an intercom announcement one evening: "Will the inmate who dropped the K2 in the canteen line please report to the sergeant's office."

Twelve-step recovery meetings are a big part of prison life, mostly because administrations force drug offenders to show up to gain privilege promotions. For some reason NA (Narcotics Anonymous) attendance at Southern was closely monitored, but AA's was not. There, the sign-up sheet gatekeeper let guys sign in and leave, in exchange for a stamp. The authorities had no idea. So only eight or ten dudes showed up to "work the steps" to help salvage their lives.

The civilian AA meeting leader was an ex-con named Jerry, a jovial black guy of around sixty. His "shares," delivered in a sing-song voice, usually ate up twenty minutes. These usually included Jerry's baby delivery story, him reading from Psalms 23, references to the size of the lines he used to snort, and how his first drink of the day came through a straw due to the shakes that kept him from drinking normally.

He told of being interned at a "nuthouse," where he defecated on the lawn while not even drunk. A Mexican guy there told him about a "tecato gusano," which is a "psychic worm" many Hispanics believe causes addiction that can never be sated or killed. Jerry was a hoot until it became clear he repeated the same stories every week.

During my shares I described a cloud of guilt that followed me around during my teen years. The solution? Drugs. Specifically weed, and alcohol. So began a vicious circle. As George Orwell once said: "A man may take to drink because he feels himself a failure, but then fail all the more completely because he drinks."

The damage caused by my chemical use was more sneaky than acute. I didn't end up in a gutter, perhaps because I still lived at home, still in high school. I smoked pot all day and aspired only to make weed money as a golf caddie. My mother eventually recognized this and tricked me into an in-patient rehab stint that lasted three weeks. I quit partying and attended many AA meetings while still living at Mom's, but resumed partying and procrastinating a few months later.

And so my life went. I spent pursuing good times enhanced by intoxicants in the short term. There'd be plenty of time to plan for the future. Then days turned into weeks, weeks turned into months, and I blew decades just screwing around waiting for tomorrow's big break that never came.

All the guys in the prison AA circle could relate to this, but they tired of hearing it even more than I loathed repeating it. Such repetition summed up these AA meetings. "I know I've done wrong, I'm going to do right, and I'm going to work the steps," can only be swallowed so many times. Few of the inmates in this small group ever had anything new to share.

I decided to read the Big Book on my own, and cough up a stamp a week so I could blow off the meeting. Before I bowed out, however, I picked up some wisdom.

The group once entered a debate about the gray areas of sobriety. For instance, is smoking a cigarette solely for the "dizzy buzz" a violation? What about getting dizzy from vigorously smoking one to trigger a bowel movement? For that matter, can't most recreational drugs be helpful until they're abused?

Much more worth attending were the NA meetings, which involved at least forty inmates and a case manager making sure no one left after hitting the sign-in sheet. These weren't productive Twelve-step studies either, but more like going to a party. The tenets of the program became the topic only occasionally, and not for long. Guys only cared about telling war stories. The civilian that ran the meeting enjoyed yarns full of dubious detail, as opposed to Jerry, who took the AA meeting protocol seriously. Hardly anyone wanted to discuss fears or feelings, anyway. Story time beat everyone staring at their shoes and not sharing any day.

Inmates told of running from the cops or evidently getting away with murder. They revealed domestic violence details as if describing a trip to the store. I learned that impregnating a gainfully employed woman is a keen career move for some guys. They seemed to find this funny. I tried to keep my brow from raising upon hearing all of this, but probably failed.

Wonderful street terminology surfaced during these stories. "Dry goods" is slang for drugs other than alcohol. If a woman is "coin operated," she's a hooker. When a man walks confidently, he is "pimp-rolling." Calling someone out for bullshit dropped during a discussion is: "You ain't gotta lie to kick it."

Once a month someone stood behind a lectern for an official speaker meeting, instead of war stories coming from the gallery. Jittery civilian volunteers sometimes spoke at these, sounding like kindergarteners compared to our usual tales. More often an inmate told his story. One time this was me. I started with a bang.

"If someone told me I'd be an inmate giving a speech in prison back when I was a pimp," I said, "that probably would've been your mother."

Huge laughs. Insults appeal to some crowds, and I'd read this one right. I spent the next ten minutes telling my story. I never really "hit bottom," my chemical abuse eroded my will. My hard partying stole the energy needed to make something of myself. The longer I went, the more eyes glazed over in the audience. Time for Plan B.

I dropped war stories of my own, including about Lauren bleeding all over a hotel floor. Smiles and life returned to the room. On a roll, I told some of my more off-color stand-up comedy bits. One described a blowjob from a toothless grandma. I was not the recipient of this, I should point out, but the story earned me the nickname *Gum Bob*. Several guys could relate, because dentures are relatively common in their worlds, and not just among grandparents.

I wrapped up my speech feeling warm and happy inside. I wasn't a total loser, at least for a while.

I met many wonderful people in the joint. One of my first, and favorites, was "Night," a happy guy in his late twenties. He rocked the body of an NBA point guard and played like one on the court, too. Those that knew him claimed he had the fastest hands they've ever seen in a fight.

Night didn't move around the barracks much – people came to him. That's how you spot who runs the block. He told me as much the first time I met him, somehow not sounding smug. Night ran the big evening card games, which is another way to spot the Ballers. They can keep the peace when disputes arise, and in prison they are inevitable.

I appreciated how he chatted up the new white guy when I first arrived, not even trying to sell me anything. This policy was hardly common among the black inmates, but Night didn't see skin color. Being that way would be both anti-Christian and bad for business. Night sold me stamps no matter how scarce they were. He answered whatever questions I threw at him and told me what was what.

He spent ten solid minutes in his locker door mirror on workday mornings, primping for his county DOT job on a road crew.

"Females out there be lookin'!" he explained, when I asked why.

"Sweet Pea" proved to be an even better pal than Night. He was a wiry black dude in his mid-twenties, a gangsta from the Charlotte housing projects. His bookishness and charm belied his background. We met as bunkmates, when I occupied the bottom one. Pea rarely climbed up to his, hopping up like a high jumper instead. The bunk stood over six feet high. The feat was cute, unless I was sleeping.

Like dozens of guys, Pea wore "state" glasses that looked like the classic Groucho Marx disguise, minus the fake nose and mustache. They prohibited metal frames for inmates with violent crimes, so the state replaced them with plastic ones. Young gangstas trying to act all hard while wearing them made me laugh. While I did my time, the Groucho frame style became popular among hipsters and fashionistas, much to my amusement. I can't take them seriously, either.

Besides both of us being chill, Sweet Pea and I bonded over music.

"Yo! Yo!" he said, after running over to me. "What song is this?"

I smiled. "That's Journey. *Don't Stop Believin'*."

"This shit's hot!" he said, walking away with his head bopping.

I found his classic rock interest delightful, and Pea dug that I liked rap. So we taught each other the finer points of each. After Pea confessed he'd never heard of the Rolling Stones, I lent him a picture book of them.

"Man, them clothes are ace!" he said, grinning. "And them old-school bitches are tight!"

In turn, he shared his hip hop magazines and advised me on current artist feuds and odds on which rapper would be next to get shot.

Pea joined in my favorite pastime at Southern: jam circles. Ice and a couple of others owned guitars, and the camp provided a set of bongos — a luxury in the prison system. When the weather was nice we'd set up in the yard to play and sing. Nearby, black guys hung out listening to a Charlotte hip hop radio station, engaging in rap and dance battles. Our bongo crew intermingled with the rappers once in a while. This immensely fun respite from prison drudgery felt like stealing time from The Man.

Pea gave me lessons in freestyle rapping, and I became decent at it. Some dudes suspected lines I improvised were written previously, which is a high compliment. Soon enough, I was a member of Pea's clique, puffing on roll-ups while freestyling on someone's bunk. They taught me how to turn my "chop" into "flow."

Spitting rhymes in a prison rap circle makes doing live stand-up comedy feel as easy as talking into a mirror. The audience senses nervousness. Bring game quickly or get the fuck out. After stumbling for weeks, I survived by focusing on two keys to success: 1) Rap slower, to allow time to think up lines, and 2) boldly talk major trash even when you're a pussy. One of my rap stanzas went like this...

Don't think 'cuz I'm Whitey you can take me lightly,
Truth is I'll fuck you up, both daily and nightly.
Now you don't wanna fuck with me, or mess with my reach,
Face it son, you a student, and it's time for me to teach.

Sweet Pea, in addition to rapping like a pro, labored as an entry-level soldier in a nationwide street gang. Many weeks passed before I figured it out. One day at the bunk he said: "I guess I'm a weed dealer now!" and offered me some. In other words, he didn't choose to start dealing; his higher-ups put him to work, or else.

Pea became a K2 casualty around this time. He turned numb, reckless, and stopped paying off debts. Many deadbeats could operate this way with few repercussions in minimum security, at least for a while. Pea, however, dealt with hardened gang members who didn't give two fucks if they lost prison privileges for beating someone down.

His gang brothers found an isolated area in the yard and two of them beat him half to death while a couple gang bosses watched. Pea suffered a broken jaw, a severe concussion, and other beat-down injuries – fewer than three weeks before he finished a seven-year sentence. All of his assailants got identified (ratted-out) and flushed from our mostly good-vibe camp forever. Their leader was the guy I was warned not to bunk with on my first day at Southern.

Pea left in an ambulance and never returned. I never had the chance to say goodbye or exchange contact info with him, which pains me to this day. Such is often the case when in lockup. Friends get transferred to other camps abruptly or busted and sent to the hole immediately. I became numb to this. Spiritual nourishment from a friendship on the inside was always temporary. The sanest solution was to put my soul in neutral and turn off all emotions to eliminate the lows.

This approach probably made the aforementioned death of one of my best friends in the world easier to handle. I missed his funeral, but got over it quickly. My whole life was a tragedy that could hardly be sadder, anyway. Sometimes I sat in amazement at what my life as a slacker had bought me. And the far-reaching effects of my decision to deal molly to dig out of the hole I'd dug. I swore to never break the law again seemingly ten times a day while I was down.

CHAPTER TEN

The Thing About Inmates ...

After I started hanging out with Pea and his buddies, white guys started joking that I was a "wigger." White dudes that didn't know me well looked at me sideways as I smoked and bullshitted with my new pals. I often heard racist tropes like: "If you didn't hate blacks when you got here, you will by the time you leave!" While this is nonsense, the notion doesn't come from nothing, especially among long-timers.

Many contend African-American culture is louder than white. A prison that's majority black literally amplifies this opinion. Every room consists of concrete floors and cinderblock walls. Sound waves run wild. Even games of chess involve shouts and trash-talking, and dominoes participants would slam them on the table, not caring who they disturbed.

A sweet middle-aged black guy called "Pudge" mingled with whites more often than not. He spoke in a shout, even in the close quarters of the barracks while people napped. One time a white buddy called him out.

"Bro, *inside voice*."

Pudge's face scrunched up: "What?"

A black kid nearby chimed in. "He means your *church* voice!"

Everyone laughed, and Pudge piped down a little in the barracks from then on.

Eventually it became clear that socioeconomic class dictates loud and inconsiderate behavior more than race. I learned that the jerk yelling in my ear at Southern was usually black because he was part of sixty-five percent of that camp's population. Flip those percentages and the loud guy would probably be white.

One thing was for sure: Hispanics were quietest. Practically none of them did time in minimum security because the state saw them as high escape risks. They stayed in medium, regardless of good behavior and short time remaining on their sentences.

I felt a kinship with the Latinos. We stayed quiet, enjoyed soccer, and we were starved for good conversations with relatable people. The guys that spoke little English had fewer than ten potential friends that spoke Spanish. If they proved to be unlikeable duds, they were fucked.

My penitential odyssey debunked many inmate stereotypes. For instance, prisoners rarely claim to be innocent to each other. They do, however, all swear not to return to prison once they're sprung. Statistics show sixty-five percent of them are full of shit. Bullying and exploitation aren't rampant, either – at least in minimum security. Again, the lure of privilege-level promotions keeps toes on the line.

Besides the child molesters, inmates don't particularly care why others are locked up. Asking usually prompted a long story which meant less time for guys to talk about themselves. I didn't want to know, either. The ability to carry a good conversation and decipher a joke was more important to me than some sordid past deed. We were all on the same gargantuan prison bus, just trying to get along.

Names are overrated, too, especially at first. Too many names to learn, and the population turned over too quickly. Only after becoming pals did it seem important. Once I tried referring to a kind young fellow a few bunks away.

"What's that dude's name?" I asked a neighbor.

He shrugged: "I usually just call him 'Hey, Dumbass.'"

Since we lived one long day anyway, greeting inmates in passing – even friends – was strictly optional. No one took offense when small talk didn't happen, an aspect of prison I loved. Everyone knew a prison mood could hit at any time. Lots could trigger them: bad news from home, women troubles, or dwelling on their station in life. On the lighter side, conversations with pals were ongoing, picking up days later without greetings or preface. We lived in a time warp.

Accurate inmate stereotypes included copious tattoos and maniacal weight training. I noticed the upper bodies of most lifters seemed out of proportion. I suspect they built everything else up so their guts looked smaller by comparison. Achieving sculpted abs, after all, is a tedious task that doesn't involve the glory of lifting impressive weight. Like me, most inmates were strangers to persistence and hard work, otherwise they wouldn't be in prison.

"Getting ripped" at the weight pavilion was all a lot of guys cared about. Many of them spent more time in front of mirrors than Tom Cruise. Bodybuilding magazines were the most prominent on the camp, by far. I couldn't understand why none were titled *Meathead*.

Workout supplements such as creatine were no-no's in the joint, but this didn't stop dudes from using them, of course. The aptly-nicknamed "Blockhead" was one that did. Someone cracked that perfecting his physique would be like installing $3,000 rims on a $1,000 car. He wasn't the brightest.

Blockhead enjoyed the highest privilege level – including weekend furloughs – but evidently needed more self-esteem than that. One day at the canteen window he dropped multiple creatine powder packets onto the ground, right in front of a sergeant. Bye-bye weekend furloughs.

"Someone told me these were vitamins, I swear!"

I planned to tone up with weight training before my sentence expired, but I couldn't handle it. Not the weights, the people. Weight pavilion conversation was miserable; a bodybuilding magazine come to life. The incessant grunts, barks, bleats, and groans reminded me of the vulgar world I lived in. I'd almost rather read a David Baldacci book than hang out there.

On the other hand, watching "Lift-offs" between huge motherfuckers who *warmed up* on the bench with 225 was highly entertaining. And once I overheard a guy encourage his workout partner to make one more lift: "Bitches already have pussies! They don't need another one!"

Prison is a great place to see rednecks preen and bloom. Starting in early March guys returned sunburnt from outside jobs or playing in the yard all day. I'd ask why.

"I hate fucking with sunblock. Besides, once you get a base tan you're okay."

This was nonsense. I saw more category five sunburns above inmate collars all summer long than at a Florida spring break. I once bought sunblock from the canteen and the clerk took forever to find it. He'd previously sold the same number of them as pocket dictionaries: zero.

Since inmates wore uniforms, they made personal style statements with hairstyles and tattoos. Mullets were alive and well inside prison gates. They spent many man-hours maintaining long dreadlocks or intricately sculpted buzz cuts. The "cop cut" prevailed for white guys: head shaved tight on the sides, leaving what appeared to be a rodent pelt on top. Why inmates sought hairstyles that made them look like police remained unclear. If the canteen sold mirrored sunglasses, they probably would've sold out, too.

I learned of a fresh twist on the comb-over style. Picture the bowl cut of Jim Carrey in *Dumb and Dumber*, except shaved tight on the sides. Hair loss wasn't obvious from a front view, but from the side it looked like a claw clamping down on a hairless dome. It reminded me of wide tassels found on golf shoes of yesteryear.

Hairstyles done with clippers could be criminal, but traditional scissor cuts were often worse. Prison barbers were "state certified," but how to cut white people's hair clearly didn't weigh heavily on the final exam. Most of the cuts appeared hacked out with landscaping tools. My only real choice was a straight buzz cut, for zero maintenance. The less time I spent in the bathroom looking into a mirror, the better.

The Thing About Inmates ...

Even worse than the haircuts were inmate tattoos. Amazingly, the huge swastika on my first bunkmate, John, proved to be far from the worst.

Neck tattoos seemed almost as common as arm ones, almost always featuring a female name. Normally the name of a significant other, they sometimes proved to be daughters. Maybe this is why exotic dancers use an alias – it's different from the name on Dad's neck.

The backs of fingers displayed statements, and room for just four letters proved sufficient. My favorite was a threat. "YOUR" over one fist and "NEXT" on the other. Your next what?

The most confusing of these was "FUCK" on the right hand and "LOVE" on the other. Was the dude fed-up with love, or professing that he loved to fuck? I'm sure it impressed women either way.

Another chap had just a question mark about the size of a quarter on the side of his cheek, depicting my exact thought upon seeing it. Someone else, doubtlessly a proud Duke University alumnus, had its logo etched above an eyebrow. I failed to ask what he majored in.

During an eerie walk down a corridor in The Hole, I saw an inmate in a cell. A tattoo across his forehead shouted DISCIPLE. I stared at it in amazement as I passed by, drawing a spiteful glare. This reminded me of buxom women who wear plunging necklines, then scold those that look: "Um, my eyes are up here!"

One poor guy invested in large block letters across his upper back: "THOROGHBREAD" (sic).

Finding the worst tattoo overall took nearly three years. I assumed choosing just one would be difficult, but not so much. It graced the back of a massive powerlifting guy that happened to be the camp baker. Part of that job was working in the chow hall service line, handing out the items he baked. His bulk limited his ability to reach with his arms, so he had to pivot his torso back and forth instead. An Oompah Loompah came to mind.

Anyway, huge block letters across the top of his back spelled: "WHITE." Below this was an exquisitely crafted

141

color Confederate flag, and under that the word: "POWER." My buddy Louie observed that this ink could be more offensive only if a pit bull burst through the middle of the flag with a severed arm of a black guy in its mouth. Baker was lucky that prison administration wasn't dumb enough to assign him to a prison near the N.C. coast, population ninety percent black.

Baker's nod to racial harmony was the talk of the camp for days after he arrived. I found not staring at the tasteless monstrosity to be impossible. Even old-timers struggled to recall such brazenness. Many agreed at least Baker deserved credit for commitment. I also gave him props for chutzpah, but no one else knew what this meant. No one dared address him directly about it.

Given all the tattoos, I expected to see more ink work in progress around the barracks. Apparently the majority got etched on the street, which is amazing considering most of them looked like jailhouse work. My entire time down I saw only one makeshift ink gun, using a motor from an electric shaver and ink made from soot from a candle flame, mixed with water.

Early in my sentence I indulged anyone in conversation, but after a few months I avoided people like a sorority pledge that failed to make weight. The novelty had disappeared. Bad tattoos served as warnings: chat this guy up at your own risk, because it will probably suck. Every third guy seemed to be doing time for being a bad conversationalist.

To discourage chatter I started wearing earbuds all day long. This withdrawal, even though I looked like a dick, also meant fewer guys bummed coffee, stamps, or oatmeal cakes with no intention of paying me back. Even better, I suffered less small talk. I eventually didn't give two fucks if they thought I was an asshole. The book I was reading loved me just the same.

I'd still talk to some lonely souls, however. Guys kicked out of the world, dying for attention and relevance. Prison is the endgame for those who can't figure life out. The easily impressionable that fail to consider consequences before a dumb move gets them arrested. The people barely above the IQ cut line that defines the mentally retarded. Those forgotten by society and suffering from bigotry against stupid people.

I felt worst for those smart enough to know they're dim; the flip side of ignorance being bliss. Many of these dudes don't necessarily mind the downsides of prison.

"It's a lot easier in here than out in the world. Out there all I do is fuck up," a neighbor once confessed.

Prison gave me a new sympathy for these unfortunates, and I met scores of them. One was Bernard, a gentle guy of around fifty. He'd ask me to pronounce or define words, often simple ones. He once asked me if "enter" started with an "e" or an "i". I felt awful for him and helped all I could.

Many inmates considered me, the bespectacled nerd, to be a human Google. I once settled an argument over which ocean surrounds Hawaii. I settled complicated legal questions, like: "Since I gave my bitch power of attorney can she sell my car and keep the money?"

I sympathized with the less-intellectual guys, but on bad days I'd bristle because no one seemed interested in bettering himself. Multitudes watched TV all day long with nothing to read during commercials. Remedial reading books like *Today I Will Fly* were available if they wished to read it. Anyone could enroll in basic education programs, but most didn't try.

Dimwits could be entertaining, at least. One long-term inmate once took exception to being bossed around by COs. Once they were out of earshot he'd loudly proclaim, "I'm nobody's puppet."

He repeated this ad nauseam until a sizable neighbor became fed up. He laid out reality for Puppet Man. "Hate to tell you bro, but you're in a puppet show, and the state of North Carolina has its fist directly up your ass!"

Another guy babbled incessantly about his fighting prowess. He once mentioned that he'd taught his daughters how to fight. I said: "That's cool. So they'll be ready when they go on Jerry Springer!" Not only was the guy not insulted by my crack, he smiled and nodded with pride at the prospect.

North Carolina law considered gay sex to be a "crime against nature." I openly mocked the term, but a nearby inmate set me straight. He explained that "nature" referred to sex outdoors, like on a picnic table at a park.

My favorite story of stupid was when a guy took cell phone pics of himself and his crew in the barracks, with people around. Showing off a phone was dumb enough, but he also failed to delete the photos after sending them to whomever. The guards inevitably found both the phone and the culprit, because cheap flip phones don't require log-in info.

As with most busts, COs learned of the phone from an informant. Guys with phones often rented out air time for stamps. They'd also tell dudes trying to bum free phone time to get lost. They soon learned how easy it is to trigger a snitch.

Snitches placed more people in danger in honor grade facilities than physical violence. Many times the guy ratted out would get yanked from the camp, often headed to the hole followed by medium security. Rats dropped notes to administration into the mailbox, usually stating their enemy harbored contraband. These were de facto shankings – no blood flows, but an adversary gets fucked up all the same.

Reasons to set someone up could be as simple as wanting an annoying neighbor moved out or to settle a running beef over the TV. Debtors could get rid of creditors by ratting them out. Snitching could also create a desirable job opening that a rat was next in line to be assigned.

Unless the informant was too stupid to cover his tracks, retribution for snitching was unlikely. This aspect of minimum security disgusted many career inmates. Some swore they preferred medium, at least until they left for the weekend on a home pass or enjoyed some other privilege.

The administration loved snitches. They helped root out cell phones, scourge of prisons everywhere. An inmate could use a phone to coordinate outside criminal enterprises, arrange for contraband to be tossed over the fence into the yard, or even to plan escapes. Dire consequences greeted anyone caught with one. Wise users kept them on the super down-low, but

The Thing About Inmates ...

nothing is foolproof when crafty COs are milling about. An old codger of a guard named Bowers fit this description.

Unlike most of the COs, Bowers liked to keep moving. He also seemed to enjoy sneaking around corners in attempts to bust people for smoking, looking at porn, or whatever. Several dudes warned me about him early on. "You gotta watch that motherfucker. He pulls some real ninja shit!"

One morning Bowers slipped into the only bathroom on the camp that featured a toilet surrounded by a real stall, like those found in public buildings. His sixth sense must have led him there. He pushed the stall door open (no latch) to find an inmate texting away on a flip phone. The culprit showed enough sense to flush the phone down the toilet and enough agility to juke his way past Bowers and out the door.

"It don't matter if you run or not, you're still goin' to the hole!" Bowers yelled after him. This was assuming he could retrieve the evidence or the charges against Phone Guy might not hold up upon appeal. So Bowers and another guard, named Smithers, went to work.

Smithers was disrespectful and humorless. He also rankled people because he was the size of a Kenyan distance runner, yet he pimp-rolled around as if built like a linebacker, trying to look all hard. Few guys liked or respected him, so the show that unfolded for us outside the window proved especially satisfying.

A manhole that provided access to the camp's outgoing sewer flow stood thirty feet away. Within its depths was a grate designed to catch items that had gotten flushed down the toilet – like phones. So as four or five inmates gathered at each of several windows to watch, the guards manipulated actual ten-foot poles, fishing around down there.

At one point Smithers peered down and the stench hit him. He reeled back as if someone had kicked him in the face. This caused his mirrored sunglasses (that he often wore indoors) to fly off his head and into a valve apparatus for a nearby propane tank. The peanut gallery roared with approval. Not a bad way to kill time on a lazy Monday morning.

Soon, backup authorities appeared. These including the

warden and the maintenance boss, who brought a flashlight-equipped hardhat. Still, after nearly thirty minutes of poking their poles around like Jim on Huckleberry Finn's raft, the guards found nothing.

As those of us watching began to tire of the scene, a fun dude called "Gamer" voiced a bright idea.

"Hey, y'all! Let's fuck with them! Let's start flushing the toilets over and over again!"

Before anyone could debate the wisdom of this plan, soldiers had raced away to flood the pipes. We eventually learned that this action, a) only diluted the odor the COs had to endure and, b) hastened the phone's arrival into the filter grate due to the heavy water flow.

The group of officials surrounding the manhole became animated, and Bowers soon applied the flashlight helmet and climbed into the hole. He emerged a minute later and raised the phone skyward with a latex-gloved hand like it was an offering to the correctional officer gods. He had found the evidence, sure as shit stinks.

In prison, I paid my penance with day-to-day hassles more than anything. With minutiae like waiting for a bunkie to move so I could simply climb down out of bed. Such tickytack aggravations chipped away at my sanity as much as the near-constant auditory rape.

It began at five each weekday, with sinister fluorescent lighting that plagued me eighteen hours a day. Mankind should not suffer illumination this way – I swear it causes brain damage. Or at least fucks with a person's internal clock and will to live. Hell uses fluorescent lights in areas away from the roiling fire, I guarantee it.

Brutal lighting had a partner in sensory torment: the intercom system. It started blaring before dawn and continued until evenings, running roughshod over conversations like a competition leaf blower. COs bluntly barked orders, almost never with style or grace. "Please" or "thank you" came only when the chaplain spoke, which was hardly ever. As an additional kick in the balls, Southern's PA system featured auto-repeat, so every alert came twice in a row.

The intercom occasionally provided unintentional humor, though. Once, during toilet paper distribution time (inmates kept their own), a guard issued a final warning: "If you ain't done went and got it, you need to now."

The Devil's alarm clock started off days by alerting "special diet" inmates of breakfast time, an hour before regular breakfast call. Getting back to sleep for that hour usually proved futile. After I woke up for real, I was quickly reminded of freedoms lost, specifically the choice to fart at will and take a leak without hassle.

Going to the bathroom was such an arduous task that I'd just wait until fully dressed and headed to breakfast. The other option was to walk two hundred feet round trip while barely clothed. I usually occupied a top bunk, so a bunkie on the same schedule as mine made every step of dressing a chore. I'd do so while still on my bed to stay out of his way.

Once dressed I'd walk to make my bladder gladder, often having to pee with a dude taking a crap three feet away. During warm months a pedestal fan blasted gale-force wind off the cinderblock walls. Sometimes I looked in the mirror afterwards, raccoon-eyed and cursing my plight. Meanwhile, some shady yet brightly lit convict behind me belched while pissing. Welcome to the new day!

Next I sulked to the chow hall for woeful dining after waiting in line with guys equally miserable. Loud conversations of Morning People assaulted me often, which was like being probed by Satan's pitchfork and pushed into the inferno. If I were a fighter, they might have extended my sentence because of assault charges. I could probably live in a Buddhist monastery for a decade and still not fully recover.

Upon return to my bunk I'd listen to *NPR News* with the din of inmate activity in the background. An hour later came the mandatory three-hour barracks exodus. Sometimes I'd fall asleep again before this happened, so I got to wake up in prison twice in ninety minutes. As those with jobs headed off for the day I began my game of dodging COs to settle into a quiet writing area. Sometimes I thought Jason, my buddy from processing who preferred the serenity of maximum security, may have been correct after all. Travel for a free hernia surgery soon rid me of this notion.

I can thank the Asheville DA and North Carolina for a free hernia repair, a mere three months into my sentence. I'd needed it for months prior, but couldn't afford it. I feared the prison solution, assuming I'd get cut on in a Soviet-era clinic, by a surgeon one error away from a stripped medical license.

Instead, I visited a gleaming hospital, staffed by real professionals. First came an examination by the surgeon that drew my case. This required a van ride to Raleigh, the state capital. I sat on a cushioned seat for the first time in months. I gushed about the comfortable seating to a fellow passenger.

"Sure beats steel benches in a paddy wagon with no windows while handcuffed," he declared.

He'd once suffered extradition for a trial in these conditions. An eighteen-hundred mile round trip that included stops at county jails for overnights. One-way took five days, and sometimes the freeway paddy wagon filled up with other defendants. Medium security inmates I encountered that day found transport uncomfortable, too. Even non-violent-crime inmates got bound in cuffs and shackles and required two accompanying guards when traveling.

An old-time con called Red joined me and three other medical cases in the holding cell waiting to see the doctor. A southern boy of about sixty-five, "Red" was now a misnomer given his fully-gray combed-over hair. He was so short in stature that he plopped *up* on a bench, his feet then dangling above the floor. For some reason I asked Red what he was in for, and after a pause he admitted rape. This made him the only guy I heard 'fess up to a sex crime the whole time I was down. I quickly steered the topic to our health issues.

"I'm kinda worried because they gave me a colored doctor,"

he explained. "But at least he seems like he knows what he's doing."

He said this while sitting right next to a black dude who was older too. He let the comment slide instead of turning the cell into a mini race riot. Red seemed oblivious to his racism, or at least didn't give a shit about anything anymore. Like admitting to rape, for instance.

Not much later I moved to an exam room and met my doctor, an affable guy fresh out of UNC medical school. He fondled my balls. He promised my surgery was imminent, but gave no specifics for security reasons. About a week later Southern's cute and efficient head nurse — who wore vast swaths of clothing to thwart ogling inmates — told me not to eat or drink after midnight. It was on.

Painfully before dawn, Officer Portis (the skinny old NASCAR driver lookalike) and I embarked for Raleigh and my outpatient hernia procedure. Contrary to regulations, Portis allowed me to ride shotgun in the transport car, not even handcuffed. No cramped-up legs in the back seat cage for me — I reclined and rode in style. Life was good until I realized riding with Portis sucked.

The guy chattered endlessly and one-upped stories like a frat douche. He babbled on about nothing and "topped" my quality anecdotes with boring ones. Worse, I was both caffeine and sleep-deprived, stuck humoring him for favorable treatment. At least the cartoonish cop spilled camp gossip, including sexual flings among staff and which COs were boozers.

Portis complained of a sinus infection at one point. I asked if he'd tried the Nettie pot remedy of flushing with a saltwater mix. "

"Yep, but I don't need to buy 'em," he explained. "I do it the old-fashioned way." He simulated dumping salt on the web between his thumb and index finger and snorting it up. "When you do it right, the salt drips down into your throat."

"Yes, I'm familiar with that process," I deadpanned. "I just didn't know people did it with shit that's legal." This comment confused the CO, and the subject dropped.

Portis didn't know precisely where to deliver me when we

arrived at the nearly new Rex-UNC hospital. We parked in a remote corner of a parking deck, far from any activity. I briefly considered ramming Portis' head into the driver's side window, throwing him into the trunk and driving away. Then I realized a) I'm not a violent criminal, and b) I'd need to reschedule my hernia surgery, and it might not be free next time.

Instead, the CO and I meandered into the main reception area of the hospital. I enjoyed real life for a minute. I walked on carpet. I inspected art on the walls. I saw a woman wearing a skirt.

Wary glances shot my way from concerned waiting-room occupants. Portis and I probably looked like a hostage situation waiting to happen: my sizable self in a prison uniform, uncuffed, standing with a CO that could pass for Barney Fife's offspring. I could knock out Portis and take the old lady at the information desk hostage. Then she'd probably be even *less* capable of answering a basic question.

This pleasant detour ended with Portis being directed to a holding cell near the loading dock. There, I learned another downside for inmates in medium security custody: an honor grade dipshit like me asking stupid questions. A guy next to me in the cell wore the cuff and shackle assembly. I pointed to it.

"Man, they make you wear that everywhere in here?"

"Nah," the dude managed, annoyed. "Once I get to a bed they just handcuff me to that."

"Damn, that sucks. I got to ride in the front seat of the car on the way here with no cuffs."

I tend to blab before thinking in strange social situations, but this was the worst. So bad I nearly offered to punch *myself* in the face on the poor sap's behalf. Worse, my call to the pre-op area came first despite his arriving an hour earlier than me. I gave a *sorry about this* shrug as I moved out, met with a glare.

Next I enjoyed an absurdly comfortable adjustable bed – a quantum leap from my past few months. I couldn't stop smiling as I messed with the controls. Additional amusement came from Portis being outfitted for the OR in powder blue scrubs, footsies, and a paper hat. He seemed like a nervous father with a son about to receive a sex change. I asked him to apply his surgical mask early, so he might stop talking. He didn't laugh.

An orderly chatted us up at one point, describing his contractor job in Iraq. "Yep, I worked six straight months with no days off."

Portis replied, "My cousin worked on power lines after an ice storm once and went three days on no sleep."

Counterbalancing Portis' lame one-upmanship was a gift from above: beautiful young females everywhere. Evidently North Carolina law requires hospital personnel to score seven or higher on the hotness scale. Seeing the beauties — and even exchanging smiles with them— was bittersweet. I had no shot whatsoever. Was it better to have lusted and lost than never to have lusted at all?

Portis ruined this too. He brazenly stared down the lovely passersby, nearly standing *in* the hallway as he did so. I cringed on behalf of those poor girls, at least until the sodium pentothal took hold.

Next came the operating room. I counted down from one hundred until the gas kicked in. A minute later, seemingly every beautiful nurse in the building greeted my awakening in the recovery room. I slurred compliments towards them, but they probably dismissed it as the Dilaudid talking. Especially after I requested a second blast, triggering an opiate la-la land more for pleasure than painkilling. Soon nausea befell me and my urinary function failed.

"Go to the bathroom and give it one last try, otherwise we'll have to put in a catheter," a nurse explained.

I'd never had the pleasure, and even while drug-addled I knew to avoid a tube in my dick if possible. Public urinal "stage fright" was child's play compared to this dilemma. I needed to piss ... *or else.*

Too dizzy to stand, I staggered to the toilet and plopped down. The pressure to perform was so great that I ... passed out.

I came to still seated and leaning against the wall. A puddle of urine surrounded me, which made me think of a scene from *Infinite Jest*. But hallelujah, my problem was solved. And thanks to the dope my pool of pee didn't even embarrass me.

I spent more time nauseous. I dry-heaved, and learned this reflex may be partly psychological. The lurching made my hernia repair incision burn severely, prompting my subconscious to speak clearly.

Okay, fuck this. *No more dry-heaving or your sutures will rip!* Miracles, the spasms ceased.

I needed to stay overnight, but hospital personnel strongly suggested we head towards the door, like closing time at a bar. I also felt bad for Portis, who was fourteen hours into his day. Despite how I whine about him, the man has a good heart. Having him assigned to me that day was a great break.

Portis rewarded me for ending his day by letting me pick the radio station on the drive back to Southern. This meant he heard *This American Life* for the first time. The final segment described an anti-gay activist who ended up gay himself.

"Now just what the *fuck* are we listening to, Phillips?!" the cartoonish cop exclaimed.

I laughed, which brought breaktaking pain to my groin area despite the dope. Any humor and merrymaking for the next couple of weeks cost me dearly. Avoiding it proved a lot harder than you'd think, and reminded me that prison wasn't all bad.

CHAPTER ELEVEN

New Place, Same Tricks

"Damn! Motherfucker look like he seen a ghost!"

Someone shouted this at Southern during my wheelchair ride from Portis' car to a segregation cell that served as my recovery room. Thanks to our benevolent warden I enjoyed room service for three days, with COs serving as butlers and a nurse on call. This time of pampered solitude inspired the essay: *My Greatest Achievement*, which I later submitted for an inmate writing contest (detailed later).

The slightest movement felt like a blowtorch to my groin. Once I moved back into the barracks, I often slammed coffee with a Lortab, which produced a dreamlike, active buzz. I'd shuffle back and forth past bunks because my nurse insisted I move around. My fellow felons detected I was high, of course, and made obscene offers to buy my pills. One junkie offered ten bucks for a single one.

"You don't seem to understand," I'd explain. "Look at me. I need these for pain!"

The prison life of being around people all the time worked in my favor for a change. Someone was always around to grab things or otherwise help me out. Sometimes I gained a tingle of gratification from this, which may have helped my recovery go better than expected. Nice people are everywhere.

Another example of this, one of my most memorable, came following an argument I had with some dickhead over the TV. The guy acted like he'd punch me, although I never felt in real peril and didn't dwell on the incident. A bit later, as I lounged on my bunk with my mind elsewhere, a buddy who witnessed the scene stopped by.

"Hey man, don't take that thing too hard," he said, giving my shoulder a squeeze along with a look of sympathy. "Some people are just assholes."

"Thanks, man," I managed as he walked away.

Even though I was over the incident, my buddy's version of a reassuring hug made me weepy. His emotional kindness took me totally by surprise. It reminded me of how lonely I was, and how much I longed for tenderness in any form.

Soon a bunkie switch left me paired with a guy named Greg, who looked like a bad guy in a '70s TV detective show. He and I were neighbors and chatted in county jail three months earlier, yet he didn't recognize me. In Greg's defense, alcohol withdrawals were savaging him. His body was accustomed to three gallons of vodka every week.

Greg and I got on famously. We shared a sense of humor, which was no small favor. Unfortunately, he suffered from spastic leg syndrome. He randomly jerked and flopped as he slept, waking me up all night long. Even during lulls in this, I lay half-awake, waiting for the next bed quake. Good friends or not, one of us had to go.

Also, the agony of prison living without air conditioning during a southern summer bore down on me. That time of year when taking a shower didn't cleanse so much as it just changed out layers of sweat. When accidental glimpses of repulsive inmates lying around scratching their nuts while wearing only boxers happened. When fans cooled only guys within ten feet because of humidity, and the building imitating a brick oven. And, house flies.

Flies treated me like the piece of shit the Asheville DA thought I was. They made me pick my poison when trying to sleep. Sleeping without a sheet over me was cooler, but then flies would land on me all night. Then it became personal. In retaliation, I used a flyswatter for eradication missions. I could kill a dozen or more flies in five minutes, sometimes two in one magical swat. Flies were also oppressive in the chow hall because they love roadkill. Somehow fly-killing strips or other control solutions weren't in use there, either.

Luckily I had a plan to avoid all of this. A couple of weeks earlier I'd written a letter to prison administration.

Dear Boss Person,

I am a drug offender, listed to enroll in the prison drug rehab program during my sentence. I am trying my best to remain sober in the meantime, but the temptations available here are shaking my resolve. I would greatly appreciate prompt admittance to the program, if possible. Please help me speed up the process of improving myself.

Sincerely,
Biff Buckhead

I knew they held the ninety-day rehab program only at air conditioned facilities, so I timed my request accordingly. My call to move out came two days after I decided to "break up" with my jerky-legged bunkie Greg. If not for the searing pain in my crotch area I would have leapt for joy.

I bid a bittersweet farewell to Greg and my other Southern buddies, a blow softened by the knowledge I'd return after rehab. One fine May morning I boarded another prison bus. Stage four of my big adventure was underway.

The ride to Rutherford Correctional Center in Spindale nearly killed me. And I'm not even referring to my fellow bus passengers this time. My hernia repair region felt like its stitches were ripping apart with each bump. My teeth stayed clenched as back roads twisted and turned and I absorbed shocks with my butt raised off the seat as if riding a galloping horse. Luckily I sustained no damage beyond pain and worry.

My new camp proved far less spacious than Southern. At

first glance, I assumed the yard was around the corner of one of the buildings. Cramped conditions meant only a half-court for basketball and just one horseshoe pit instead of two or three. The barracks and dayrooms were equally tight. Thank god for the camp's stunning hilltop setting.

Sweeping Blue Ridge Mountains views to the west took my breath away, and a wide valley panorama to the east added to the beauty. Sunrises and sunsets painted brilliant, shifting colors on a huge sky – a rarity in the heavily forested American South.

Of some two-hundred and forty men on the camp, perhaps six gave the spectacular sunsets a second thought. One guy even asked why I watched them so often. "The sun sets every day," he said. The best viewing spot juxtaposed nature's beauty with a line of inmates, chatting on benches just below the horizon, facing me.

Soon into my stay, I compiled a pros and cons list for Rutherford to show the fellas when I returned to Southern. Reports about other camps ranked high on the list of inmate conversation topics.

Personalized laundry service didn't exist. Instead, inmates suffered twice-weekly lines, usually in the hot sun. Kitchen workers offered no food for sale. Not enough dayrooms were available, and they offered only old tube TVs and a crappy channel selection. Walking on the grass in the yard was prohibited, as was wearing shorts or going shirtless. Daytime temperatures exceeded one-hundred degrees for two straight weeks in summer 2012, when I was there.

A surly staff enforced rules usually ignored at Southern, like book limits. The head sergeant, Godfrey, acted like he ran a boot camp instead of a warehouse for fuckups. He raised tensions instead of tempering them. For instance, in response to offenders caught smoking, Godfrey restricted canteen purchases for everyone.

Many old-timers had never seen ridiculous rules like Godfrey's. Luckily the air conditioning made all the downsides worth it, along with hot and cold controls in the showers. No more pushing a button every twenty seconds to dispense one-temperature-fits-all water. Crafty inmates figured out how to adjust the thermostat, too, even though a locked steel encasement covered it.

They'd microwave a cup of water to boiling and then hold it under the steel. Soon the thermostat figured it was summer in Death Valley and the system cranked out frosty air for a way longer time period. In truth, the barracks temperature was fine as it was. I figured the cup holders just felt like getting away with something and being inventive.

Much to my delight, the canteen sold three-ounce bags of instant coffee, as opposed to the expensive packets of dust offered at Southern. I spooned too much into a cup at first, which left me awake half the night. The blessing of good, strong coffee would prove to be a double-edged sword in more ways than one.

A mere four months of lockup made me somewhat "hard." Even though I limped from my injury, I conveyed a cocky aloofness on my first trip into the barracks at Rutherford. Instead of introducing myself and seeking approval I laid low. A couple of weeks later a heated argument near my bunk drew my attention from a book. I didn't bother moving and simply watched the show.

Jack of Hearts approached the bunk of Ace of Spades and began arguing about poker. Jack claimed Ace cheated and cost him money.

"Make it right, man." Jack urged. "You know I got ten more stamps comin' my way."

Ace dwarfed people with both height and width. Fuck You size, some would say. He looked at Jack: "Fuck you."

Jack's voice raised an octave and his arms flailed as he moved towards the door. "This ain't right! You know this shit ain't right!" And he was gone. This incident alarmed me so much I decided to take a nap. Like I said, they had hardened me.

BOOM! I awoke to a shower of white powder, bits of glass, and large shards of clear plastic flying onto my bed. I heard heavy thumps and the awful screech of metal on smooth concrete. I raised my forearm from my eyes and saw Ace ramming some dude's head into a bed frame, two bunks away.

The head being rammed was Jack's. He'd returned to adjust Ace's attitude with a classic makeshift weapon: a Master lock inside a sock. Jack had whipped his weapon towards Ace's head, but the toe seam of the sock gave way. The lock rocketed directly into a bank of fluorescent lights nearest to my bed.

Several bystanders managed to pry Ace off of Jack, who had become an unconscious lump on the floor. "You still wanna try me, punk-ass bitch?" Ace yelled while heading out the door.

Two nurses and three COs soon rushed in, breaking an eerie silence and looking for answers. Remarkably, no one nearby claimed to have noticed an assault. Strange how a pool of blood, a possible corpse, and fluorescent light fallout can just happen. I'm ashamed to admit I was more concerned with the glass shards and powder on my blanket than a possibly dead guy five feet away.

The administration interviewed everybody in the area over the next day, including me. I told them I was showering at the time and saw nothing. Someone sang, however. Three COs came in two days later to cuff Ace and take him to the hole. Jack reportedly suffered a fractured skull. I doubt the poker dispute ever got settled.

Besides near manslaughter, other chaos reigned in my new bedroom. All drug or DUI convicts had to enroll in rehab, but they could opt out after two weeks. The only personal growth many guys cared about was weightlifting, so lots checked out. Inmates shuffled in and out based on the rehab's schedule, too. I felt like I'd entered the processing camp all over again. The Cricket Syndrome stayed in full effect.

By contrast, I eagerly awaited A New Direction. Comparing prison rehab with the private rehab I attended a year earlier would be interesting. They might as well be on different planets. At Caron, I learned about rich people's problems. Here, I'd learn about real criminal thought processes. My embedded reporter task began in earnest.

Hazelden, the notable Minneapolis addiction treatment foundation, developed "A New Direction: *A Cognitive Behavioral Treatment Curriculum*: mapping a life of recovery and freedom for chemically dependent criminal offenders." In other words, a fancy version of the AA saying: "fix your stinking thinking." To end vicious circles. It looked great on paper for those who wished to change.

Each rehab class day lasted three hours or fewer. The program normally included an afternoon group session, but a staff shortage made this impossible during my time there. I try not to dwell on the excellent writing fodder I missed out on because of this. The morning sessions provided plenty, followed by copious nap time.

They held two classes of twenty inmates in neighboring barracks dayrooms, which consisted of cinderblock walls and concrete floors. Only a whiteboard up front and temporary table arrangements resembled a real classroom. Alert and engaged inmates kept most sessions lively, which surprised me. I suspect fresh caffeine buzzes helped with that. The counselors seemed like actors in a bad sitcom.

The flighty and attractive Ms. Wyatt led my class. She was a trim, sharply dressed woman in her late-fifties who flowed around the room rather than simply moved. She often adopted sexy poses as she sat on a table and spoke, absent-mindedly twirling her hair or slipping a foot in and out of her shoe. Guys shot looks to each other, eyebrows raised. Ms. Wyatt seemed oblivious to her effect on men full of pent-up sexual desire.

I delighted in watching Ms. Wyatt, but the chaos in her class annoyed me. Students took advantage of her kindhearted nature. She tolerated tardiness, eating, and talking out of turn. No stern taskmaster, she once instructed: "If you don't feel like doing the exercises, at least read chapter six." She never graded work anyway.

If the class bogged down, Ms. Wyatt sometimes asked

"why are you so dead?" like stimulating discussion and rapport was our job.

The primary tool of the program was Thinking Reports. These exercises laid bare the thought processes that lead offenders into trouble. First students identify an incident that pissed them off and describe their initial reaction. Once they recognize their knee-jerk reaction as destructive, they consider better ways to deal with the problem.

In other words, a gangsta should pause and think shit through instead of just smacking a nigga.

A typical class session required several students to write their thinking reports on the whiteboard for group analysis. Ms. Wyatt then clumsily analyzed each point and corrected errors, with the class joining in. Opportunities to counsel inmates arose often, but Ms. Wyatt only tossed psych buzzwords over their heads, often reading from the workbook. She wouldn't recognize a teachable moment if it prison-raped her.

I felt bad for those that asked for help in class. I'd seek them out later in case they wished to discuss it, working AA's twelfth step. I tried to help based on what I'd learned from Caron and AA, in street terms. A few guys serious about recovery even sought me out after a while.

These interactions often sent a tingle up my spine – a wonderful feeling. Perhaps I ended up in the penitentiary to assist my brethren in this fashion. "Maybe the universe planned this," as my Mother would say.

This optimism helped a lot because A New Direction exercises taxed me emotionally. Compiling lists of money blown, people wronged, and opportunities squandered – yet again – could bog me down. I lived a seemingly endless fourth AA step, just like in Caron and the halfway house. At least class time could be fun.

The bumbling Ms. Wyatt provided light moments. Once she utterly failed to explain "empathy" – a foreign emotion to inmates if ever one existed. I took up the task instead, and the class felt me.

"A fine example of empathy can be found on the Snoop

New Place, Same Tricks

Dogg track *Ain't No Fun*," I declared, as snickers arose from classmates familiar with the song.

"The sage Warren G says: 'It ain't no fun if the Homies can't have none.' This shows empathy for his crew. He felt bad for them and wanted them to feel like Ballers too. So dude shared his weed and bitches."

After laughter and hooting subsided, a bemused Ms. Wyatt managed: "Yes, I suppose that's a good example."

Workbook lessons in the class started over again after six weeks. The only difference was half of the class had graduated, replaced by different guys to annoy me. Then, just as the redundancy of A New Direction nearly broke me, a savior arrived.

My last couple of weeks in the program coincided with Ms. Wyatt going on vacation. We all dearly missed her sexiness, but the class received a different gift: Head Counselor Norm Carver as the substitute counselor. Short and stocky, he would be perfectly cast as an older brother of *Breaking Bad* actor Dean Norris. We'd heard great stories about Carver's wackiness from his students in the classroom next door. Now we got to live them.

On his first day, he wrote a lesson topic in large letters on top of the whiteboard: Generational Addiction Patterns. He began with a rhetorical question: "How did you come upon the thought process that put you here (in prison)?" Ignite engines – we had lift-off.

The first generation analyzed were "The Veterans," born between 1920 and 1945. According to Carver, spouses stayed together no matter what back then, and citizens would have been ashamed to accept government assistance had it been available. He also professed Germany invaded Ireland, and Japan took the U.S. by surprise in the Pacific since we were busy fighting in Europe at the time – with Italy on our side.

I began taking detailed notes of this flurry of inaccuracies that had nothing to do with addiction rehab. Carver noticed, and gave me a wink of approval. He glanced at me several times after this, following points he seemed particularly proud of.

The next generation was the Baby Boomers, 1946 to 1964. As Carver told it, this period saw Henry Ford present the Model T to the masses, women entering the workforce (which caused a divorce epidemic), and everyone trying to keep up with the Joneses. Marriage licenses in Vegas included divorce applications on the back, and California was the center of the LSD scourge. Carver explained that families ate dinner together during this era, whether the siblings got along or not.

I intervened at this point, assuming a class discussion was underway. My raised hand clearly annoyed Carver, but he humored me.

"I thought LSD didn't really kick in until the Summer of Love, in '69?"

"Yes, that's true as well," allowed Carver. "Despite what you may think, I'm not all-knowing."

I assumed he was kidding and chuckled, which peeved him further. No humorist, I'd bet he thinks self-deprecation means pooping one's pants. From there I struggled into "listen-only" mode. This lecture was not to be sidetracked. The usual disrupters of the class lay low, too, sensing Carver would steamroll them if they piped up.

Next up for analysis was my wheelhouse, Generation X, 1965 to 1980. Carver explained this was when couples began cohabitating without bothering to marry. "But, if these sinners lived together long enough," Carver explained, "a common-law marriage could result."

The relevance of this went unexplained, as usual. It did, however, lead to another touchy subject: mixed relationships. Carver lamented that whites in the U.S. will be a minority by 2050 since mixed-race individuals will exceed fifty percent of the population.

"Mixed marriages will take over, but you won't tell any difference anyway," the instructor said, shaking his head.

Carver claimed Generation X's science scores in the U.S. rank twentieth in the world. This, of course, explained why

New Place, Same Tricks

a former inmate pupil of his sustained injuries in a crystal meth-cooking explosion.

"I told him to drop his drawers, right there in class, 'cuz I didn't believe him," Carver said. "He did, and the son-of-a-bitch had scars you wouldn't believe. And one of his calves was completely gone."

Following the meth lab explosion, the guy's dog — a regular modern-day Lassie — alerted distant neighbors, saving his master's life. I dearly wished to point out that the concussive blast drew attention just fine, but I stayed out of it.

"I used to work in illegal manufacturing myself, although it was a lot less risky," Carver admitted. "When I was a kid I moved bottles of the family hooch from the still to the log pile, using an old flour sack." The class learned this was a better option for the small lad since a heavier "toe sack" could've caused a stumble, breaking the bottles.

Equally relevant to generational addiction patterns were — you guessed it — female reproduction issues. Carver noted with alarm that "girls these days can menstruate as early as age nine," and he knew of a twelve-year-old who "already has nice titties and a pretty butt."

The counselor drew an hourglass figure on the whiteboard for clarification, complete with nipples on the boobies (mercifully, no pubes or vagina). He claimed the daughter of an acquaintance required an abortion to avoid giving birth, otherwise "her hips would split her apart." His point being — I have no fucking idea.

Most of the class seemed oblivious to this farce and took it at face value. This only made not laughing more difficult. A guy next to me appeared bored somehow and knocked out workbook exercises instead of listening. Then again, he may have been silently protesting an earlier Carver reference to "colored-only water fountains" in the fifties, apropos of nothing.

I exchanged glances with buddies who appeared equally baffled, took notes, and felt like I'd entered a David Lynch movie. I stared at the whiteboard, noticed my reflection in it, and questioned reality. As if I'd smoked weed minutes earlier, and the THC had just kicked in hard.

My dissociation faded just in time to comprehend Carver's take on Generation Y, 1981 to 2000. He cited the Columbine shootings as "the event that changed the world forever, along with 9/11. Because we all remember where we were when that went down."

Carver professed 9/11 had been triggered by a ninety-three cent box cutter converted into a bomb. "And even worse, terrorists are even more creative these days. They have bombs surgically implanted in their bodies!"

The class learned that the U.S. lacks Australia's security. There, you must enter a second line at customs if you're carrying antipsychotic medication, as Carver once did. Also, the U.S. has never won a war below the 38th parallel, "even though we had laser-guided bombs that could hit a three-foot square from one hundred miles" in Vietnam.

I had to grab my wrist to keep my hand from going up on that one.

According to Carver, America's breakdown means "China is going to wipe us out and there's nothing we can do about it." He lowered his head for a few beats before continuing.

"We are literally running out of gas, and solar panels won't help because they're manufactured in China, for god sakes!"

Suddenly the counselor appeared ready to cry.

"We had a great run, but empires fall about every three-hundred years, so we're forty years overdue."

As if things could possibly turn darker, for no apparent reason Carver claimed to own "a long rap sheet," but admitted he'd never done time.

A bold classmate piped up upon hearing this: "So you sayin' you was a snitch?"

Carver took a step back. "Define snitching", he yelled, face reddening. "Is it snitching if you tell them you didn't do something?"

"Depends if you beat the heat by naming names or not," came the cool reply.

Snickering arose, along with veiled calls of "Sniiitch!" and "Narc!"

"You weren't there, I was!" Carver sputtered. "And I can

promise you as clear as I'm standing here that I never ratted anyone out."

"Then you was the *powe*-leece even back then."

Carver closed in on his questioner, spittle flying. "If I was a rat, why would I help inmates now?"

"Maybe you feel guilty enough."

Had a judge been present, a gavel would have been abused. Whoops and laughter meant order had left the court. A rat was on the ropes.

Carver turned his back and slowly returned to the front of the room. He shakily gestured toward the whiteboard, at the generational timeline he'd written. He tried to steer back to the point of the lecture, such as it was, and abruptly checked his watch. Luckily for him, the class had entered overtime.

"We'll pick this up tomorrow," he said, through a clenched jaw.

Carver moved to a corner opposite the door as the class rushed out into a day full of joyously rehashing the instructor's disgrace.

My remaining lessons with Carver kept a similar aimless but entertaining vein. For fun, a few classmates and I asked questions that sent him off on tangents. We made bets on this game, with bonuses paid if he ranted about China. Carver never brought up Generational Addiction Patterns again. Perhaps his accidental mission as a counselor was mystical – to provide unintentional comedy for beleaguered prisoners like me.

While I rip on Carver, he saved me from living without air conditioning in August for a couple of weeks. My term in the rehab class was ending, so a transfer back to Southern loomed. To buy more time, I praised Carver's wisdom and begged for a couple more weeks to learn at his feet.

He seemed surprised at this request but smiled widely. "You know, it's not often someone appreciates what I'm accomplishing here. Especially an inmate."

I attended his class over two more weeks, but none as entertaining as that first one. Cool air in the barracks on those hot summer nights helped me get over this, though. Favorable trade-offs such as this are rare inside penitentiary gates.

My favorite inmate at Rutherford, a twenty-something named Farell, happened to be gay. His prowess on the basketball court and masculine manner fooled others, but my twenty-eight years in Atlanta had honed my "gay-dar." He and I enjoyed reading gossip magazines like *Us Weekly* together while making fun of the celebrities.

I never asked him outright, but our commentary eased into it. I'd ask him if he thought certain male actors were hot, and he always answered without protesting. I suggested Farell stop hiding it, to no avail. He'd change the subject immediately.

I madly respected inmates that were out of the closet, but being "out' appeared easier than I thought it would be in such a den of masculinity. I expected gays to lie low in fear, but tons of them actively socialized, played poker, or lifted weights along with everyone else. Turns out some inmates "fronted" like homophobes, but mostly treated them respectfully. I could hear derisive remarks behind their backs but direct insults were rare. We were all on the prison journey together.

This tolerance from career inmates perhaps stemmed from familiarity with Out – and I mean really Out – gays they encountered in medium security joints. There, guys wore makeshift makeup and ultra-tight clothing and rocked sculpted eyebrows and fancy hairstyles. And of course, blatant sex acts in the bathrooms and even on bunks took place late nights. The Queens (their prideful term for themselves) in minimum were low key by comparison.

Medium security was notorious for late-night trysts, effectively closing bathroom access until they finished the dirty work. Such common-area sex never happened in honor grade; it happened in off-limits and out-of-the-way areas. Only once did I see two dudes making out, in a dayroom when I ran late for a chow call. One of them noticed me but didn't even hesitate. He knew most inmates didn't care how they got their kicks.

Certain camps were known for a propensity of Queens, and inmate arrival days were major events. Resident gays and those "gay for the stay" assembled in the yard and assessed incoming prospects as they paraded off the bus and through the camp. Successful couplings could result in makeshift weddings, complete with a cake known as a "Bigfoot Pie." Primary ingredients: melted honey buns, Oreos, Kool-Aid powder, and other sweets from the canteen.

I adored gays in lockup. I found them a welcome relief from typical inmates. We enjoyed civilized conversations and made fun of the barbarians. Also, gays rubbed me the right way.

Most everyone had a "hustle" in prison. Enterprising gentlemen cleaned shoes, made beds, and even tended to someone else's dreadlocks for stamps. But no one offered massage therapy. Sore and knotted muscles went untreated beyond Ben-Gay. At least until a pal of mine briefly massaged my shoulders, in a friendly way.

"Dude. I'll give you five stamps to rub my back."

You'd think I tasered him. "Fuck that, bro! That's gay as hell!"

I didn't care. An epiphany that would soothe my endlessly knotted muscles had arrived. I marched over to two of my gay friends and interrupted them blowing each other (just kidding, they were talking).

"Guys! Want to make some money?" The rest is history. I learned gay dudes were happy to give massages at every camp they assigned me, hiding from the COs like smokers after one accused us of engaging in foreplay. A few other inmates saw me getting a rubdown and bought one for themselves, too.

CHAPTER TWELVE

The Bible Belt Bites

Rutherford on the whole sucked, but it did feature charms beyond good coffee, air conditioning, and sunsets. Field Day was among these when inmates invaded a normally off-limits grassy area to play games. The concept tickled me because this activity usually involves actual pre-teens, not a bunch of guys who are, emotionally speaking, twelve years old.

Since the injury report listed me as out (hernia), they assigned me to officiating duties. In other words, appointed me to snitch on those who stole competitive advantages. I didn't need new enemies, so I "let them play," as they say in the sports world. Someone got tripped? I didn't see nothin'. Refereeing a race of grown men carrying eggs on spoons with their mouths was hardly what I expected to do during my incarceration.

The camp programs director oversaw the games. Her gawkiness reminded me of Olive Oyl, except with a nice ass. She seemed as naïve as Popeye's girl, too, surprised when everyone refused to run the three-legged race, which requires sharing a burlap sack with another dude. Inmates are hyper-sensitive this way. They also never tell someone when their fly is open, for fear of looking gay.

Field Day was just the beginning of a May Day celebration. Guys laughed and smiled everywhere, and not just because Sergeant Godfrey had the day off. Excitement ran high for a cookout, followed by a live Christian rock concert.

On the visitor's patio at Rutherford, site of the cookout and concert. Pic taken by my dad.

COs worked the grill, and inmates devoured normally unavailable fixings like onions and relish. Baked beans and genuine iced tea completed a dinner worthy of the real world. "Real" food for inmates was rare, so beef hot dogs and fresh burgers felt like stealing. The highlight of the day for me, however, was the concert.

A four-piece band called Messenger played, fronted by a pretty brunette singer and keytar player in her early twenties. She lacked charisma and sexiness, which made me picture Bible study leader Olive and prison administrators meeting to decide what band to book for this occasion.

"I'm afraid she'll cause security problems because she's too attractive. Is she sexy too?"

"Not at all, really."

"Okay, fine. Book them."

The show was supposed to be free, but the lead guy in the band made us pay dearly by ranting about Jesus before they started playing. He also addressed the audience as if he were playing for an elementary school.

"I heard y'all had a big day today!" he exclaimed, drawing out every word.

He thanked the inmates for sitting up near the stage, not realizing we just wanted to be close to an attractive female. A crate of ice cream about to be offloaded at a steamy refugee camp couldn't be desired more. The raven-haired singer kept her sunglasses on well into dusk and rarely dropped her eyes lower than the horizon.

"Okay, this next song is called 'Break Out,'" she announced, reluctantly.

Hearty laughs from a bunch of convicts filled the air. Once the singer got the joke, she laughed along. She asked that we not take the song as an excuse for a jailbreak, and her mood lightened noticeably. The band found its groove, such as it was, and played solid Christian rock.

The singer unleashed a flexible, powerful voice. She invited three inmates up for a little funk jam, punctuated by excellent singing by a dreadlocked dude from my barracks. Guys whooped and danced, briefly not caring if they looked gay or not. By the end of the show, our girl had ditched her shades, revealing striking blue eyes.

The band chatted with inmates from the stage after the show ended. I stood torn over whether to talk to the singer, if only to gaze into her marvelous eyes for a minute. Since it was a Christian gathering, I wondered What Would Jesus Do? I decided he would've ignored the girl and returned to the barracks, cursing His dad's name on the way. So that's what I did, goddammit. Where I lived, fresh reminders of feminine charms would only cause me pain.

About a week later I found a gift richer than Field Day, a cookout, and a concert combined. I learned of the Inmate Creative Writing Contest. Sweet! What do I win? I figured this challenge would be like fighting a UFC match against former Olympic ice skater Johnny Weir.

Alas, the only "prize" was a certificate: "Winner, Bureau of

Prisons Writing Contest." But forget Pulitzers and other self-important awards – my name on this document would be an unsurpassed credit. I'd proudly display it right next to my Associate Degree diploma from Georgia State University, which shows I may associate with people who have real degrees. (Joke credit to my late friend Brian See.)

The contest included three categories: essays, short stories, and poetry. Offenders could submit one entry in each. Flush with writing topics from my past couple of years, I entered all categories. Three winner's certificates would bring triple the validation. God knows I needed it.

I browsed the guidelines for the contest. My work wouldn't pressure COs or cause tension, nor would it be defamatory, obscene, or injurious to anyone. And I certainly would avoid writing about sex. That would be too cliche. I'd write about prison-ish topics like bodily functions, drug rehab, and downscale exploits that carried street cred. No way I'd lose.

So I wrote my ass off over the next week with a knock-off Bic pen purchased at the canteen. The words flowed like runny gravy from the chow hall despite many interruptions from neighbors asking for help writing letters. The stories wrote themselves.

My essay entry, *My Greatest Achievement*, detailed a recent episode in the wake of my hernia surgery. The piece came straight from my heart.

My short story factually described my rehab stint as a teenager, except for a twist at the end. It went a little something like this...

A Stab At Rehab

Biff Buckhead loved watching football, and the day of his high school's first game of the season had finally arrived. He'd been looking forward to it since well before his senior year had begun. The skinny kid arose for the school day as usual and found something most *unusual*: His father, Homer, emerging from the guest bedroom.

He had moved to Atlanta following his divorce four years earlier, and had shown up late the night before, unbeknownst to Biff. After the two shared a hug, Homer spoke.

"Hey, wanna take a trip to Minneapolis with me?"

"Uh, I dunno. Tonight's the first game. Why are you here, anyway?" Biff replied.

"Business trip! I know you like going on those, so I stopped through to see."

This proposition would normally be a no-brainer for the kid, but football is very important in Ohio – almost as vital as the partying that surrounds the games. One of the happiest social occasions of the year was on hand, and many of his friends played on the team he wanted to support.

On the other hand, blowing off a day of school with the blessing of his parents and taking a plane ride to visit a new city was a tempting alternative. Joining Homer on business trips had always been fun, and Minnesota sounded exotic to the seventeen-year-old. Besides, ten more football games were to follow in the season.

"Okay," Biff finally said. "Let's ride!"

Biff quickly packed a travel bag and bid his mother farewell for the weekend. She insisted on a long hug, which seemed odd considering he'd see her again two days later. Biff quickly forgot about it, though, and father and son enjoyed an uneventful flight north.

Upon arrival, Biff emerged first from the jetway. He immediately faced a man who was a dead-ringer for Ned Flanders from *The Simpsons*.

"Are you Biff?" the squirrelly character asked.

"Yeah, that's me," Biff replied before looking back to his dad.

"Then you must be Homer," Flanders said, looking to the elder Buckhead.

"Wait, you two don't know each other?" Biff asked his dad. "I thought you were coming here for business."

Homer turned somber and suddenly looked weary.

"Son, the reason we're here is your mother and I feel you have a drug problem. We're going to a place that will help us find answers. This man works for a treatment center."

Flanders seemed taken aback at Homer's deception and said nothing. Becoming upset, Biff finally filled an awkward silence.

"Wait, how in the hell can you assess a drug problem from nine-hundred miles away? Don't you mean *Mom* thinks I have a drug problem?"

Homer had no reply ready, so Flanders piped up. "Fairview is here to help both of you during this trying time."

Biff looked at him sideways and wandered away. The two adults then quietly conversed as the kid pondered his predicament. Biff figured he would spend the weekend convincing these people he was no junkie and return to his happy life, thank you very much.

Just then another teenager emerged from the same plane. Impossibly, it was Jim Linder, a fun high school classmate of Biff's that hadn't been to school yet that year. He wore his usual impish grin and a big cast on his wrist.

"Linder?! What the hell are *you* doing here? Where have you been?" Biff nearly shouted.

The friends slapped hands as Jim explained: "I'm coming from one drug rehab, going to another one. What about you?"

"I guess I'm going to rehab too. This guy here said Fairview or something?"

"Yep, Fairview," Jim replied. "Me, too."

Flanders introduced himself to Jim, and the foursome began walking to ground transportation, the teenagers trailing.

"So what's up with the cast?" Biff asked, pointing to Jim's wrist.

"Oh, I was just in a rehab in Akron — Edwin Shaw. I punched through a window at the security desk," he explained, "so they're sending me to a more secure place."

"What?! Why did you do that?"

"They pissed me off," Jim replied, matter-of-factly.

Okay, this is getting too weird," Biff replied. "I don't need to be in any secure place. All I do is smoke weed! How long is this going to take, anyway?

"Oh, at least a month."

"No, I mean for someone non-violent like me," Biff said.

"Don't matter, dude. This ain't no weekend thing. You're going to be here for a while. Get used to it."

Fairview Deaconess was a rehab institution of high repute that drew clientele from across the country. The kind of place worthy of John Wayne's daughter, or the son of a professional drug counselor — like Biff's mother, for instance.

Upon arrival at Fairview, Homer Buckhead sat through the orientation spiel, offered words of encouragement and general bullshit, and bid farewell to a despondent Biff after a couple of days. The kid was happy to see the asshole leave. He was livid with his parents for screwing up his life — his senior year! Biff was now alone in a daunting alternate universe.

The rehab facility was part of an extensive hospital complex, and the evaluation wing for adolescents did not screw around. Thick screens guarded the windows of the locked area, acting as jailhouse bars. Patients were clothed in backless hospital gowns, pajama bottoms, robes, and slippers. The authorities restricted movement to one wing of the floor. Going outdoors was forbidden, and they banned both cigarettes and music. Patients were to concentrate fully on conquering their addiction demons, not distractions.

The evaluation wing, where Biff and Jim were assigned, assessed a patient's addiction status, based on "drug histories," which were presented to a group of peers and two counselors sitting in a circle. The patients on the hot seat each day placed written pages in the middle and verbalized their content, followed by an up or down vote on their honesty from the group.

"In the fall of '82, I drank three nights a week, usually to the point of being drunk. That winter I drank a lot also smoked weed every few days...."

"Bullshit," a counselor would often interrupt. "Go re-write this honestly and get back to us."

Some might call this tough love. Coercion and head games could be another way to describe it. Biff presented his drug histories a couple of times, the second of which was accurate, but the group roundly rejected both of them.

"Who are you kidding?" they'd bark at Biff. "You wouldn't be here if these are all the drugs you've done!"

"Look, my mother is a drug counselor. She knows heroin addicts usually start with smoking weed. She wanted to stop me from doing that and blew the whistle too soon."

"Bullshit. Don't present to the group again until you're serious."

Meanwhile, those who failed to offer a "truthful" abuse history became outcasts, and Biff joined them – stuck at the starting line of the program and bathed in shame. By contrast, patients deemed "open and honest" got rewarded. They received warm hugs and praise after their histories were accepted, practically getting carried around on the shoulders of the counselors in celebration. These winners advanced to the "treatment wing." There, patients wore their own clothes, smiled a lot more, and even got to listen to music, smoke, and go outside now and then.

Biff could see them in treatment wing, through a small window in a hallway door. He wanted in more than anything, to join the "cool kids." So he started making shit up despite himself. He pretended to have an addiction problem since no one bought that he just smoked pot every day and binge drank on weekends. That was the truth.

Cocaine? Biff had never even seen it, but for his current purposes he'd spent the past two years wired. As far as these people knew his friends called him "Hoover." LSD? In truth, he'd never indulged but the "new" Biff, who wanted to wear real clothes, had eaten it like Pez since the eighth grade. He also claimed he drank so much he probably had cirrhosis of the liver at age seventeen.

"You've come such a long way!" the counselors gushed after Biff "came clean." "We're so proud of you! What you've done isn't easy." Actually, it came easily to Biff because making up stories was fun. But whatever the case, it was time to break out his suitcase, listen to some music, and have a smoke. Hello, treatment wing!

Of course everything comes with a price. In exchange for his new privileges, Biff was required to confront the pesky first step of the twelve-step recovery program: *We admitted we were powerless over chemicals, and that our lives have become unmanageable.* No way was Biff getting past that one. He needed something more personalized, like: *We believe our parents jumped the gun and we haven't lived long enough to know what an unmanageable life even means.*

So began ten days of utter failure coming to terms with the first step. Try as he might, Biff found faking it to be increasingly pointless. The only instance of powerlessness he knew was an inability to hide pot-smoking from his mother.

Also, "family week" was fast approaching, and his parents and sister were about to pay for expensive travel for no good reason. Appealing to their frugality and general logic, Biff finally talked his parents into calling the entire thing off. No more tedious group meetings, insolent counselors, and trying to convince strangers he was something he was not. He was finally going home after twenty-two days.

Biff may have continued through life fully vindicated, but the world will never know. In a crazy coincidence,

The Bible Belt Bites

Biff's high school friend Jim was in Fairview's "coping with jealousy" group when he heard the news.

"That son of a bitch! Why does he get to leave instead of me? This is bullshit!"

Unfortunately for Biff, the "processing homicidal rage" group wasn't scheduled to gather until two days hence. So Jim proceeded to carve a shank from a hardcover Alcoholics Anonymous book. When Biff dropped by Jim's room to bid farewell, he received a shank to his aorta for his trouble. The wound proved to be mortal despite an emergency room being a quick elevator ride away. Perhaps it was all a success, though: Biff's daily pot smoking problem came to an end.

Getting back to the writing contest details, a thoughtful meditation on my broken life served as my poetry entry. This was my weak link because I don't "get" poetry. To me, iambic pentameter might as well be an obscure Olympic event. No subtle wordplay exists in my poems. I rhyme lines like a seventh-grader. Nevertheless, given my competition, I expected a three-category sweep.

Once I finished editing, I located the aforementioned Olive Oyl, the dowdy programs director, and handed her my labors of love

"Oh ... great!" she said, beautiful blue eyes blazing.

"Thanks for dealing with this," I brown-nosed. "Feel free to critique it if you'd like!"

She chuckled awkwardly and ambled away. Based on her surprise I may have been the only one to enter the contest. This seemed odd, and later I wondered if everyone else knew something I didn't.

I swaggered through the next couple days, buoyed by a sense of accomplishment and feeling less like a loser. I began thinking about frame styles for my winner's certificates. Then one lazy afternoon as I lounged on my bunk the intercom sounded: "Garrett Phillips, report to the sergeant's office."

My heart entered my throat, transported back to being called in front of a school principal. In prison this call is often harmless, usually to receive legal mail or a box of books someone sent. Sometimes, however, unwanted bunk switches are revealed, or disciplinary action described. The worst case is a notice of a death in the family. I trudged with dread across the camp to learn my fate.

Rutherford's sergeant office featured a walk-up window, occupied by Olive. I exhaled, assuming she intended to congratulate me on my fantastic writing. Behind her, a sergeant sat at one desk and a CO at another, both studying me with eyebrows raised. Olive abruptly shoved my writing contest pages through the window, into my face. She spoke with a southern accent common among stilted witches.

"You cain't be serious with these, and you should be ashaymed of yerself!" she spat. My jaw dropped.

"There's profanity in awl of them. And you cain't write about bowel movements!"

The officers behind her laughed, so I wondered if Olive was joking. I began a reply. "You know, the contest guidelines don't prohibit writing about bodily –"

"No one wonts to read about your duuump bein' a slot machine jackpot!" she huffed.

Far from joking, she'd somehow taken my contest entries personally. I guess she held a black belt in Southern Baptist.

Confused, I asked if the problem lied with the slot machine or the dump. Alas, Olive closed the window on the episode – both literally and figuratively. She slammed it shut. Rattled but undeterred, I buzzed back to my bunk and began the required revisions.

As I changed words like "hell" to "heck" and "shit" to "stuff" I heard "Yo, Biff!" shouted from around the corner, followed by dramatic murmurs. I waded through my fellow felons to the CO desk by the door. There stood Olive, face still red. She'd made a house call instead of calling me on the intercom. Her baby-blues sliced me with a glare. You'd think I sold her dog for parts or something.

"Give me those entries back," she commanded, through clenched teeth.

The Bible Belt Bites

I zipped back to my bunk and grabbed the pages, thinking someone had talked sense into her. As I placed my writings into her trembling hand, I said: "By the way, the contest guidelines don't ban profanity either, you know."

"I doubt that's going to help yew!" she spat, and stormed out the door.

I assumed this meant they would enter my work into the contest, despite her disapproval. Or Olive's co-workers insisted she retrieve them so they could read an entertaining story about some inmate's creative dump.

I absorbed good-natured shoves and elbows from the assembled barracks crowd. "Whoooo! Damn, Biff! Bitch was pissed!" So much for me staying low key at this camp.

Word of my dilemma quickly spread and repeating the story felt like holding a dozen separate press conferences. Guys were dying to read it too, but I had already mailed the first drafts back home for safekeeping. Even COs wanted to see. I learned most of them considered Olive to be uptight and enjoyed watching her freak out.

As I sat signing autographs the following day I again heard "Garrett Phillips, report to the sergeant's office." Once more Olive stood at the window, only slightly more composed than last time. She explained that not only were my contest entries rejected, but they would write me up for obscenity and use of profanity.

"Obscenity?" I sputtered. "With all due respect, my essay lacked taste, but it wasn't obscene at all."

This sent another surge into Olive, one she had probably prayed to avoid. She grabbed the offending pages and applied her reading glasses. She quoted.

"'My body – or more specifically, my sphincter – screamed 'No!' Uhh, that's clearly obscene!"

"Probably not to inmates," I countered. "And it's our writing contest, right?"

Olive ignored me and continued quoting aloud, much to the delight of two COs seated behind her, laughing.

"And your short story has a murder in it! How … how can you think that would be okay?!" She yanked her glasses off.

"This is a writing contest for prison, not a garden club."

This cracked up the peanut gallery further, which made Olive even redder. To her, no discussion or negotiation was needed. She had a godless sinner right where she wanted him.

She told me to expect a formal write-up and slammed the window closed with authority. No "Good day, heathen," and no compliments on my paragraph structure or for my snappy phrases.

The farce continued two days later at my arraignment in the mailroom/disciplinary office. An affable young CO named Hastings had this paperwork duty dumped on him. At least he enjoyed comic relief as he recited and typed up my charges.

The official indictment referred to a "dangerous weapon (hunting knife)," and contained the phrase: "comparing his bowel movement to inanimate objects." Nonsense. I had compared a human being – or at least Rush Limbaugh – to the result of my bowel movement, not the physical act. I smelled a strong legal defense based on semantics.

Denial of a winner's certificate worried me far more than official punishment. Almost everyone figured I'd draw a suspended sentence, to be struck from my record if I behaved for a few months. I assumed that someone during the appeal process would stop laughing long enough to dismiss the charges.

My persecution progressed at a meeting with the warden, a portly gentleman equal parts pompous and humorless. His doughy index fingers pecked out my "incident report" on a keyboard while I told my side of the story. I might as well have been addressing a church pew. One that could roll its eyes.

The warden barely paid attention and found facts and logic unimportant. He had no plans to side with a smart-ass like me over his programs director. He pronounced me guilty, so I took the next step: an appeal to a Disciplinary Hearing Officer, employed by the same state agency as Olive and the warden.

Two days later I sat in the same room, talking to the same guy only with a different name. I wondered if they attended the same church. Any hope he would stop this debacle quickly vanished. He read aloud: "a turd frozen and fashioned into a hunting knife" through a smirk. His beady eyes narrowed as they drew me into focus.

"I can offer you a suspended sentence for a profanity charge. If you decide to appeal further, I will add charges for insubordination and obscenity."

I had planned to appeal all the way to the top. Perhaps even alert the media as a last resort. I envisioned my story becoming a cause célèbre among creative minds. The Man not only took my freedom via the War on Drugs, but now artist creativity came under the pressure. Tasteless topic or otherwise, this oppression could not stand. Someone had to go to the wall for shit jokes. Otherwise, where would the tyranny end?

Instead, my resolve crumbled in the face of escalating penalties. If my appeals failed, I'd go to the hole, followed by medium security instead of honor grade. And some honor I showed. The Man broke me. Fyodor Dostoevsky spent four years in a Siberian penal camp for publishing anti-government pamphlets, yet I wussed out over this. This shame shall sully the rest of my days, even though my ride through prison rolled much smoother for it.

The next day I accepted a suspended sentence for the flimsiest inmate violation imaginable: profanity. Turns out official prison regulations forbid "profanity of any kind," so its absence in the contest guidelines was irrelevant. At least I obtained the official document that includes numerous quotes from my disqualified works. I display it with pride – my poor man's winner's certificate.

A nice guy I often chatted with was doing time for necrophilia at the funeral home his parents owned. He didn't tell me, but barracks events required research to confirm it. Specifically, he got caught creeping around bunks at night, rubbing on young fellows. He was shipped away, and prison administration responded with a Sexual Abuse Awareness initiative. All inmates assembled at the basketball court one evening to hear about it.

The sourpuss warden and programs director Olive stood on a high point of the yard in front of everyone. Despite the touchy subject, the man on the scene didn't deliver the rundown. He made Olive struggle through the task instead, which raised the awkwardness even higher. The warden seemed to be there only to sneer at the crowd and dare offenders to laugh.

Even worse for Olive, no PA system or even a megaphone was available for use. Her thin voice struggled to shout loud enough so two hundred men could hear her read from a pamphlet. She began by defining "sexual" as "the sex organ or mouth of one person and the sex organ, mouth, or anus of another person."

Olive clarified, "we consider any sexual contact between an inmate and staff sexual abuse, whether consensual or not."

Convicts later agreed that we'll judge what's abusive, should we be so lucky. After all, one man's abuse is another man's dominatrix expenditure.

Next, she listed rape prevention tips, which gave inmates way too much credit. "Don't let your manners get in the way of keeping yourself safe. Don't be afraid to say no!"

Upon hearing this I asked those near me: "Manners? Who the fuck has manners around here?"

The lecture suggested ways for would-be rapists to come correct. Helpful hints for those who felt The Rapes coming on included breathing exercises, working on a hobby, or writing to a friend. Perhaps: "Dear Donna, I'm happy to report my appetite for raping was due to a lack of healthy diversions. Who fucking knew?"

Finally, the floor was opened for questions. I was dying to ask: "Does all this mean the mandatory circle jerks are discontinued?" but thought better of it. To do so would risk a write-up, and perhaps a beat down from inmates ready for the meeting to be over already.

I found widespread farting more sinister than sexual assaults. Seemingly everyone subscribed to my Grandmother's theory: better an empty house than a bad tenant. I was no exception. I constantly calculated how much gas I could pass without getting detected because you never want to be that guy. I'd hold fire or meter out gas in small doses if people were around – test flares to determine if the fart was a "shirt-puller."

Especially putrid farts forced guys to pull their crew neck collars over their noses. You could watch a bad one move down the line of bunks, dudes deploying their makeshift gas masks like slow motion dominoes falling. Alas, my long neck made getting my collar that high a stretch, so I usually weathered the invisible menace by breathing through my mouth.

Occasionally I'd shirt-pull anyway, to shift blame. When I dealt it, my collar came up immediately. This shifted the suspicion to a neighbor. Some blacks battled dangerous methane levels by shooting "smell good" (their term for cologne) into the air as they walked down the bunk row. So much cheap berry aroma hit the air that I suspected retaliation more than an effort to make the room smell better.

If religion is the opiate for the masses, television is the speedball, especially on the inside. I avoided it except for certain sports because most of the programs chosen were dreadful. Many others watched seemingly twelve hours a day, sitting on hard plastic chairs. A TV that quit working at Southern was replaced immediately since they stored brand new flat screens on-site. By comparison, a broken microwave often took weeks to replace. The ovens were a convenience life could go on without; TV was a babysitter.

A blatantly race-based inmate committee determined what programs hit the screen. This unofficial panel required an equal number of whites and blacks to hash out weekly schedules – a victory for logic. These schedules could change on the fly, however. Some COs enforced them more than others.

When guards didn't care, a show of hands in the room usually determined viewing choices. Sometimes black dudes chose the channels unilaterally. They knew white guys didn't want trouble based on TV and took advantage. This sort of nonsense made reading or doing something else instead an easy call for me.

TV sparked conflicts, too, involving seemingly benign programs. *America's Next Top Model* once prompted a heated discussion over which chick was hottest. I nearly joined in, even though I was only in the room to write on a table instead of my clipboard. I learned to stay out of it a different time when a debate over the hottest female on *Vanderpump Rules* resulted in a brawl. Tables got tossed over, fists were thrown, and ribs got kicked.

Keeping up with the Kardashians caused no similar disputes. Kim was the consensus hottest, and the show was #1 with practically everybody. Reality show formulas kept inmates transfixed. Scantily clad babes, glimpses of luxury, and petty conflict among vapid souls spoke to them. In other words, the programs depicted both the fantasy and actual lives of most inmates.

Old-timers insisted on watching *Little House on the Prairie* — the TV equivalent of a color-by-numbers Western novel — every day. The Lifetime Movie Network (aka Lonely Man's Network), featured simple, salacious plots and half-naked young actresses, and drew hordes of horny viewers.

Family Guy provided a secondary level of humor. The prison audience loved the slapstick and blunt jokes, but sharp humor and satire shot right over most heads.

"Man, I ain't watchin' no cartoon!" some guys huffed as they walked out. "Shit is stupid!"

NASCAR ruled the sports viewing. North Carolina loves little men driving in circles as much as college basketball. "Ricin'," as they pronounced it, was my nemesis in the joint. Any race took the top priority, and could last five hours, delaying football viewing in the process. Once a NASCAR race popped on the TV during the 2014 *Wimbledon* Men's final, which I'd bribed a guy to put on the schedule.

"What the fuck?! Who changed this?" I shouted, looking around a nearly empty dayroom on a Sunday morning.

"Me," replied a race fan. "Last night got rained out. You know ricin' comes first."

Equally unwatchable to me was the WNBA, which inmates love. They relish anything that makes young women sweat, sometimes at the expense of big events like major golf tournaments. Guys loved college softball, too. The general chunkiness of the players and the jiggle of the pitcher's ass during delivery prompted many to exclaim "Ooooo-wwweeeee!"

The dayroom always became electric for the women's competition in the *CrossFit Games*. These featured sturdy, spandex-wearing ladies – several very attractive – bending over, raising legs, and so forth. Convicts stayed transfixed during the deadlift, when failed attempts dropped girls onto their asses, legs splayed out. If only we'd all concentrated as hard in school as we did for those.

At Rutherford, the TV committee in our barracks suddenly consisted of no one, probably because its meeting took place at 7:30 Sunday mornings. I leaped at the chance to fill the void, eager to watch some of what I liked instead of standard prison fare. What could possibly go wrong?

Enter a career inmate known as Mophead, his derisive nickname that referred to his gray, poorly maintained dreadlocks. His face reminded me of looking at a turd, and his attitude matched it. No one liked him because he always pulled shit like cutting in line or just being a general asshole.

"Whoa, hey! What the fuck is *Family Guy* doing on the sports TV?" he shouted one day, to no one in particular.

"No good sports are on right now," I replied. "So I scheduled other shit, just like it's always been done."

Mophead looked like he'd never seen me before. "Wait, you're on the TV committee? With who else?"

"No one right now."

Mophead marched straight to the CO desk and ratted me out for TV-scheduling shenanigans. Never mind the committee guys before me pulled the same trick. I avoided official trouble by feigning the ignorance of a novice, but a feud was born. As soon as the CO moved out of earshot I erupted.

"What the fuck are you, the *powe*-leece?" I shouted at

Mophead. I nearly grinned from my pronunciation even though I was livid.

"I don't make the rules, man," he replied, backing down. "Shit needs done right."

"That's bullshit, and you know it. Damn snitch." I headed to my bunk before I did something worse.

"Yeah, you better walk," Mophead taunted. "Who made you boss, anyway?"

Hours later I learned Mophead was the new black guy representative on the sports TV committee. Suddenly, I had to decide how important watching *The Open Championship* golf and *Euro 2012* soccer was to me. Could I stomach sitting at a table with this scoundrel, sullying my Sunday mornings for televised sports? I decided to try it for a week.

In the dayroom again, my mild-mannered buddy John got into an argument with his friend and bunkmate "Moon." I'd failed to schedule the *X-Games* on the sports TV that night, and John thought Moon, a huge bald black guy, was responsible. Since Mophead minded other people's business, he joined the argument.

No fan of Mophead, John turned to him, "Man, shut the fuck up!"

"I ain't gotta," he replied. "The sports TV ain't no place for white boys no how."

John's eyes bulged as he reddened. "What did you say?" he spat. "What the fuck did you just say?!"

"You don't run this place, man. We got rules for the TV," Mophead replied as he stepped backward.

Moon turned on Mophead: "Yo, man, this ain't your shit. Go the fuck away."

The career inmate was dumb, but he wasn't stupid. He slithered away, mumbling to the floor as bystanders laughed at him.

Once I figured out what they were arguing about, I explained the *X-Games* oversight was my fault. John and Moon cooled off as real men do it – no COs involved. Not even two hours later, John faced a rare locker search.

The well-liked CO assigned the case didn't try very hard.

As he idly flipped through items, he confessed to searching for "dip" (smokeless tobacco). "Sometimes they tell me to search so we don't get a grievance filed about racial favoritism," he told John.

Mophead, emasculated in a packed dayroom earlier, had obviously snitched. Not only was he too stupid to delay such revenge, but he blew the whistle when a CO who hated rats as much as anyone was on duty. Otherwise, he wouldn't have shared that information with John.

This episode left me incensed. I get emotional about snitches. I stayed restless most of that night, struggling with the urge to respond on John's behalf. I'd see Mophead again in mere hours, at our first TV committee meeting together. He needed to pay.

The TV committees from ten barracks met in the chow hall. Blacks and whites sat in pairs and hashed out that week's viewing options. I arrived early, tense but also foggy from sleeping poorly. I passed a CO at the doorway. He moved to patrol elsewhere, leaving only inmates anywhere nearby.

Soon Moon arrived and sat with me and his co-scheduler, an old coot called Dingbat. I simmered until Mophead showed up ten minutes late. He moved toward our table. I remained seated but wasted no time.

"Oh look, it's the *powe*-leece!" I loudly declared, prompting all heads in the room to rise.

"What choo mean?" Mophead replied.

"Well, you go to the police about everything, right?" I said, coming to a boil.

"Man, you know the sports TV side is the sports side, ain't nothin' 'sposed to be ..."

I cut him off. "Nevermind that bullshit. You ratted out my boy for dip!"

Conversation in the room stopped. Moon's jaw dropped and his eyes bugged out. He knew me only as easygoing. He made no move to chill me out.

"I didn't do nothin' like that shit," Mophead insisted. "And I oughta beat your ass for sayin' it."

I sneered and yelled: "Why don't you just pull out your pepper spray – after all, you're the *powe*-leece!"

This drew laughs from the rapt gallery.

"I'm just tryin' to make the schedule here, man," Mophead replied.

I'd already filled in *British Open* golf on the sheet, so I slid it across the table towards him.

"Have at it, motherfucker!" I shouted. "I don't work with snitches!"

I stood abruptly as the gallery howled. Mophead raised fists to defend himself. I headed straight to the door wearing a sneer. My point had been made, and Mophead humiliated. That's my kind of violence.

If Mophead were bigger or had allies on the camp, I would have been less bold. Then again, frustration overcame me like never before. Annoyance with snitches. With ignoramuses. With the exasperation of being locked up. I'd been "institutionalized" to the point of nearly fighting a two-bit career inmate. My goal of getting through thirty more months of my sentence physically unharmed did not look good.

Rutherford's tight watch on kitchen food stock benefited me now. I harbored no illegal oatmeal, or any other contraband. If Mophead ratted me out in retaliation, I'd be fine. Instead, he and I settled into an uneasy truce. In other words, we ignored each other. We'd part ways in two weeks, anyway.

CHAPTER THIRTEEN

Unplanned Reporting Assignment

After three months I bid farewell to the cramped confines of Rutherford and returned to Southern, which felt like home. Shouts of "Biff!" echoed through corridors as old pals welcomed me back. For the next day or so I marveled at how guys I knew were still locked up three months after I left. It struck me as strange and pathetic.

Even stranger: one of them was me. *Like, how the fuck are we even doing this?*

I felt like a celebrity upon my return, oddly enough. Everyone wanted a piece of me, or at least information about the camp I'd just been to. I answered the same questions for two days while still physically drained from the move. I wished to hold a press conference to get it over with all at once ...

Q: *What about the female CO's? Were they hot and did they have fat asses?*

A: None of them attracted me much, but I like to think I don't yet have "dumpster dick," like most inmates. No offense. But yes, a couple female guards did swing nice, big asses.

Q: *Did the canteen sell coffee in bags you can spoon out or just the packets like here?*

A: Bags, but the camp kept a strict per-day limit on canteen purchases.

Q: *Did they have real toilet seats, or do you sit right on the bowl like here?*

A: Real seats, but the toilets are like a bidet when you make a courtesy flush.

Q: *What the fuck is a bid day?*
A: Never mind. Press conference over.

Soon after my return, I paid an inmate ten bucks – a fortune in the joint – for his back-corner bunk spot in the quietest barracks. We swapped bunks. The extra serenity was worth it, especially since Southern allowed us to hang sheets from bunk frames for privacy. Being inside felt like being a little kid under the dining room table again. I decorated it with artsy *Vanity Fair* ads featuring hot chicks. I considered it a private cabin on the worst cruise ship ever. I enjoyed life again, at least for a minute.

I returned from Rutherford with eight bags of brown gold. Coffee rules the lives of many people, but especially inmates. The coffee available at Southern sucked, so I could trade a spoonful of the good stuff for a stamp, and a whole three-ounce bag for practically anything. My drug dealer mind went to work for a way to import more.

I recalled bidding farewell to Carver at Rutherford. "If there's anything I can do for you, let me know," he said as we shook hands.

A pal I met in the rehab program, Blade, planned to transfer to Southern in a couple of weeks. I wrote to Carver, asking him to pass a note:.

> *"Hey Blade, Please buy me ten bags of coffee before you leave and come to Southern. I will have my people fund your account when I get a letter from you confirming the buy. I'll tip you later for the effort.*
>
> *Thanks! Biff"*

A couple of weeks passed without a word and I'd nearly forgotten about it. Perhaps Blade changed his transfer plan or didn't want the hassle. Whatever. Then one afternoon while enjoying a nap I felt my bed shake. "Phillips! Wake up!"

Unplanned Reporting Assignment

There stood Warden, a middle-aged guy who both dressed and looked like a golfer: A tan white guy. We'd talked college basketball in the past, and he seemed nice, albeit gruff. Most inmates respected him as a "straight shooter," as one put it. He rarely ventured into the bunk area, so seeing him at my back corner startled me.

"I need a handwriting sample from you," he said, skipping any pleasantries.

"Sure," I said as I scrambled to my feet. "Give me a second."

I extracted an unimportant page from a stack in my locker and handed it to him.

"This is pretty random. What's up?" I asked.

"Nothing you need to worry about," Warden mumbled and strode away.

I assumed a staff member received a threatening letter, and Warden was narrowing down whodunit. No biggie. I whistled through the rest of the day unfazed, not thinking twice about the visit. Then I awoke in the middle of the night, with an adrenaline shot in the pit of my stomach. *My letter to Carver!*

I asked old-timers like Billy what to make of it all. I learned that asking a prison official to pass a note to an inmate is a big no-no. From that moment, all of the emotions I suffered between my MDMA arrest and prison intake returned. My life upended and the dread of a dead man walking. Every laugh that arose was tempered. My name could blast over the intercom at any moment. As these anxious days crawled by, however, a beacon of happiness appeared.

Tip, who was my inmate barber and a chow hall gospel singer, came by to smoke a cigarette with me as I sipped a cup of coffee at my bunk. His optimism brightened up Southern, even though he'd been locked up for over four-thousand days on a gun violence charge.

"I'm fucked, Tip," I whined. I described my predicament and finished with, "I'm getting browned-down for sure."

"Shit, I did five years in medium. You'll be fine, just like you are here."

If Tip had endured his plight and still smiled constantly, I might be okay. He even left me with several draws remaining on his Newport – a luxury compared to a roll-up. My despair lifted, at least for a few minutes. Gifts of human kindness can be found in the strangest places.

During five days of stewing and wondering, I consulted veteran inmates for strategic advice.

"Pretend to be an ignorant dumbass. Should be easy enough for you," Ice joked. "Go look in the mirror and practice looking shocked."

"Garrett Phillips, report to the Sergeant's Office." My stomach plunged, and I trudged to the nice part of town. You'd think I'd be used to this shit by now, but not so much.

I drew a deep breath and entered the office. A captain occupied a big desk, the only one in the room. Officers of his rank rarely came around, so this signaled deep do-do for me. He looked like an actor playing a prison administrator, miscast because he was attractive.

"Good morning! You must be Mr. Phillips," Captain said, warmly.

"Yessir, that's me," I managed. I shook his hand with my clammy one and sat down.

He slid the letter I wrote to Carver in front of me, wasting no time.

"What we have here is a level-three bribery attempt. A serious issue and an 'A-charge,' as a matter of fact."

Gape-mouthed, I stammered: "I … Oh, man, I had no idea I couldn't ask for a favor like this!"

Captain chuckled. "That's interesting, Mr. Phillips. But it says here, in your writing to the counselor: 'Sorry if I'm asking you to bend some silly rule.'"

Oops.

Trying to ignore that inconvenient fact, I played my best card immediately.

"In my defense, Mr. Carver often described himself as a 'guest of the prison system,' never as an *officer* of anything," I explained. "In fact, when I left he said: 'Let me know if there's anything I can do for you.'"

Captain pleasantly explained that rehab counselors are

considered officers of the system, and said Carver's alleged offer changed nothing. Also irrelevant was coffee causing the fuss. "Could've just as well been heroin, doesn't matter."

"I'll be honest, I was sure someone set you up," Captain offered, still smiling. "That's why I needed a handwriting sample to analyze."

He was nice enough not to add "because I never thought someone could be this stupid." Whatever the case, they hit me with a weighty "A-charge," for bribing an officer, and a less serious "C-charge" for improper use of the mail.

Next, I met with Warden, a good guy at heart and the main reason the camp treated inmates so well. My bribery charge baffled him since I made no promise of compensation to anyone besides an inmate. Nevertheless, since a major infraction was pending, they moved me directly to off-camp segregation – the hole. Both Warden and common sense suggested I'd beat the charge on appeal, but this was hardly a given. As my writing contest debacle showed, logic sometimes doesn't mean shit in prison.

The benevolent Warden let me pack up my belongings myself before heading to jail, a job almost always performed by COs. This major courtesy allowed me to pass off items like clipboards that otherwise would've been confiscated. My pals would give them back upon my return.

I was soon moved to a cage in a backseat for an unpleasant car ride to the hole, about an hour away. My long legs suffered tight quarters, and the oblivious CO at the wheel tortured me with weak radio broadcast signals of gospel preachin' that intermingled with rock music. Back and forth the stations faded, creating a bizarre mash-up. This seemed a perfect soundtrack for such a surreal episode: "You go back, Jack, do it again ... and JEE-SUS said ..."

Despite events turning sour, I stayed optimistic. I loved reading and writing, so I welcomed a break from myriad distractions in the barracks. My insane previous sixteen months since my arrest had yet to break me, and I didn't intend to collapse then. Warden seemed to have my back, too, which helped allay my fear. I tried to focus on the process; to embrace my new assignment as an embedded reporter. And talk about great source material.

If Southern Correctional was a miniature idyllic town, Piedmont Minimum was the shitty neighborhood on the other side of the tracks. The building that contained forty segregation cells was aptly dark, dingy, and timeworn. I barely noticed at first, though. My spirits were oddly high, possibly because I'd arrived at a private suite in which to masturbate with impunity.

At first, the worst part of the hole seemed to be the unacceptable bedware – a floppy, lumpy mattress on a steel slab. Underneath the bed platform was a shelf for belongings, and a stainless steel toilet/sink combo stood next to it. Neither a writing surface nor a chair was provided. I could stand in the middle of the space and touch both walls simultaneously, just like I can in a passenger elevator.

My new home consisted of three cinderblock walls and bars forming the fourth. Picture an indoor storage facility, only storing people instead of extra household items. While bleak, the cell block wasn't the dungeon suggested by the term "the hole." The single light bulb in a cage high on the wall too dim to read by felt kinda medieval, though.

At least a window to a courtyard across a corridor allowed glimpses of grass and sky and provided light during the day. I folded my mattress in half to create a poor-man's recliner, the window at my back for reading and writing when light was available. At night I changed ends, my head at the wall. This made the cell seem like two rooms and helped separate day from night.

Upon my arrival, COs examined two plastic tote bags containing my personal effects. Only certain items were permitted in the cell. Happily, my books and journals made the cut, along with snacks I'd stockpiled back at Southern. They took my real pens to prevent stabbings, so my writing instrument became a flimsy "safety" pen, basically the thin stick inside a Bic. My *A New Direction* workbook passed and served as my

Unplanned Reporting Assignment

desktop. This small victory mattered little, though, because my radio didn't make it.

I learned radios are forbidden for A-charge offenders in segregation. Losing this lifeline to intelligent life almost made me break down and cry. I sat and stared blankly, grasping this tragedy when an affable middle-aged CO named Lukens stopped to chat while on his rounds.

"I noticed you came from Southern."

I could only nod while staring at the floor.

The CO continued: "I transferred from there a year ago. Is a guy called Gage still there? He was the tobacco kingpin."

"Yes, Gage is still there," I allowed. "But I have no idea what you're talking about besides that."

Lukens chuckled. "Of course you don't. But I'll tell you, that son-of-a-bitch is crafty," the CO gushed. "We knew he ran the tobacco, but could never pin it on him. It's only a matter of time, but not with him."

This livened me up a bit, and I steered the conversation toward others at Southern. We discussed other mutual acquaintances. This reminded me of the classic *Looney Tunes* cartoon scene when the sheepdog (Sam) and the wolf (Ralph) greeted each other at the time clock, starting another workday. Guards and inmates are natural enemies, yet close brethren in a way. I heard multiple COs over my time sum it up: "The only difference between you and me is I never got caught."

Lukens and I chatted for about fifteen minutes. Before he moved on with his mundane day, I took a shot: "Say, I looked through my stuff here and I noticed my radio is missing. Who do I need to talk to about getting it back?"

"Uh-uh. You're here for an A-charge, so you can't have a radio."

"I have charges pending," I pleaded, "but like I said Warden is convinced I'll beat them!"

"Sorry, I can't do anything for you there." He sauntered away.

I felt like I'd been hit with a brick all over again. I faced a grim thirty days with no sports news, right as football season started. I lamented the loss of *Sound Opinions*, the excellent rock music review show. Then, just as I mourned losing *Fresh Air* with Terry Gross, Lukens reappeared. He slipped my radio through the bars and quietly said, "You didn't get this from me, and some other officer is probably gonna take it back anyway."

He winked and headed on his way. Not all cops are dicks!

This victory aside, depression and despair from segregation descended quickly. I was a reject from a population of rejects – the sediment at the bottom of the barrel. I tried to tell myself I didn't belong there and wondered how much I'd rot. Concentrating on anything besides this negativity proved a constant struggle. Especially since my confinement wasn't exactly solitary.

Modern jail cells comprise four solid walls. Piedmont's only had three, which allowed for an auditory assault that would turn Gandhi vindictive. Guys shouted inane questions and stories to buddies many cells down the corridor – often repeating themselves to be heard – disturbing neighbors near and far. Earplugs barely helped. Daytime relief came only when the temperature rose high enough to run large cooling fans, which drowned out other sounds.

Otherwise, the worst part of experiencing the hole is tough to pinpoint. Hot water was not available for cooking noodles. They had banned coffee. The meal schedule was ridiculous, with dinner completed by 4:00 pm. I usually set aside bread or a biscuit for evenings so I didn't blow through my limited snack supply during the thirteen-hour gap between meals.

Unlike in the general population, substituting the meal entrée for beans or something was not an option. I either ate the "meat" or went hungry. I employed a competitive eating strategy, basically inhaling the awfulness and slamming water as a chaser. I'd then brush my teeth immediately and have a cough drop as a finishing mint to manage the wretched taste.

Also difficult to digest were trips to the shower, which involved being handcuffed and escorted by a CO. This strange dance was such a pain that I normally showered only every third or fourth day. Daily recreation time, in a twenty-foot square pen, usually came in the chilly pre-dawn that begged for a long-sleeved shirt that inmates couldn't have. Luckily I endured only one of these mornings because God had an alternative exercise plan for me. One that allowed The Hole to work for me.

My cell came pre-stocked with several Jesus pamphlets, up high on a small shelf. A few days into my stay an epiphany hit: the Lord wanted me to create juggling balls from His paper. I pressed multiple pages into three crude juggling spheres. God then drew an errant ball into the toilet, triggering a second revelation: a wet paper ball can be compressed more effectively and, once dry, keeps its shape better. Hello exercise props!

Juggling provided a workout, especially under-the-leg tosses that require high knee raises. Even better, my bed was at thigh-level so drops usually settled on it. Patience to learn new tricks was easy to find because I had nothing better to do anyway after reading and writing until cross-eyed. And I stole time from The Man.

Most COs seemed surprised by my hobby – like I was the first captive to turn tricks in this fashion. Most of them were nice and accommodating, even retrieving balls that rolled out into the corridor. One guard, however, tore up a ball in search of contraband. She claimed stranger hiding places had been discovered. No problem, though. I had endless time to craft a replacement and plenty of paper on hand. *Thank you, Jesus. Thank you, Lord.*

Juggling also allowed me to vent frustration with the loudness that enveloped me. The main culprit was my next-door neighbor, who I'll call Curse. (I never asked his name, lest I encourage him to talk more.) He kept a running dialog with his pal two cells down on the other side of me. Bravado-packed stories of complete bullshit besieged me all day long. If not yelling in conversation, Curse usually thought out loud, rapped, or sang poorly. No human mouth has ever run as much as his.

Even worse, most of his declarative sentences ended with a mindless "yeah." An innocuous enough tic, I suppose – until heard for hours on end. Equally charming was his penchant for saying "shit" three times in one sentence, like "They saw my shit and got on my shit; shit's crazy!" Or, if you prefer: "I mean, shit, it was shit you could see happening in real life and shit!" I suddenly understood why suicides in the hole are so prevalent.

My only relief besides the occasional fan noise came when Curse had a book to read. In his case, this was like stuffing a pacifier into a fussy baby's mouth. Unfortunately, he could only read pop fiction with spoon-fed plots – basically bad TV for readers. This became clear after I lent him *American Psycho* and *Everything is Illuminated*, both of which he rejected despite no other options. He started babbling endlessly soon thereafter. I never engaged him again.

On the plus side, Curse provided a force-fed anthropological study; a glimpse inside a dense criminal mind. He had fathered six kids by age twenty-eight, by three different women. He landed in the hole (this time) for a fight over a card game, which delayed his release date by four months. Proving this idiocy was no fluke, he continually insulted a kitchen guy who delivered our meals. Who knows what ended up in Curse's food.

My neighbor's finest work, however, was descending into an extended scrap with "Old School," the assumed nickname of any older inmate. He was a sixtyish janitor who I loved because he sold me canteen items forbidden in segregation and supplied extra clothes and bedding. Anyway, the janitor screwed Curse on a tobacco deal, pocketing his stamps instead.

The two of them kept a running dialog of insults and threats. Old School once told Curse: "I coulda been your Daddy, but I didn't want to wait in that long-ass line!"

Their differences came to a head when Curse threw water at Old School as he mopped – not exactly the best plan when one is cornered in a five-by-seven cell. Old School left and soon returned with his mop bucket. With a smile on his face, he dipped a cup into the mop water multiple times and doused his opponent with it. Hearing Curse cuss and knock around trying to dodge the fetid assault brought a smile to my face.

Even better, the conflict escalated into a fistfight even with Curse behind bars. This prompted me to stick a hand mirror out of my cell to watch. Old School bobbed and weaved, occasionally slapping what appeared to be two disembodied arms. Curse responded with strained insults, repeating: "I live this shit!" presumably meaning the Thug Life. Or maybe he meant engaging in ill-advised altercations.

The janitor moved close enough to get slapped a couple of times, but never took a real punch. This didn't stop Curse from trying. He feverishly jabbed through the bars anyway. Only in the post-adrenaline aftermath did he realize his forearms were scraped, like he'd run them through a potato grater. Of course, then he whined about it for days to no one in particular. I've never needed Sam Harris' *Waking Up* meditation app more desperately.

It's okay, only a few more days, and he's gone.

I must have told myself this a hundred times. I started counting down the days until they sent Curse packing. I practically counted his final hours and minutes on my shitty Casio wristwatch. Just before he left, Curse announced he would ruin his mattress, just to fuck with the next guy.

The cell Curse occupied stayed vacant only a couple of hours. I called his replacement "Jinx." He looked like Nic Cage's dumbass boss in *Raising Arizona*. He refused to work his prison job, so thirty days got added to his sentence and thirty in the hole.

His booming voice terrorized all within earshot, which means probably the whole fucking jail. Jinx continued my neighbor's tradition of shouting in conversation to someone several cells down, too. Even worse, five or six times a day he emitted an ear-splitting roar while shaking his cell bars. He'd then laugh it off with some dim witticism like, "Just wanted to make sure y'all are paying attention."

Like most inmates, Jinx was devoid of empathy and oblivious to his own disruptive behavior. He incessantly complained about how loud the other guys were. I longed to tell him to shut up but refrained. The less potential nut-job enemies down the road, the better. Swallowing my anger may have come at a cost, however.

Unlike in the general population, segregation offered nowhere to hide from the likes of Curse and Jinx. I felt like a cornered ant, with my cell as a magnifying glass and my insufferable neighbor the sun. This aggravation triggered the emotional nadir of my prison stay. The wall I'd built to hold back pain, regret, and remorse came crashing down.

With Jinx's shouting as a soundtrack, I looked past the bars of my cell, out old, foggy windows into the barracks across the way. Oh, to be there instead, in that happier place joking around with the fellas. I thought back to a similar situation from a short rehab stay during my teen years. I'd traveled so far in the subsequent decades, yet my station in life was even worse.

Was I truly this level of a loser? I neared a complete emotional breakdown that night, with self-pity joining a feeling of utter and complete loneliness. I wept like a little kid, with no one to comfort me. A slacker had found his comeuppance. That night I lacked the will to even promise myself to do better.

Besides nervous breakdowns, a general dread plagued my first two weeks in The Hole. My meeting with Mr. Holsinger, Disciplinary Hearing Officer (DHO), loomed like a final interview for a crucial job. I constantly felt like I'd wrecked my Dad's car while he was out of town and had to wait for his return. An unfavorable ruling meant medium security, likely costing me teeth and any chance of transfer to the honor grade camp in Asheville.

Officer Lukens often stopped by to say hello over the course of these days. During these chats, he allayed some of my fears about the meeting. He told me Holsinger, a former prison guard himself, was a good friend of his. I learned that talking Carolina Panthers football and rock music would earn me suck-up points. I nearly asked Lukens to put in a good word for me, but that kind of mess got me in the hole to start with.

Jailhouse rumor suggested that Holsinger was fair and lenient. And if inmates, with their entitlement complexes and twisted fairness standards, think a guy is okay he probably is. Whatever the case, after eight days of worrying and projecting worst-case scenarios, a CO appeared to escort me to Judgement Day.

Once again I felt like a movie actor, this time playing a murder defendant fitted in full shackles, hands locked at my waist. This felt more surreal than joining in a prison rap circle with eight black guys, and more like a Halloween stunt than a punishing reality. I passed inmates wandering on the yard on my way to the judgment. They seemed to regard me as a homicidal cannibal, unaware my most recent fight was in fourth grade. The absurdity of it all nearly made me laugh.

Lightness aside, the ankle cuffs were tight on my Achilles. Trundling to the hearing office was an uncomfortable chore. My last girlfriend Laura's wounded foot debacle came to mind, specifically her crack about returning her dignity should I find it. Worse, I couldn't scratch seemingly constant facial itches. I briefly considered bringing a lawsuit for cruel and unusual punishment due to unscratchable itch.

My first stop was a large room, the office for the sergeants and a breakroom for guards. Pop music (and commercials) blared from a radio. Three COs had to raise their voices over the likes of the song *I Kissed a Girl* to discuss NASCAR and pro wrestling. I might as well have been invisible. After fifteen minutes a door opened and a fellow felon shuffled out of the hearing room, nearly in tears.

A guard emerged from another room. "Phillips!"

I made my way through the doorway and, because of limited agility, basically fell into a chair next to Mr. Holsinger. Someone closed the door behind me.

In his early fifties, the DHO officer resembled the actor Oliver Platt. He wore poorly-balanced reading glasses, which he removed often. I waited patiently as he wrapped up notes on his previous meeting, wishing he'd scratch my nose.

"Okay, let's see what's up with you," Holsinger said, skimming through my file. "Um hmmm, mmm, uh, huh …"

"Officer Lukens tells me you're a Panther fan," I said after a couple of minutes, breaking the brown-nosing ice.

"That I am,' he muttered, without looking up. Sixty seconds of silence followed, which felt like five minutes. Eventually, he removed his glasses and spoke.

"I saw the Panthers get blown out by the Giants the other night," he said. "I wanted to drink away the pain, but beers cost damn $8.50."

"Hey, next time just smuggle in a flask. Take it from a convict!"

Holsinger laughed, and my white privilege networking gambit began. We talked about football, the sad state of rock radio, and Iron Maiden concerts.

"Damn. It sure is nice to find a good conversation for a change," I remarked at one point.

"Tell me about it," he replied.

I wedged the details of my writing contest debacle into the conversation. Holsinger laughed at the absurdity of it.

"Yeah, that Western (part of the state) bunch isn't pleasant. They're one reason I'm glad to be retiring soon."

Finally, we got around to my disciplinary action. According to Holsinger, whether I offered Carver compensation to pass the note to my buddy was immaterial. "Or influence" was the phrase that mattered. Even asking for a favor was punishable.

"Be that as it may, I still plead not guilty," I declared.

"Now why would you do that?" Holsinger asked, good-naturedly as he removed his glasses for the tenth time.

"Because I didn't bribe anybody, and I had no idea asking for a favor was a big deal. I'm new at this, after all."

Holsinger lowered his voice and slowed his speech as if speaking to a child: "New or not, you attempted to influence an officer. You will not shake this charge. This isn't complicated."

"But ..."

"And this mess activates the suspended sentence from your writing contest bust," he added.

He offered a plea bargain, which would avoid an appeal to a "less understanding" judge. "This is the best you'll do," he promised.

"Look, all I care about is going back to Southern. Can that happen?"

Holsinger looked at his computer screen and started pecking. My beard grew an inch before he finally declared: "That's doable, assuming my boss goes for it. He kind of lets me do whatever since I'm almost retired. We should be good."

The bad news was I still faced another fifteen days in segregation, followed by a canteen purchase sanction for six weeks. But at least I'd stay at Southern.

The DHO officer printed out shit for me to sign as I decompressed, thrilled to have a resolution. I thanked him profusely and bumbled to my feet. We exchanged farewells before I tottered out the door. But this wasn't the last I'd see of him.

As a CO arrived to escort me back to my cell, Holsinger emerged to hand somebody paperwork. He saw me and continued our conversation, unconcerned with numerous CO and inmate bystanders.

"Hey, I forgot to mention, Alice Cooper played with Iron Maiden when I saw them."

I stifled a laugh at his continuing our chat there, but managed: "Wait, played with them, or opened for them?"

"Opened for them. And don't laugh, Alice was great!"

"Oh, I don't doubt that at all," I assured him, heading out. "Did he also have the snake?"

"No snake," Holsinger replied, deflating slightly.

I practically got shoved out the door by my escort before I could reply. On the walk back to my cell I dwelled on fifteen more days of discomfort ahead of me. I'd all but packed to leave that day, so this felt like a loss. Worse, my record now showed an A-charge. So much for a good transfer.

Everyone near my cell knew my meeting happened, so everyone asked about it when I got back. I shouted the result into the corridor from my cell so they could hear. "You still in honor grade?! Damn, you got off light!" one guy commented.

This brightened my spirits. My paperwork showed that I carried a whopping twenty-three demerit points, yet I remained assigned to minimum security. No one I told of this over the rest of my sentence had heard of such. The prison justice system taketh away, yet it also giveth. Seemed about right.

CHAPTER FOURTEEN

Rough Times for a Rookie

The bed I made for myself (the hole) hurt. Literally. The hard surface bruised my bony frame and threw my muscles into knots. I'd wake in the night with a limb asleep and choose which side to sleep based on which hurt the least. Mornings felt like I'd slept on the floor after a party and woke to find no coffee anywhere. At least I finally finished *Infinite Jest*.

Another positive was time slowed down, in a good way. I listened to sports on the radio, for instance, something I'd done little of since my teens. Local stations carried pro football and baseball games. Following along required painting a picture in my mind, like reading a book. Like the old days. I'd forgotten how enjoyable it could be.

Also fun was being only three cells down from the shower. This provided a nightly parade of jailbirds passing by, including an old dude I knew from Rutherford. We always exchanged pleasantries, showing how mindless polite greetings can be. The guy always asked how I was doing as I stewed in my dim cell.

"Good!" I'd reply, "And you?"

"Can't complain!" he'd reply, shuffling along with a CO escort, shackled and wearing only boxers.

A Barking Guy sounded off many times a day, often shouting a string of obscenities from at least ten cells away. He'd let loose plaintive wails, sometimes howling like a hound dog. BG cursed and barked so impressively that I couldn't tell if he was playing around or not.

"Let me out of here, you yellow sons-of-bitches!" he'd moan, in a heavy Midwestern accent. "Ohhhh," he'd groan. "I can't take it anymore! You hear me, you rat bastards?!"

Other times he presented threats. "I'm gonna bust out of here, you motherfuckers. And when I do, I'm comin' back for each and every one of you! I can't take it anymore! Ohhhh!"

After two weeks, BG was obviously lying. He *could* take it more. His barking became more refined — six or eight short bursts, then a long howl, followed by more barks. Other cons bayed and yapped along with him just for kicks. It sounded like being in a kennel.

A few guys, including me, enjoyed mimicking BG's rants. This always drew laughs even though mocking a brother in pain was cold-hearted. He sounded too whimsical to be suffering, anyway. He lived at the Ritz-Carlton compared to hardcore solitary confinement, too.

BG's outbursts reminded me of typical prison stories that describe inmate meltdowns. I expected to see crying fits many times on my prison tour, but hardly ever did. Again, honor grade has its privileges.

A relative calm settled in as my time in jail wound down, even though Jinx remained as my neighbor. A couple of his buddies moved out, and he stopped shaking the bars in his cell and screaming. I suppose it was all theatre meant for them. My strategy of ignoring Jinx paid off, or he might have kept acting the fool.

"Pack it up!" a CO yelled into my cell one morning.

"Uh, I think you have the wrong cell," I replied.

After the guard confirmed he meant me, I felt like the last day of school came ten days early. I was so happy I tossed oatmeal pies and other snacks into neighboring cells on the way out. I tried to find Barking Guy, to put a face to the howls. Sadly, the CO escorting me rushed things, so I failed. In my mind, he'll always look like the late pianist and troubadour Mose Allison.

Arriving at Southern again felt like coming home — almost too good to be true. I felt like a five-hundred-hour car trip had finally ended. I slowly reclaimed the comfort level I enjoyed before my vacation. I spent many stamps for a good bunk spot, reassemble my wardrobe, and so forth. Life was good.

Inmate Christmas package ordering was all the rage the week of my return. This annual opportunity allowed inmates access to myriad items not available from the canteen, coffee pouches included. Had I known this was coming I never would've written my letter to Carver. But I had to be "crafty" and not run my plan by veteran inmates before doing it.

The supplemental orders were delivered in large clear garbage bags. Dudes looked like overgrown elves as they crossed the camp with their goodies slung over their shoulders. Celebration filled the barracks, but I also noticed those who got nothing. They had to watch others bask in the riches.

I pulled in twenty-five three-ounce bags of coffee, enough to last a year. But I soon resumed trading it away. Getting goods and services this way meant my canteen account needed replenishing less often. I'd leech less from my friends and family that way. But my coffee would never last twelve months at the rate I went through it.

In my excitement, I didn't think that everyone saw me cramming my locker full of coffee and all my new snacks. Simple me didn't even worry about it. This invited the have-nots that I originally pitied to start begging. My generosity ran low fast.

"Dude, this shit needs to last me a year," I explained. Soon this became, "I told you what's up. Quit fucking asking."

In other words, I gave a green light to some criminal minds. I later learned experienced inmates plan ahead for goodie-bag days. They kept their best items concealed before even starting the walk to the barracks and waited until no one was around to unpack. Some even recruited friends with spare locker space to hide long-term items like coffee for them, just to be safe. I couldn't have played it worse.

Sure enough, two weeks after delivery I discovered fourteen coffee pouches missing from my stash. At least the thief was thoughtful enough to leave six bags behind, and nothing else had gone missing. He must have been a friend of mine.

Given the rarity of theft at Southern, this stunned me. Guys occasionally howled about something stolen only to find they misplaced it. But coffee is very much a drug, and prison is full of drug addicts. Kiss honor among thieves goodbye in this case. I took the loss in stride and moved on. Even if I identified the culprit, getting revenge would risk another trip to the hole. Had I listened to a crafty veteran called "Junkyard" when I first arrived I could have avoided my loss.

The dentally challenged Junkyard always looked like he'd just rolled out from under a car. He also smiled all the time. A larcenist, he claimed to harbor thousands of dollars worth of stolen copper, stashed in an old school bus buried in the ground. Talk about a retirement account. He loved reading dreadful Western paperbacks. Sample passage: "Melissa was delicious, sweeter than the sweetest fruit, more sugary than a fresh-baked pie."

"You need to buy a good lock," Junkyard slowly explained. "Not the Master brand everyone else has. Buy one from someone goin' home soon and get it when he leaves."

But sometimes having the same lock as ninety-five percent of your neighbors pays off. One time some dumbass (me) locked his key in his locker. Step one to open it was finding out if any of my neighbor's keys worked. A line formed, waiting to take a turn. Some jiggled and finessed the lock, others rammed the key home with authority. None of the keys succeeded, but it did look like a porn gang-bang scene and that made me laugh.

Another option was to pry open the locker door with a broom handle, wide enough to reach in and grab the key. I felt like a lion tamer, sticking his head into a huge yawning jaw. If the guy holding the broom pulled it out I'd lose an arm. A guard using bolt cutters seemed the only solution, at least until a hero appeared.

"Hold up. I got this!" said a burly dude that had just returned from work. "Back up."

He held his steel-toed work boot above his head with both

hands. Down came the boot onto the lock, like a sledgehammer. The lock gave way on the first try. I'm sure it wondered what the fuck happened. No one around had seen such a thing. Lock Buster played it cool, as if he performed that trick every day. The lock still worked, too.

Anyway, months later I learned two guys stole my coffee. Both of the shitheads had transferred elsewhere by then. One was notable for always holding a cup of coffee, despite not having much money. He smiled constantly, at least when he saw me. No wonder. The other culprit, Kenny, who looked like a thirty-something brother of the actor Woody Harrelson, could be funny and friendly but carried the aura of a real scumbag.

Reasonably intelligent, Kenny somehow never learned to read. He didn't care about sports and didn't play cards or watch TV. He filled his time lifting weights, socializing, and bumming things, usually nicotine, without saying thanks. Frequently in trouble, Kenny once got busted for tobacco, which would earn him a brown-down if convicted. To solve this problem, he joined forces with Loober, my dryly hilarious bunkmate.

During a break in Super Bowl 47, I scooted back to my locker to grab an oatmeal pie. There on the floor lay young Loober, on his back and wide-eyed. Far from panicking at the sight, I sensed shenanigans. The kid was generally full of shit, and he looked fine to me. I ignored him, but practically every CO and the nurse on duty didn't have that luxury.

They flooded into the barracks, and in the meantime, Kenny raided the sergeant's office to steal the evidence they had on him. Reports were he succeeded, too, at least for a minute. Administration shipped him out anyway, based on multiple suspended sentences for previous offenses. They had tired of his shit.

I figured Loober was ripe for an accessory charge due to this stunt, but not even close. His hospital visit and subsequent tests — based on *faked* chest pain — revealed a legitimate medical condition. Too many enzymes in his system caused his kidneys to start shutting down. Had Loober not joined in

Kenny's plan he might have died from it, undiagnosed. My fellow felons and I learned a valuable lesson: *Dishonesty and deception could very well save your life!*

This episode made me laugh and recall my first job, as a teenager. Paperboys collected subscription payments door-to-door back in those days, usually in cash. I'd typically delay this pain in the ass for many weeks, then appear seeking payment for up to three months of deliveries. Basically, I treated these customers like ATMs before they were invented. Whenever I wanted cash to blow I'd go collect a few accounts.

When my boss came to collect my money, I never had enough. This crookedness got me fired, followed by collection proceedings against me. For better or worse, a family friend was a partner at a high-octane law firm, and he saved (enabled) me. He argued they routinely issued and charged me for more newspapers than I had customers, which was true. The newspaper soon dropped the matter.

While an excellent result at the time, paying reparations for my larceny would've been a better lesson. Instead, I learned that powerful connections and dumb luck trumped rules. Laziness and dishonesty could pay.

Most of my inmate brethren were stuck at middle-school age emotionally. They worried most about "street cred" or "prison pride," which inevitably drew trouble. "Pooch," a thirty-ish native of Atlanta housing projects, personified this. We became pals and bonded based on our hometown and doing time for drug trafficking. Funny that the drugs we dealt with and our Atlanta experiences were almost entirely different.

Pooch and I discussed this, and the different ways we regarded life. He mostly talked about hustling on the street and people who'd disrespected him. In his mind, everyone else was doing it wrong, and he wasn't to blame for anything. He was a prime candidate for the criminal thought therapy of *A New Direction*. I wish he'd gone through the program before we met.

My buddy's negativity and complaining soon led me to quit hanging out with him. Pooch was a lone wolf, so he soon noticed I'd ditched him as a pal. He also took it personally when I bought roll-ups elsewhere because they were cheaper. Sarcastic trash-talking was his style of humor, but he started taking me seriously when I threw it back at him. Whatever.

One Sunday morning a dozen or so inmates lounged about in a dayroom, reading the paper and watching NFL pregame shows. I leafed through the sports page, and a couple of other newspaper sections sat in front of me on my table. Pooch strode up to me and spoke in his tough-guy style. "Yo, lemme see the sports."

I didn't look up, but said, "Ain't happenin'." I waved at the table. "Looks like the Lifestyle section is all you, though."

This was standard playfulness between me and most inmates. They'd push me around, I'd basically tell them to fuck off. Pooch sat down without comment.

About a minute later he asked for the sports again. "Uh no," I replied, probably with a smirk.

Next thing I knew I held a mere scrap of the sports page in my right hand and Pooch sat down with the rest of it at the next table over. He'd snatched the paper and left me stunned for a second.

"What the hell is wrong with you?!"

Pooch didn't look up. He mumbled "you ain't shit, mother-fucker" as he pretended to read. My heart rate rocketed as I weighed my poor options.

Pooch was well-built, but over a foot shorter than me and at least sixty pounds lighter. Prison annoyances had built up my wrath, so I'd win a fight if I turned it loose. If the authorities caught wind of it, however, I'd have a ticket right back to the hole. Followed by a trip to medium security. My adversary probably carried a shank, too.

So I did what any real man would: I wadded up the small paper in my hand and tossed it at him, saying: "Man, that's bullshit."

My nemesis caught the paltry projectile and threw it back at me, hitting me square on the tip of my nose. No one laughed at this slapstick. Drama like this usually drew silence, and my punking was not a laughing matter. I felt like a little bitch, albeit one with well-considered priorities. My street cred among the gallery matched the number of sports pages I held in my hand: zero.

Word of my humiliation spread. My "ruined" rep bothered me more than I expected. I liked to think I didn't need prison pride, but for the next few days, I felt like a punk. Any swagger in my stride had disappeared. I recovered quickly, though. I felt lucky such petty concerns didn't nag at me. And, unlike with most inmates, no one back home on the street would hear about it.

Pooch and I ignored each other after that despite sleeping only a few bunks apart. A few days later he made a clumsy attempt at normalcy between us, but I didn't play along. A couple of weeks later a CO randomly frisked somebody, which was rare at Southern. Then a phone began vibrating – in the friskee's ass crack. Talk about a fateful call. To my delight this inmate was Pooch, so he got shipped out of my life forever. My prison frustration remained, however.

Southern's administration had its priorities straight. They provided a deluxe TV package that eventually added a channel carrying UFC events. Fans of the sport were psyched, and the fights got sprinkled into the TV schedule. Fast forward to the evening of an NFL Divisional Playoff game. A big deal. Since NFL was second in TV priority only to NASCAR, everyone assumed football would be scheduled as usual. So no one bothered doing it.

A guy new to the camp, I'll call him Big Redneck, exploited this opening and got UFC slipped onto the schedule in the typical NFL slot. This was ludicrous for two reasons. First, the program he scheduled was a replay from the previous week, so fans knew the outcomes. Even the usual group of UFC viewers didn't care about watching it.

More importantly, only seven games remained in the whole football season. The UFC events could be shown for many weeks after this, unopposed. And last, WE WERE IN GOD-DAMN AMERICA, where football is king.

As luck had it, the by-the-book CO crew worked this fateful evening, so they required a unanimous vote for any TV schedule changes. The voting results: NFL - 20, UFC - 1. People howled and tried to reason with Big Redneck. Some dudes begged and pleaded, but to no avail.

Defeated, guys slowly walked away to wedge into the other sports TV room or stand in the hallway to watch through the windows. I remained in the first room, simmering to a boil. I finally unloaded on BR.

"Listen," I snapped. "this is fucking America. And in America, real men watch the fucking NFL playoffs!"

A peanut gallery gathered as BR slowly processed my insult but said nothing. He'd turned down a dozen pleas to change his mind by then – he had dug in.

"And since everyone else will be watching football," I spat, "this would be a good time to host a circle jerk with the other closet homos!"

BR had heard enough. He sprang to his feet and "bowed-up," as they say in the South. Thankfully cooler heads held him back, so they didn't send me to the hole for hitting BR's fists with my face. I scampered down the hall to watch football from the hallway. Thank god BR didn't follow me there.

MMA fighting annoys me anyway, so after this I *hated* it. To me, the fights look like homosexual overtures in a trailer park gone horribly wrong. Not coincidentally, the fights drew keen interest of probable closet cases that hardly ever watched sports otherwise. And many of the "out" gay guys sat front and center, of course. They loved watching nearly naked dudes desperate to get horizontal and grind on each other.

Not that there's anything wrong with that, of course. Unless it's taking up a prison TV during the NFL playoffs.

I could hardly stand the zoo surrounding me in the main barracks building by this point in my sentence, about a year in. So I finessed a solution, not a moment too soon. I moved into the Mod (a modular structure), an extra-long double-wide trailer outfitted with extensive creature comforts, at least for prison. Inmates there enjoyed a lap of luxury compared to the usual warehouse.

The Mod was the only air-conditioned barracks at Southern, and the inmates controlled the lights. This meant no fluorescent assaults at 5:30 a.m., and civilized lighting the rest of the time. The bathroom and shower areas boasted features found "out in the world," such as hot and cold knobs. The two TVs were also free-rein and scheduling was simple thanks to the relative maturity of the residents. A church retreat camp would be less luxurious, although the other campers there would probably be more annoying.

Even better, the COs appeared only for inmate count times and other predictable intervals each day. This meant risk-free smoking, and a big exhaust fan in the bathroom spared non-smokers the annoyance. The atmosphere in general was more civilized because childish types rarely qualified for a bed there. Mostly work-release and other top-privilege inmates did, not those that acted like idiots. I secured my spot by talking the warden into giving me a Mod janitor job that became available.

My regal new home faced a park-like setting on three sides, with a pond on one of them. Views outside were unsullied by a perimeter fence, and wildlife like fox and deer could appear from time to time. I once saw a full mini-rainbow over the pond. Living in the Mod felt like getting away with something. It reminded me of a toast Hugh Hefner was known for: "Gentlemen, gentlemen, be of good cheer. For they are out there, and we are in here!"

The setting for the Mod (upper right) at Southern.
(Imagery © 2019 Google, Maxar Technologies)

The barracks I slept in before moving to the Mod included a group of friends that lived in Lexington County before their arrest. Ten of them had transferred to Southern to reunite. The result was basically a cookout party every night for them – *really* stealing time from The Man. They seemed to like me, and I found them to be fun company. For kicks, I posed in one of their group photos one day. I tried to look prison hard, sporting my buzz cut and bushy beard. What could possibly go wrong?

Turned out these fellows couldn't just enjoy their endless block party; their greed and criminal urges led them into a tobacco turf war. Mere days after moving in I lay on my Mod bunk reading when eight of the Lexington crew showed up, game faces on. They aimed to set some business straight. The meanest of them spoke: "Hey Stitch! I think you got some 'splainin' to do!"

Stitch never had time to talk, because two impatient gentlemen began pummeling him. I stayed on my bunk, a good twenty feet away. Sadly for Stitch, no one leaped to his defense. He'd recently been caught sniffing a guy's underwear. Allegedly.

While this ass-kicking progressed, a Mod resident called Brody plunged into turmoil on the side and earned a punch in the eye. While no boxer sniffer, Brody annoyed people by minding everyone's business while bitching about how no one minded their own business. This meant no one had his back either, even though he ended up in dire straits. The Mod is a bad place to find backup – no one wants to lose their bed in it. Gear, the tobacco kingpin, was an exception, however.

Gear got into a third fight within twenty feet and enjoyed plenty of help. Bunk beds got pushed out of place and lockers nearly toppled over. A small gallery watched, a couple of them getting in a kick here and there. Stitch became a kickball, closed like a turtle in his shell on the floor. Brody got stuck in a headlock. Gear occupied the center of chaos involving five dudes.

"Man down!" shouted one guy, followed by three others. "Man down!"

This is the universal prison warning for here comes a cop. Bystanders detected a CO walking down a forty-foot path from the main camp area to the door. The mayhem ceased immediately as if the leader of an improv troupe had barked "scene!"

Ten seconds later the CO sauntered in to find a curious number of chaps standing around and breathing heavily for no clear reason. Someone occupied this *powe*-leece with small talk, lending cover for guys to slip out the door or disappear around a corner to assess wounds. The guard seemed suspicious but said nothing. And, of course, no one told him anything. He took a stroll through the place and exited before he had to work harder.

The fallout from the donnybrook began the next morning, starting at the post-breakfast headcount. Inmates normally remained on their bunks for this process, but this time we had to stand at the foot of our beds in a line, like they do in medium security. The guards counted us and then doubled back to inspect faces and knuckles, hoping to identify fight participants.

The administrative investigation – a search for more snitches, really – began. And not eight months after my first visit to the disciplinary room, I found myself there looking at Warden behind a desk again. After I sat down, I noticed what felt like an ambush behind me: an asshole sergeant and an old-school CO known as the "Hatchet Man".

"We really need to stop meeting like this," I began. No one laughed. Warden didn't greet me besides with a slight nod. He looked like a disappointed dad, and I felt like the kid.

"What do you know about the fight?"

"I heard a ruckus, but I was on my bunk napping on the other end of the room."

Warden rolled his eyes while taking hold of a photo. The one I posed in with the Lexington crew for a goof. I was in the middle back row, looking all hard.

"Why are you in this picture?"

"I'm just friends with some of them from the barracks," I explained. "I don't know any of them very well."

No reaction.

"What do you know about this crew and their involvement in the white supremacy movement?" Warden asked.

Only then did it click with me. All white guys. Most of them with shaved heads. Everyone scowling, and some making weird hand signals.

My face must have shown my obliviousness to all of this. I imagine I looked like a Kardashian on *Jeopardy*. "Honestly," I managed, "I don't know about any of that. I wouldn't be in the picture otherwise."

Warden read the expressions of his two henchmen behind me, then pointed to the photo again.

"Who in this photo came down to the Mod yesterday?"

I needed to finger someone.

"Well, like I said ... my bunk is way on the other end ..."

Warden threw me a steely-eyed glare that said *don't fucking bullshit me.* The kind of look that gets a guy a job as a warden. Now I faced a gray area of The Code.

I couldn't plead ignorance. That would be like telling Warden to fuck off and inviting him to sabotage the rest of my prison tour. I could kiss an Asheville transfer goodbye. It's circumstances like these can turn a decent man into a Rat.

I parsed levels of snitching in my head. Joseph Warren Jones was fifty times worse a Rat than I might be here. And the Lexington crew were doomed, anyway. Sacrificing my prison juice for them would be idiotic. That's how I rationalized my sin. I took a deep breath and pointed out three of the instigators I didn't like, pleading ignorance about the friendly ones.

Warden seemed satisfied with this pound of flesh. He moved to the next order of business.

"OK, what about Brody? Did you see him get in a fight?"

Disgusted with myself and resentful of Warden, I blurted. "Maybe I did, maybe I didn't."

Warden didn't miss a beat: "And maybe I'll ship your ass to Caledonia!"

The prospect of moving to that awful medium security camp adjusted my attitude, and quickly.

"He may have been scuffling with someone," I hedged. "Like I said, I was pretty far away."

Warden looked to the ceiling and sighed, probably as weary of this charade as me. "All right." He asked the CO standing behind me for the next name on their list.

"Go back down there now and send Bailey up here," Warden ordered.

I dragged ass down to the Mod to notify Bailey, and to lie to everyone about my testimony. I'd become what I reviled. A snitch.

The Lexington County party dissolved, shipped off to various other facilities. Brody avoided the hole for fighting, despite his two black eyes. This led many to suspect he ratted everyone out for leniency. No one suspected I also snitched, but probably wouldn't have cared due to the minimal info I spilled anyway.

I had to live with myself as a rat, though. And that hurt.

CHAPTER FIFTEEN

There I Go Again

"If the others knew how good we had it in here there'd be a goddamn riot."

My bunkmate said this to me one weekday morning in the Mod. We'd both just woken up and got moving at around nine o'clock. We didn't get kicked out into the yard at 7:30 like everyone else on the camp. No one had even turned the lights on yet. I lived in the best prison ever. I heard the Sinatra recording of *That's Life* on the radio around this time, featuring the lyrics "riding high in April, shot down in May." May had begun two weeks earlier.

About a month into my time in the Mod a tendon in my shoulder started hurting. It affected my sleep and physical activities like juggling. A cortisone injection didn't solve the problem, so the doctor suggested physical therapy. I visited a therapist at the hospital a couple of minutes up the road, and he agreed this would be my best option.

No one told me if I underwent the therapy I'd need to move to another prison. My shoulder hurt, but not enough to give up my comfortable new life to heal it. Next thing I knew they scheduled me for another bus ride, this time to a dreaded medical prison. At least COs informed me early enough for goodbyes and settling affairs. Many camps don't disclose transfer information until the middle of the night, only a couple hours before the bus boards.

Word of me leaving spread, so everyone tracked me down to find out to which camp I was headed. Guys that knew of Greene County usually winced and said "Ouch" when I told them. Or, "Oh fuck. *You're gonna love that place!*" One guy grabbed his nuts as if they'd been kicked, then described Greene's horrors. I felt like crying.

After a sleep-challenged night, I lumbered onto a bus. COs at the transfer depot forced me to wedge into the medium security holding pen because the minimum was full. Now an accidental sideways glance could conceivably earn me a shanking from someone doing twenty-five to life. I pretended to yawn a lot to feign fearlessness. In truth, I stood on a red alert.

The steamy ride to my new home twisted down two-lane roads, past small farms and trailer homes and into the North Carolina Coastal Plain. Five minutes into the trip I started sweating through my heavy canvas pants. And two loudmouths yelled in conversation across three rows of seats instead of moving together and talking quietly, of course. I dearly missed the Mod already.

One talker "Didn't get nothin' but twelve years" for an unspecified crime. The other guy explained: "I did a hundred twenty months, was out ninety days – actin' crazy the whole time – and they locked me up again." This chat continued nonstop for nearly five hours as the temperature rose, but neither of them paused for water. I found their camel-like durability astounding.

The bus stopped in the middle of nowhere: Greene County Correctional, in Maury, N.C. Twelve of us disembarked and paraded into a relatively new classroom for intake procedures, where three COs didn't bother to inspect our bags. Hunger and exhaustion from the journey made me loopy. This made an orientation speech from a middle-aged Crazy Woman especially surreal.

CW was an inmate caseworker at Greene and mentioned her approaching retirement several times during her short speech. She even pumped her fist in celebration of thirty years behind her, almost like she was an inmate, too.

"Breaking rules around here carries consequences," she said, stating the obvious. "And I should mention I performed my share of 'nightstick work' back when I was a CO."

Offenders exchanged *this bitch be crazy* glances, and a CO in the background struggled to keep a straight face.

About then I noticed a small sign on the wall, intended for the shop class: "Stay alert; don't get hurt." Again, I felt like I'd entered a scene in a bizarre movie.

CW slowly paced in front of her captive audience, sneering. "To best get along here at Greene, you should walk a fine line." She liked butchering the saying so much she did it twice more. She meant "walk the straight and narrow," but I didn't correct her. I needed her performance to end fast because my hunger had me eyeing chalk to eat.

Seemingly a century later our group moved to the chow hall. I noticed a sign: "No hat's [sic] or skull cap's [sic] in the dining hall." We dined on sack lunches because the kitchen had closed. Soon thereafter we dispersed into the run-down camp to find our bunks.

I immediately grasped why inmates avoid prison medical camps if possible. My neighbors in a sixty-eight-bed barracks were mostly senior citizens or the sickly. Some even required bunk side portable toilets. Guys in wheelchairs made the tight quarters feel even smaller. A couple of them zipped around like entitled criminal Battlebots and seemed to appear on my heels out of nowhere. I feared being run down by Gary Sinise's character in *Forrest Gump* at any moment.

The barracks held the aroma of a nursing home, and a reminder to be careful what you wish for. For sixteen months I bitched about commotion and rowdiness in my living areas, but at least it was alive. I didn't realize that energy helped me stay somewhat optimistic. Joking around or socializing for the fun of it seemed rare at Greene. Most seemed beaten down by the system, old age, or both. Hell's waiting room couldn't be much worse.

Practically every conversation involved either how oppressive the camp was or strategies on how to get out. But some dudes appeared too dim to realize how bleak Greene was, and others so downtrodden they didn't bother trying to transfer. Even if they wished to, many lacked outside advocates to raise hell with prison authorities to expedite the process.

The camp's drab physical plant matched its dismal atmosphere. Low-slung, decades-old buildings mostly offered window views of the other gloomy prison structures. Multiple interior lights needed to be replaced, old paint peeled, and rust grew on lockers. Cramped dayrooms featured nineteen-inch tube TVs receiving only over-the-air channels and audio that lagged behind the video. And, Satan's megaphones.

Bullhorns designed for outdoor use served as intercom speakers indoors. They sat inside steel mesh boxes, lest they get muffled or destroyed by traumatized inmates. They seemed loud enough to blow hair around and warp facial features, like an amplified belch of an elephant. The camp's capacity of over six hundred meant they sounded off fifty times an hour every weekday. No one got used to it. Even longtime residents jolted straight when the sonic cattle prod hit. Worse, those using the microphones often shouted their announcements, distorting southern drawls that were hard to understand to begin with.

"What the fuck did he just say?" was a common question in dayrooms. Those who'd been around a while sometimes understood and translated, like parents to a toddler.

Getting to know COs proved difficult because a couple of dozen worked each shift and constantly rotated posts. I worried about suffering a write-up for the slightest transgression. The camp's size required rotation of mealtimes for eighteen barracks. They served breakfast anywhere between 5:00 and 7:30, depending on the day of the week. The kitchen routinely ran out of entrees, so those last in line often ended up with the likes of two slices of bread instead of pancakes.

The chow line, usually in the hot sun, required at least a ten-minute wait. Guys routinely cut in next to a buddy because they knew no one would bother calling them out. I initially smoldered and fixed a stare on the shameless offenders but eventually, I just accepted it. That was the wrong battle to fight. I noted who they were, however. I'd later refused to help them with writing, spare envelopes, or anything else they'd ask for. I was gangsta that way.

Two canteens that served the camp were usually closed. It

seemed like the GED math class did the management of its stock. The most popular items sold out in less than a day when lines of over sixty dudes extended far outdoors. Enterprising indigent inmates waited at the front of lines and sold their spots when the canteen finally opened.

The yard featured more bare spots than grass, no plants or flowers, and exactly one shade tree on ten acres. A mere eight benches and three picnic tables – all unshaded – were available for hanging out. Weightlifters had only a few semi-operational workout machines to work with, exposed to the elements. No pavilion stocked with free weights existed, or even jump ropes. A full-size basketball court graced the area, but rules prohibited full-court games. Horseshoes got tossed at the bare ground instead of sandpits. Only an excellent sand volleyball court met any standard of decency.

Most inmate "recreation" took place as we walked on a wide path that circled the property. Part of it allowed for delightful sunset views over livestock farms and an immense soybean field. This came at a cost, however, as the scent of a mule often wafted over the camp. Much of the walking path led past grim buildings and alongside a daunting, multi story medium security facility next door. Nearby pens full of baying bloodhounds seemed to taunt inmates.

The tiny library – the only safe harbor from intercom speakers – kept short hours and limited visits to fifteen minutes even when no one was waiting to enter. A newspaper from a small nearby town was always a day behind. Against all odds the library carried several decent titles, including *The Great Gatsby*. This being Greene County, however, over twenty pages were missing from it. I laughed.

Few jobs allowed inmates outside the fence unsupervised at Greene, so tobacco was always scarce and expensive. Some were so desperate for nicotine they'd place the very last of a roll-up on a table and inhale the lingering smoke through a straw.

Lighters were impossible to find, so guys improvised. They'd scribble a patch of pencil lead onto a paper towel. The paper ignited when cooked in a microwave for a few seconds.

Another ignition source involved threads of steel wool, a key, and a fresh AA battery. To thwart this, the canteen kept a monthly limit on battery purchases. COs actively sought to bust smokers instead of looking the other way.

I tried to avoid being a buzzkill by bitching about the camp to other inmates but surely failed. One time I whined to a middle-aged fireplug who called himself "Frankie Biggs." He wore his t-shirt sleeves rolled up to his shoulders. He'd done time for trafficking weed in his native New Jersey, and in Texas and Florida. He laughed off my criticisms of Greene.

"Fuhgetaboudit, this is the best place I ever done time!" Frankie claimed in a thick accent. "You got good clothes, good sheets. And there ain't no Spics and all the race bullshit here, neither."

I took care not to describe how nice Southern was compared to Greene. Blissful ignorance served Frankie well. Prison camp quality was all relative. "Unless you don't have relatives, in which case you're fucked," as he would say.

So most of Greene was a disaster, just like my buddies had warned. But they had transferred me to benefit from the medical expertise and resources. Surely "medical camp" meant more than just being a dumping ground for the ill and infirm.

Turned out only one full-time doctor and three part-timers served hundreds of medical cases. Over a hundred inmates required controlled medication, which they had to wait in long lines for, outdoors and with no shelter, up to three times a day.

Over-the-counter pharmacy items also involved a long queue, often endured only to learn items were out of stock.

Despite the nightmarish medical care stories I'd been hearing, I figured a cure for my lame shoulder was near. A PA blast summoned me to an administrator's office on my second day at Greene. I assumed we'd discuss my physical therapy schedule. I entered to find a grim middle-aged woman seated at an old steel desk. She was known among inmates as the "Job

Witch". A framed warning hung on the wall: *"Don't Mistake My Niceness for Stupidity."*

"We have you scheduled to start work at the laundry plant tomorrow," Job Witch declared.

"Oh, there seems to have been a mistake," I said, chuckling at the mixup. "I transferred here for physical therapy on my shoulder, not for a job."

"First of all, you need to adjust your tone," JW warned. I shut up and tried to change my look from amused to serious. The bureaucrat read my file for a minute, then spoke. "Nothing here says you are ineligible to work. And if you ain't got a doctor's note, you're signing this job release form. Either that or you can walk on over to the hole."

She slid a paper in front of me, which I ignored. I said: "I'd say a doctor sending me here for physical therapy serves as a note, doesn't it?"

JW's dark eyes lanced me before she finally spoke. "This office isn't about what *you* say. I care about what the *file* says. And it tells me you qualify for this job."

Just placate this bitch and go over her head later. And try not to snicker again. I signed the form and returned to the barracks with my copy.

Naively assuming I'd never work at this off-site laundry processing facility, I read about its hazards with good humor. Descriptions included "sweeping and blowing down lint as necessary," "conveyors," and "soiled linen rooms." Happy it didn't apply to me, I sat in the dayroom chuckling and explaining this mixup to a fellow felon sitting nearby.

"That's actually a pretty good gig," he replied, unamused. "Especially after you do it a while and they double the pay to twenty-six cents an hour."

I learned laundry workers woke up for breakfast at 4:15. An hour later the workers departed via prison bus. They endured Satan's transport for eight hours a week. Workday nourishment consisted of a bag lunch: a white bread sandwich of one "meat" slab and "cheese" slice, an apple, and a cookie. This for ten hours operating the likes of industrial clothes dryers and ironing machines. I'd rather stick my head in the bullhorn enclosure all day.

My physical therapy was supposed to start the next week. Certainly then my therapist would get me out of the laundry duty. In the meantime, I tracked down Job Witch's boss, another dour woman who repeated their requirement for a doctor's note. Experience in other camps told me this would take about three days. At Greene, getting a doctor's appointment took weeks.

This doctor's note delay forced me to seek a captain or even the warden. Anyone capable of understanding. This produced a lot of: "Fill out this form, put it in that box, and they'll call you." A different call came first. The next day a PA announcement blared.

"The following inmates need to report to the clothes house for work boots ..." My name came around twentieth in a list of thirty.

I was issued this footwear at Southern, but the COs didn't care if I wore them, so I didn't. And once I realized that shankings and rape weren't threats in honor grade, being forced to wear the state-issued boots became my biggest fear. They were barely cushioned, and made of the least pliable faux leather known to man.

After forty minutes in the boot line, I encountered an unsmiling, bellicose female CO working the shoe store duty.

"Hi! Um, I don't really need boots. I'm here for physical therapy, not a job."

"Tell it to someone else. If your name got called, you're getting boots."

I followed her into the shoe area of the clothes house. The CO brought out a pair of 14s, my usual size.

"Oh god no. Not even close," I said after trying them. "Gonna need fifteen." At this point, I knew from my experience at Southern that size 16 required a special order. That was my out.

The 15s fit perfectly. Even so, I winced as I took a few steps. "See, I have really long toes," I whined. "Can I try a sixteen?"

The CO clearly wanted to feel where my toes were to prove

they fit fine. Thank god for steel toes on these things. She rolled her eyes with disdain: "We have to order size sixteen."

"How long will that take, two or three days?" I asked, probably too cheerfully.

"About six weeks," she replied in a monotone. She sounded like a firing squad shooter who knew she loaded dummy bullets.

"Well, can't I just work while wearing my sneakers in the meantime?" I asked, fully aware the answer was no.

"All jobs require work boots," she mumbled, looking to her clipboard for the next poor bastard to throw boots at. I'd bought time to set these people straight about my shoulder. I began repeating the Eminem line "feet fail me not!" to myself as I floated back to the barracks in victory.

Sure, a lap of lameness was still my home, but I had pushed the sweatshop job off the table. My lone obligation would be a sixty-minute physical therapy session three days a week. I suddenly felt like I lived at the Four Seasons. Misery is relative.

My physical therapy sessions began when promised, which surprised me given how Greene operated. A large, modern room full of massage tables, exercise bikes, and various stretching apparatus hosted roughly a dozen ailing inmates. Several electronic pulse devices sat available to speed up the healing of tendons like mine.

A young, athletic guy named Brad introduced himself as my therapist. He was there as a civilian contractor instead of a state employee, which probably explained his pleasant disposition. Brad was definitely homosexual, a fact that bothered several of my fellow patients. I relished it. The more tender loving care, the better. I loved Brad's soft hands, excellent taste in fragrances, and a fantastic sense of humor.

I couldn't decide which made me happier: finally receiving therapy or stimulating conversation with someone who got my jokes. A typical session involved Brad rubbing and finessing my shoulder as I regaled him with crazy tales of lockup. In turn, he filled me in on pop culture buzz and news from the outside. Our meetings soon felt like a date. I even adjusted my grooming schedule to be fresh for them. I harbored no gay sex fantasies, but I relished the ritual of preparing for close human contact. A taste of real life.

At first, I downplayed the seriousness of my inflamed tendon even though I couldn't lift my arm properly or sleep on my left side. That's how bad I wanted a quick transfer back to Southern. Brad saw through this immediately. "This place sucks. I get it," he said. "But if you're already here, you would be stupid to leave early. Toughen up!"

My shoulder began improving, so I resumed juggling for exercise and amusement. Grateful audiences proved easy to find in the yard. Among these were what appeared to be menacing bands of convicts, and I felt an intense pressure to impress them. Juggling already made me feel like a narcissistic dweeb sometimes, and these street hoods increased my self-consciousness.

One time a crew stopped walking around the yard to watch me. One of them asked to take a turn and proved to juggle well himself.

"I ain't done this since I was little," he sheepishly admitted. "It fucked up my street cred."

Good thing I had none of that to begin with. I lived the dork life, not the thug life. Getting better at juggling gave me a sense of accomplishment and provided good exercise. I continued playing with my balls often.

Besides spreading good cheer, juggling meant "ball" puns dangled for the taking. Tons of guys abused them. "Hey Biff, you sure are handy with balls!" was common. I always enjoyed saying: "It's warmer out than I expected today. I'm going to take out my balls!" Perhaps I got put in prison to polish my juggling skills and provide fellow felons with low-hanging comedic fruit.

I juggled mostly in the same spot at Greene, in the shade in a low-traffic area. Sharing this space on most mornings was a wheelchair-bound black dwarf called "Shawty" and his inmate orderly/caretaker, a dude who looked ready to enter a game in the NFL at any moment. He performed one million push-ups and sit-ups every five minutes.

Shawty was down for dealing coke. He wore Blues Brothers shades, even indoors, with the "polarized" sticker remaining on one lens "so niggas know they be fresh off the shelf."

He watched me often while feeding the birds and came to know my tricks. He became something of a circus ringmaster, directing a juggling giraffe. "Okay, behind the back," he'd shout, gleefully. "Two with one hand!" and so on. We became pals.

Despite being stuck at Greene, Shawty stayed positive. Especially as a paraplegic. Or so I thought. One morning Shawty jumped up from his chair and ran over to break bread into smaller pieces for the birds

"Hey, what the fuck?" I yelled in astonishment, dropping my balls. Shawty cackled, waddled back and hopped into his chair.

I yelled to his orderly, who stood about twenty yards away with his back turned. "Hey, don't let him fool you, this motherfucker can walk!"

"Yo, why you tryna rat me out?" he shouted, chuckling.

I later learned he suffered spine disorders from diastrophic dwarfism, but could still walk short distances.

My first bunk position at Greene was at the end of a row in the heaviest traffic area, five feet from the bathroom/shower room doorway. It felt like living in a pup tent next to a porta-potty in a leper colony next to a freeway. An air conditioning vent blew a polar vortex directly onto my bunk, and they allowed only one sheet and one thin blanket to cover me. I slept fully clothed and just stayed cold during the day. I almost longed for Southern's heat and humidity because at least that wasn't physically painful. I practically felt like shanking someone to earn a warmer space in solitary confinement.

Constant passersby and bathroom activity made concentrating on reading practically impossible. Seeing inmates showering in my peripheral vision didn't help, either. Catching dudes looking past my bunk into the shower for an eyeful of dick sucked even worse. Had I gone gay for the stay, my spot would've been perfect. I had to get the fuck out of there.

Moving bunks required an agreeable sergeant to approve it. Greene had none. Every lazy one of them declined multiple requests to take two minutes to help me out. I became more miserable with each passing day. Then, a guardian angel appeared, in the oddest form: some asshole passerby shouting right next to my ear to someone forty feet away. He prompted my epiphany. *Go to the hole on purpose!*

All I had to do was claim I'd been threatened. I already tempted fate along these lines by barking "do you mind?" to fools who yelled in my ear. Odds were good I'd soon yell at the wrong guy. For relief I'd head to "protective custody" for at least forty-eight hours, then get released into a different barracks.

I knew a large, air conditioned segregation unit was on site; a newer facility with cells comprised of four solid walls. This meant I'd enjoy a respite from the general chaos. And take a break from Satan's megaphone.

I stocked up on snacks and supplies and slithered to see the lieutenant on duty the next day. He shared a name with a cousin of mine and seemed pleasant, which I took as a good omen. I presented a look of sweaty concern, slightly out of breath.

"Lieutenant, I fear for my life," I claimed, and added a few details.

"It would be best for the camp and your fellow inmates if you identify this guy." the CO said.

"No way I'm fingering anybody, lieutenant. The guy talked about slitting my throat already. I don't need a bigger target on my back."

He accepted this logic and sent me to the office of the segregation sergeant, across the camp and yet a world away. This stoic gentleman read my statement describing terroristic threats aloud, to confirm he had it straight. "Whereupon" may have been a new word for him, and "veiled" baffled him. I felt superior despite sitting there in handcuffs. Small victories.

"We'll keep you here for at least seventy-two hours," the sergeant said. *Perfect!*

I quickly learned they treat protective custody offenders the same as those segregated for serious infractions. Like sneaking into first class on a plane flight, except on the complete opposite end of the spectrum. One meant the denial of shoestrings and other personal items; the other included free alcohol, gourmet food, and a tricked-out plane seat. As long as I made it to either I got treated accordingly, no questions asked.

Upon entering my cell, I noticed a nearly ruined mattress there. My CO escort allowed me to swap it out for a better one nearby while still in handcuffs. And all the while my pants were falling off, thanks to the belt-confiscation policy. Only a wide-legged shuffle kept my trousers off the floor. Had a video of this hit YouTube a new dance might have been born. The CO sure seemed amused, which may explain why he didn't help carry the mattress.

I settled into my private suite, thrilled at the prospect of solitude. The cell was clean, the lighting good, and a sizable window afforded views of the walking track and the soybean field beyond. Not dealing with the wack chow hall lines and changing meal times pleased me. I also enjoyed access to my radio, coffee, Raman noodles, and other snacks.

This experience in the hole proved wonderful compared to my first one. No disturbances, and no worries about pending charges weighing me down. But I missed physical therapy sessions while there, despite being told I could attend them. I didn't need to foist my greasy physique on Brad anyway, though. I showered only once in eight days, because of water that was *lawsuit* hot.

No hot and cold knobs in the shower stall meant scalding water heated me into a flushed mess. I looked in the polished steel mirror in the aftermath and considered the lobster. After that, I bathed and shampooed beside my push button sink using the convoluted process of pre filling disposable cups to rinse with. I felt like a survivalist or a fugitive on the run.

I rarely heard voices in the corridors of the segregation unit, so several at once roused my attention one day. I looked out to see a group of prison higher-ups wandering around with a guy in plain clothes carrying a clipboard. They soberly pointed at stuff and conversed. They clearly tried to ignore multiple inmates' faces pressed to door windows, watching them. The awkwardness felt palpable.

I *had* to fuck with them. It was out of my hands.

I gestured frantically until I gained the group's attention. "Sir, please!" I shouted in my best Dickensian accent while pointing to the civilian. "Can you make the beatings stop?!"

After I repeated myself, louder, the four men became slack-jawed and exchanged tense glances.

"Just kidding!"

They all laughed – probably with relief – and continued down the row. The segregation sergeant turned back and glared at me, though. A food taster may have come in handy for my next few meals.

A CO knocked and shouted "pack it up," marking the end of an eleven-day vacation, eight days longer than predicted. They either forgot about me or punished me for refusing to name my tormentor. Whatever the case, I enjoyed the respite. This being Greene, however, my new barracks assignment landed me in – the same place I had fled for my "safety." I marched to the sergeant's office.

"Yeah, this won't work," I explained to a lively young female sergeant. "I need to stay away from a guy that threatened me. He's still there."

She studied a computer monitor showing my file. "Frickin' unbelievable," she said, in a New York accent. "It's almost like no one knows what's going on here."

"Yeah. Almost," I said. Why couldn't I have found this lady in the first place?

The sergeant studied whiteboards on the wall that displayed bunk assignments, then pecked away on the computer. "F-33 then. That should serve you fine. Most offenders that sleep there are gone all day." I thanked her profusely and moved to claim my new bunk.

CHAPTER SIXTEEN

Wheeling, Dealing, and Stealing

My next thirty-four-person bedroom included a couple of dozen laundry plant workers, who left at 4:30 a.m. and stayed gone all day. Even better, no runaway wheelchairs tested my patience and no bedside potties soured my morale. Instead, a two-sided *Caution: Wet Floor* sign fucked with me. The bathroom doors swung "saloon-style," and a gap between the flaps needed covering for privacy. Allegedly. So protocol demanded the sign hanging over the doors.

Each use of the doors required sliding the sign over and back again, lest some busybody complain about it. Never mind the stupid sign barely helped with privacy, anyway. Worse, most guys moved the sign with their hands, often without washing them after their bathroom business. I never saw it being cleaned. Unsanitary activity like this was common on the inside.

Despite this, sickness among men of dubious hygiene living on top of each other stayed in check. For instance, dudes hardly ever became nauseous from the flu. Perhaps living in such close quarters bolsters immunity.

Cold viruses did make the rounds occasionally, though. Unfortunately, inmates in the past abused cough syrup, so it got banned years ago. The current era of sicklies made do with weak decongestant pills and cough drops, neither of which helped much.

I caught a nasty cold bug once that had me coughing convulsively literally every single minute. Six or eight guys joined me exchanging coughing fits back and forth all night. I took an odd comfort in others hacking away; at least knowing I wasn't alone in dying a horrible death. Misery loves company.

These coughing fits made sleep impossible. I'd move into the dayroom in the wee hours out of courtesy to my sleeping brethren. I guzzled water from the fountain while cursing my lot in life. These episodes were easily the nadir of my non-segregation time in the joint. At least rousing nearby COs from their illicit naps cheered me up a little.

Almost as vexing as a devastating cough was my new bunkie, the aforementioned not-so wheelchair-bound Shawty. I loved the guy at our outdoor juggling sessions, but sharing a rack with the popular pint-sized con sucked. Everyone adored him, so every Tom, Dick, and Tyrone in the place swung by to visit – loudly. Worse, Shawty snored, but not in a tidy rhythm. His wheezes and groans sounded like the death throes from a stomach wound.

Watching him operate amused me, at least. Especially when he "scrapbooked." Most inmates collected magazine pics of women they lusted after, but usually haphazardly. Crafty cats like Shawty spent hours cutting and pasting pics of big booty bitches into thick books. He did the same for high-performance cars. For fun, I'd make him choose between, say, a Bugatti and Beyonce. He always picked the car.

I never picked the car. A nineteen-month sex slump changes a man. A buddy of mine agreed, claiming "Whore power over horsepower."

Other light moments helped break the drudgery of Greene. One day I joined inmates hanging around outside, even as contractors performed repairs. A plumber parked his toolbox-panel truck in a busy area, removed some tools, and walked a short distance away. About ten seconds later, a bystander yelled: "Hey! Stay away from that truck!" The wide-eyed contractor scampered back to defend his rig, only to find ten guys laughing at him.

The perimeter fences at minimum camps were hardly formidable, usually only eight feet high. They stood mere feet away from local roads in some places. This invited people watching, both for inmates and playful motorists driving by. One evening while walking the loop near a road three twenty-something females passed by in a minivan, a-whoopin' and a-hollerin'.

The intercom might as well have announced: "Party girls in a minivan, northeast corner!" Word traveled fast.

The first pass alone would have made the night of most inmates. Then the ladies made a blessedly slow return pass, with the sliding door of the van open. Two girls struck naughty poses on an imaginary stripper pole, to howls of approval. By the fourth time by, they shook their asses and flashed their tits to a crowd worthy of an old-time USO show.

The CO yard patrol soon declared the area off-limits and cleared everyone out. But they couldn't erase the memories captured by horny inmates. God bless those girls. Their community volunteer outreach sure beat the more typical candy cane donations at Christmas time.

This episode reminded me of its flip side: objects of lust that stumbled across gawkers unknowingly. Parking for a town function up the road overflowed past the prison, forcing late arrivals to walk right by the prison yard. Women got leered at by inmates, some letting loose hoots and shouts that would shame even urban construction workers. Others lapsed into the stone-faced trance commonly seen at strip clubs, gulping.

I observed the fresh scenery for a few minutes but felt awful for the passersby. No woman should hear terms of endearment like, "I sure am glad your parents fucked!" Several girls loved the attention, though, and sashayed for their captive audience while talking trash. Let's face it: sometimes sluttiness rules.

Sharing a bunk with Shawty ratcheted up my desperation to transfer back to Southern — even to face no air conditioning in July. My shoulder responded well to therapy so in theory, the camp doctor would release me. I say "in theory" because many guys arrived under circumstances like mine and never left. Like a penitential *Hotel California*. A clean bill of health might only clear me for a laundry factory job, not a ticket out. Greene will do a man dirty like that. The work boots on order for me were due to arrive any day. The clock ticked.

I'd been at Greene for nearly six weeks when I finally saw the doctor – waiting ten times longer than at non-medical facilities. I'd spent much of this time worrying about the outcome. Finally, answers would emerge, but I entered the staid waiting room fearing the worst.

A wooden partition that met neither the floor nor the ceiling separated the waiting and exam "rooms." I could easily hear the voices of inmates with appointments before mine in conversation with the doctor. "I think I need some Viagras," one patient suggested. Two others complained of digestive issues.

Once I reached the other side of the partition, I found the middle-aged, shabbily dressed doctor. He offered a dead fish handshake and no eye contact. This seemed predictable considering he probably ended up there after getting fired from the Jiffy Lube and Health Clinic. Following our handshake, he washed his hands and applied latex gloves.

"Doctor, I'm desperate to transfer back to my home camp. My shoulder feels better. Can we make this happen?"

He barely seemed to notice I'd spoken and didn't reply. He probably heard similar pleas all day long. He spent about fifteen seconds on a hands-on assessment of my shoulder before he declared it good to go.

"I see notable weight loss," the doctor said, looking at my file. "Two-ten to one-eighty-five. Can you explain this?"

"Have you *tried* the food here?" I blurted, "Or tried to get oatmeal from kitchen guys?"

He smirked. "Well, whatever the case I'm listing you with the highest fitness grade."

My stomach dropped. "Any chance you can make that a notch lower?"

The doctor's eyebrows raised and his jaw dropped, probably

at my naivety. "You just said you want a transfer out of here, right?"

"Oh god yes!"

"Well, your file shows recent protective segregation," he declared. "Policy is to ship you out once your medical grade is acceptable for your next camp. Get it?"

"Oh shit. Okay, yeah!" I practically shouted. "I'm good to go!"

My bogus trip to The Hole doubled as a ticket out of Greene. Yet again: dishonesty pays.

The following afternoon they called me to receive my newly arrived work boots. I headed to the clothes house to try them on. The size 16s were so big I could almost put them on over my sneakers. I clopped back to the barracks while wearing them, laughing.

"Damn, nigga! What's up with dem clown boots?" shouted Shawty when I strolled up to the bunk. Walking three hundred feet in them had already scraped my shins sore.

"Get a good look at 'em," I deadpanned. "'Cuz I'm as good as gone!"

"Dat's what the doctor say?" Shawty asked, excitedly.

"Yep!"

"Good for you, man!"

Despite Shawty's snoring and loud social life, I loved the guy.

Two nights later a surly CO woke me up at midnight for the check-out procedure. Then one of the few pleasant COs roused me out of bed at 3:30 and watched me gather my belongings. As I packed items into bags, half asleep, I accidentally rammed a stack of magazines into the bed frame. Several spilled onto Shawty's head.

Upon impact, his snoring became choppier, like a chainsaw with a clogged fuel line. Instead of waking up, my bunkie shifted slightly, snorted, and mumbled something in his high-pitched Ebonics. Then, right back to his tortured sawing of logs.

The CO and I nearly burst with suppressed laughter, as if someone cracked a great joke during a funeral. And clumsily dumping magazines onto a sleeping dwarf is way funnier than that. I'll never forget this beam of lightness in the strangest of places. It helped me celebrate the end of a dismal period in my prison odyssey.

Leaving Greene in that humid pre dawn rivaled practically anything for awesomeness. I high-fived and whooped it up with six guys equally thrilled to leave that dump behind. The term "going green" may forever make me shudder. But I made it – teeth intact and with no demerit points added to my record. I no longer felt like a prison rookie.

Southern's colorful flower beds and friendly faces that greeted me when I arrived nearly made me cry. I had missed "home" so dearly. I again basked in the temporary celebrity status of returning, and another press conference seemed in order. It might have gone as follows ...

Q: *What about the female CO's? Were they hot and did they have fat asses?*

A: Well, Greene is three times as big as here, so a few were around. But only one was really hot – a little black chick who threw around a spectacular bubble butt.

Q: *How much did roll-ups cost?*

A: At least three stamps for practically toothpick size, sometimes even five. And the cops were on smoke like a mosquito on hot breath. I just quit smoking because fuck that shit.

Q: *I know you got some of them medical camp drugs on the yard. Bring any back?*

A: Well, "lean-backs" (Clonidine) were readily available, but I did not partake. Also, they were strict about making motherfuckers crush up and swallow pills at the meds window, so I got nothin'.

Q: *Was Greene as bad as people say it is?*

A: (Long pause ... voice cracking) No more questions. I'm traumatized.

Priority one upon my return was once again scoring a bed in the Mod. I bought my way into a janitor job there after a miserable ten days sweating it out with the masses and smelling burning K2 in the air. One of the Mod janitors suffered from the synthetic weed habit, so eight dollars in stamps was enough to get him to swap places with me. Sergeant Dellwood approved the change as usual.

I soon gained my weight back by eating oatmeal in the evenings and having access to a properly functioning chow hall. Soon my wardrobe and bedding returned to the level I enjoyed before being waylaid. Obtaining a pair of shorts at the height of summer proved challenging, however. My clothes house guy promised to locate a pair, but after several days passed I had to nudge him: "Please remember to look out for shorts." I received them a day later.

My once familiar creature comforts suddenly felt like extravagances. And with two functioning shoulders, I nearly enjoyed prison again. Then, what quickly became known as "Black Monday" came down – on Labor Day, no less.

An African-American inmate filed a racial discrimination grievance. He correctly argued that Mod barracks across the state served only inmates with top-privilege-level status, mostly those with work-release jobs. At Southern, however, they tied residency in the Mod to particular on-camp jobs, too. For instance, all the clothes house workers had beds there, regardless of privilege status. Notably, roughly seventy-five percent of them were white, which was fishy because the warden and every other higher-up were Caucasian. In short, the brothers who earned those spots called bullshit and demanded their rightful lap of luxury.

The administration relented to the grievance and created mass upheaval. Guys packed up their shit and sweatily crisscrossed the camp carrying bags, bedding, and clothes. Well over a dozen top-privilege-level black dudes happily traded spots with sullen pale faces. I was among those cast out of the air conditioning into the summer heat, despite holding a janitor gig in the Mod. Back to braving the warehouse jungle.

Returning to the main barracks building meant two new problems: wearing a constant film of perspiration, and the aforementioned Chang as my new bunkie. This muscular, good-looking twenty-something acted twelve years old emotionally. We clashed often over many months, but love-hate described us best. Chang could be pleasant, intellectually curious, and likable. But he probably resented my urbanity compared to his and realized I often found him annoying.

He'd retaliate by mouthing off to me in front of fellow felons, putting on a tough-guy façade. He knew I didn't care about that posturing nonsense; that I usually let it slide. If in a foul mood, however, I'd bark back at him. Fists could've flown a few times if we weren't both bluffing. Even so, I considered him a friend, at least for prison.

Besides suffering Chang at close range, my move back to the warehouse meant more torment from the industrial fans. My new bed stood about fourteen feet from a sadistic wall-mounted sensory assault device. No bed swaps were available for a while, so I had to deal with it. My sole defense of the gale-force beatdown was my locker door. I kept it open most of the time to provide a pocket of non-turbulent air on my bed for my remaining dignity to occupy.

Since theft was so rare at Southern, I even slept with my locker door open. Little of value was in there besides my reading material, and god knows no book thieves lurked nearby. If shit started disappearing, I'd adjust accordingly. Then a special snack order arrived – now available quarterly instead of only near Christmas. For me, this included a dozen bags of coffee.

Having learned my lesson I quietly stashed this booty deep in my locker, taking care to avoid prying eyes. Only Chang knew I harbored the brown gold, and he posed no threat since he always swaggered with assets. I noticed a K2 habit developing with him, along with Xanax and pain pills. He even showed up zonked out for weekly visits with his smoking-hot girlfriend.

Still, no one could imagine he'd go broke. The old Chang easily paid his debts, often including a little extra for your trouble. But now he owed multiple people, including me. I ignored this warning sign.

I woke up to pee one night and upon returning, I noticed my locker contents out of order. Someone had stolen all of my coffee. Chang wasn't on his bunk. He'd been the guy

I ignored taking a shower a few feet from the urinals a few minutes earlier. Seething, I waited to gauge Chang's behavior upon his return. He was the sole person awake – and obviously the culprit.

He eventually reeled back to our bunk, clearly fucked up. He noticed my evil eye and loudly slurred: "What's your problem?" This confrontational behavior gave him away immediately and caused bysleepers to stir.

"You tell me. Feeling guilty about something?" I quietly replied from the top bunk, trying not to wake up the entire barracks.

"I don't feel guilty 'bout nothin', but maybe after I beat your ass I will, bitch!" he shouted, shaking the bed frame, so it squealed on the smooth concrete floor.

I noticed heads rising up along the rows of bunks, like turtles on logs assessing a disturbance. I nearly kicked Chang in the head in fury but refrained because I just don't fight. I didn't wish to scrap with a dude dressed only in prison boxers, either. That might end up even gayer than an MMA fight.

Instead, I yelled, "Gimme back the coffee you stole, motherfucker!" Practically everyone was awake by then, anyway.

"I don't have any coffee," he claimed, head lolling. "And call me that again and see what happens."

"Bullshit," I snarled. I prepared to high-kick him and shouted: "Yo, everyone check it: Chang just stole a bunch of coffee bags from me, so watch your shit around the motherfucker!"

This sent my bunkie into action. He moved to swing at me. Some clothing on the floor caused him to slip. He hit his head on the bed frame on the way down. I loved this because Chang left clothes on the floor all the time, so his weak housekeeping habits bit him in the ass. Or on the forehead, at least.

I hopped down on the other side of the bunk and braced to kick him in the chest if he came at me. Blood from a fresh cut above Chang's eye stopped that from happening, along with guys who'd gotten out of bed to separate us.

"Damn, everybody standin' around in their boxers! When's

the circle jerk start?" an inmate cracked. In the joint, no situation is too tense for a joke.

Chang wandered out to the CO desk to tend to his wound, somehow avoiding jail for intoxication. I stayed awake and decompressed until he returned. We exchanged no further words, mostly because he passed out on his bunk in a matter of seconds.

My combatant and I ignored each other for an awkward fortnight as bunkies after that. He never confessed, but also never called me out for talking shit — a tacit admission of guilt. I gained satisfaction from seeing his head bandage and telling everyone he was a thief. As for the coffee I lost, I had the funds and wheeling-dealing ability to replace it. I considered the loss a steep fee for never having to humor Chang again.

He soon went to the hole for K2. He got his comeuppance, and my transfer to Asheville remained at least possible since I didn't get busted for fighting.

Mostly, prison fights break out due to one of three conflicts: TV channel disputes, card games, and arguments over the fans that cool the barracks. To keep my teeth intact, I needed to tread carefully in these areas. Some proved easier than others.

Poker seemed like free money when I first arrived. Finding the sucker at the table is a lot easier when three or four of them are available. Turns out restraint is not in a typical inmate's arsenal, to say nothing of intelligence. Alas, many card players in the joint carry dubious credit ratings and light regard for the rules. My perceived smugness following wins could get me shanked, too. I quit cards. But I couldn't quit air.

Large, wall-mounted industrial fans — like small helicopters — ran on the high setting most of the year, 24/7. The ham-fisted white noise machines came in handy even when temperatures were cooler. Normal conversations in the barracks often sounded like reporters shouting into microphones during a hurricane. In winter, I became addicted to Visine to lubricate against dry air pushed around at obscene force.

Pedestal fans that sounded like lawnmowers on a stick cooled dayrooms and caused the most disputes because dudes could aim them directly on themselves at the expense of neighbors. Blasts from bathroom pedestal fans rippled faces and even blew pee streams around. At least guys draped clothes and shoes to dry over fan grills, which muffled the wind a little.

Guy wires kept the wall-mounted fans stationary to avoid disputes, moving the flashpoint to power switches at the CO desk. The guard on duty fielded on-off requests. COs weren't the main hurdle to fan control, however – the toughest guy in the barracks that cared about it was. Before it reached that level, though, diplomacy usually worked.

"Hey, is everyone cool with me getting the fan turned off?"

I loudly posed this question often, usually on lazy weekend mornings during non-summer months. Few minded. The barracks were plenty cool, and the fan noise in the daytime was annoying. In the period when Chang was my bunkie, a gale-force blast assaulted me every morning despite my locker door blocking it.

Usually, no one objected, so I'd go ask the CO to turn the fan off or do it myself if he/she wasn't around. The problems arose when someone turned it back on a few minutes later. Instead of starting an argument or a fight I'd opt for passive-aggression.

Since the guard desk sat around a corner, out of sight, I'd wander out into the corridor for a minute. Then I'd get the fan turned off again and kill another five minutes before returning to my bunk. I wanted to stay stealth.

But I was kidding myself. Everyone living in such close quarters knew I was cold-natured and bunked in the polar blast path. Even GED-level math students can put two and two together.

One morning I simply wasn't in the mood for that sneaky shit. I faced making my bed in what seemed like a forty-degree windchill. Waking up in a prison barracks didn't need such added insult. So I marched out, turned the fucker off, and returned immediately.

A linebacker-sized black dude called Thor didn't like this. I hadn't bothered to meet him yet because all he did was loudly bitch about whatever. "Yo, why'd you turn that fan off?" he thundered.

"Because I'm ten feet away from it and I'm freezing my ass off!" I snapped, aiming for a maiming. In my mind, whoever was closest to the jet stream deserved the most control of the fan, and Thor slept two bunks farther away than me.

"Man, you ain't the only one in here," came the condescending response, "and you don't run the block."

"I don't care who runs what, it's fucking cold in here. The fan doesn't need to be on."

Thor slowly shook his head: "Shit, it ain't cold in here, it's too damn warm."

I laughed, probably because my *don't get killed* instinct had yet to engage that morning. Worse, my mouth shot off. "Well, if you're so warm, I suggest you take off your long-sleeved shirt and throw on a pair of shorts."

This drew a few chuckles and hoots from increasingly interested onlookers. Thor gazed crookedly and slow-walked towards me. He wore a snide grin in addition to too much clothing. He stopped a mere four feet away, just short of *now we gonna fight* territory. A peanut gallery began gathering around.

"*You* suggest?" he slowly began and paused.

"Look man, I — "

"You suggest nothing!" he boomed. "Not about what I wear, and not about the fan. It keeps germs away."

I then realized the fan was beside the point — I was looking at a longtime inmate with alpha male concerns. Thor thought I'd made a power play instead of a simple move for Sunday morning serenity and comfort. Twenty months earlier I would've backed down, but now I felt bold and "prison hard."

I felt a right to stand my ground at my home camp, where I had many allies — including the fucking warden. At worst, buddies would have separated Thor from me before I became a bloody pulp. I also knew that most guys in honor grade were all talk, no matter how physically intimidating. I spoke freely.

"Dude, germs are gonna get you if they want you in this place," I said, through a smirk. "The fan just blows them around."

More laughs from the onlookers.

Instead of taking a swing at me, Thor's face wrinkled. Surely he wondered how a block supremacy challenge became a germ debate. A couple of beats passed. He stepped back and his sizable fists relaxed.

"Man, you fucking *crazy!*"

The diffused tension invited my neighbor "Rumble" to weigh in. His bulk dwarfed even Thor's, and he carried the authority of occupying the bunk a mere three feet away from the fan.

"Yo man, I was gonna turn it off anyway. Shit ain't hot."

Game over. Thor mumbled and whined his way back to his bunk, and the day proceeded with the fan off. I suspended my policy of ignoring Rumble and gladly fist-bumped him. I hated the guy for being off-the-charts obnoxious, but I loved him right then. Politics has nothing on prison when it comes to strange bedfellows.

Thor and I became friendly despite our rough start and his penchant for complaining. He proved to be more thoughtful and emotionally available than most anyone I met on the inside. We killed time together many mornings after finishing our adjacent janitor jobs.

His openness provided some of the heaviest moments of my pseudo-journalistic odyssey. He spoke of the court system railroading him on trumped-up charges. He explained that finding adequate and affordable legal defense seemed almost impossible in his community. Reports of such plights are common, but spending time actually inside The System with a poor soul conveying his pain from it choked me up.

"Where I come from, even trying to fight charges a dirty DA throws at you means you're a bitch," he explained, as my jaw dropped. "Just do your time like a real man do."

I'm practically never at a loss for words, but I was then. How entitled and lucky was I? Thor constantly reminded me of other examples of my entitlement when he saw them. Once I bitched about the chaos of the barracks.

"That's every classroom I've ever been in," he said. "Dudes like you think they're 'sposed to be quiet."

Another time I remarked about a stupid CO.

"Man, he might be smarter than the best teacher I had in high school."

Thor enjoyed pretending to take a swing at me to see if I'd flinch. He did so at the oddest times, too, like when he spoke openly about his emotions. And for the record, I flinched pretty often. His fists were as big as cantaloupes.

CHAPTER SEVENTEEN

I'm a Sonata

I ended up sharing a bunk with forty-three different dudes during my penitential tour. This remarkably high number reflects how often I moved between camps and how frequently I changed bunks. I didn't hesitate to move away from loud neighbors, heavy smokers, wind tunnels from fans, or bad bunkies.

My worst bunkmate ever was "Vex," an affable, middle-aged guy. I hated him so much that I didn't even record his real name in my journals. Our worlds collided when I bought the bunk above him in a back corner of the camp's quietest barracks. Nearly all of its residents worked jobs outside the gates all day, which brought blessed tranquility. This brightened my outlook, at least until I realized what a pain in the ass Vex was.

When we first met, I thought he was cool, even though he sang along loudly with his radio. This is the second-worst bunkie habit to me, and it needed to be taken care of immediately. The evening I moved in he started singing, intermittently and off-key. If he didn't know the words, he'd hum them. "Mmmayybaayyy, bay-bayyyy! Hmmmm, mmmm, say you'll stay-a-ayyyay!"

"Hey! *Hey!*" I shouted, finally tapping his shoulder to get his attention. He pulled an earbud out. "I don't ask for much, but please stop with the sing-alongs. No one wants to hear that shit."

"Oh! I thought I sounded good!"

"Even if you sounded good, it's still a dick move."

"Okay, my bad. Sorry," Vex replied.

What a great guy! Then he went and filled a Bad Bunkie Checklist fuller than my list of squandered opportunities at a productive life.

Vex followed the worst daily routine a bunkmate can: he got up early and stayed up late. The guy needed only five hours of sleep, which baffled me since his mouth ran constantly the other nineteen hours, talking about nothing. Vex was almost always "home," had buddies over to visit, and smoked – a lot. He also thumped the Bible and fronted as an evangelist, yet also actively traded "jack pics." Photos of sleazy women covered his locker door, right next to printouts of scriptures and a handmade crucifix.

My plum bunk position forced me to tolerate Vex. I took many deep breaths and counted to ten often to diffuse my inner tension. That worked until one Christmas morning, coincidentally enough. Vex and his ever-present sidekick "Fast" sat in chairs at the foot of the bunk jabbering like they enjoyed a Saturday in the park. Never mind five guys within ten feet of them wanted to sleep in.

After being awoken for the third time, I sat up and yelled: "Would you shut the fuck up?!"

Vex shut up for a second, taken aback by his usually laid-back bunkie going off. Then he barked: "Hey, you don't speak to me that way!"

He had a point. I could've used a different tack, but I'd had it. "Okay. How about keeping your voice down or go to the dayroom?"

"Fuck you," Vex shouted, temporarily losing his religion. "You ain't the boss of me!"

"Look, you wake me up every fucking morning, and I'm sick of it."

Our neighbor Columbus, four feet away, bolstered my point with a faint, "I heard that!"

"It's nine o'clock (actually 8:15), so you should be up, anyway!" Vex countered.

"Oh, so now you're my alarm clock too?"

"You know what? Go back to sleep! Just go the fuck back to sleep!" Vex shouted, standing up as if ready to fight.

"I'd love to!" I exclaimed.

"So would I!" Columbus added.

I moved back into sleep position, a pillow over head. Arguing with a guy like Vex is pointless.

"Oh, and Merry Christmas!" he shouted.

"Fuuuck off!" I suggested, using a New York accent out of nowhere.

Vex continued running his mouth for several minutes, surely insulting me and my mother. I could only hear mumbling through my earplugs. I later learned that Fast joined in with barbs.

"If you want quiet, why don't you just go home," he suggested.

What a great idea. Why didn't I think of that? I arose a couple of hours later, in a foul mood.

"Merry Christmas," Vex said, happily.

I assumed he was testing where our beef stood. I chuckled and returned the greeting. My point got made, so negative energy didn't need to be kept around. Some might call this a Christmas miracle. Our truce aside, I sought a permanent solution.

Vex cherished his back-corner spot, but he liked money and tobacco more. He was among those that scrounged under lockers for the remnants of roll-ups. Fast slept fifteen feet away, and I assumed Vex would love bunking with him. He could swap with "Red," who currently shared the bunk with Fast. He didn't smoke and spent fourteen hours a day sleeping when possible. He would love a bed in a back corner. I dipped over to talk to him one afternoon.

"Hey man, I need a little help," I said.

"Sure, what is it?" Red asked, jovially.

"Vex is driving me nuts, and I need him out of that bunk. Wanna swap with him?"

Instead of leaping at the chance, Red said, "Hmmnnn, ummm, I don't think so."

I looked at him like he'd regurgitated a full water balloon.

"What do you mean? It's the best spot in the whole room!"
"Meh. I kind of like it over here. Sorry."
Stunned, I trudged back to my bunk. I described the conversation to Columbus, who also wanted Vex gone. Once I finished, my happy-go-lucky buddy spelled it out for me.
"Dude, he's working you. He wants that bunk, he's just holding out to get paid."
"The fuck? So I have to pay Vex and Red?"
Columbus laughed in my face. "Sorry, man. Red may look young, but this ain't his first rodeo. He knows a mark when he sees one. No offense."
I'd recruited good new bunkies multiple times but never had to pay one to move. These guys think I'm a goddamn ATM! Before I coughed up compensation to Red I needed to learn Vex's price.
"Oh, hell no. There's no price. I love this corner," Vex replied when I asked him how much.
"But you can bunk with Fast. He's your boy!" I countered. "And you'd be doing Red and Columbus a favor," I lied. "They're old friends."
"Sorry, not gonna happen."
I could see the wheels slowly turning in his head, however. Probably thinking about a big pile of stamps or a baggie full of roll-ups in his hands. "You know, COs can catch you smoking a lot easier on this side of the room than over at Fast's bunk," I reasoned. I walked away to let him chew on that.
Five minutes later Vex found me sitting in the dayroom.
"Yeah, about that bunk switch. What's it worth to you?
"How about five stamps?" I began.
"Shiiiiiit!" Vex spat. He walked several feet away but didn't leave the room.
I walked over to him and sat down.
"Hey, sorry about the low offer but I had to try. How about eight stamps and a honey bun?" Every deal in the joint seemed to be sweetened with a honey bun, which costs sixty cents. Who was I to dismiss this tradition?
Three dollars may not sound like much, but that's twenty roll-ups Vex wouldn't have to scrounge from the floor. He

pretended to think about it for a second then said, "Sounds like a deal! When can you pay me?"

"Not right away. First, we need to get Red to switch, and he ain't tryna hear it," I explained.

"Okay. I'll talk to him."

I returned to my bunk and filled in Columbus. I didn't even ask him to pitch in because the bargain I got out of Vex pleased me so much. He wanted the chain-smoker gone almost as much as I did, after all.

In the chow hall later that day I sat down with Red, to gauge him. He spoke before I could.

"So, you got Vex and Columbus working for you? You must want this move bad."

"Nah. Not *that* bad," I lied. "Vex and I are cool now."

"You can't bullshit a bullshitter, bro. I want twenty stamps."

Once I got back into my chair I said, "No way. I'm still trying to catch up after all my coffee got ripped off. I can't afford that."

"Ain't my problem. Let me know when you're serious about getting rid of Vex."

Red got up and took his tray to the dishwasher, leaving me sitting there. That evening I conferred with Columbus again in our bunk area.

"Listen, bro, if this is gonna happen you gotta take part of the hit," I explained. "The bitch wants twenty stamps. I almost don't even want him over here now."

"He'll go lower, and you can count me in for five."

This felt like I'd found money. I would have paid twenty stamps for such a big improvement, truth be told. Hell, sometimes I matched buyout offers that quality bunkmates received just to *keep* them. Avoiding shitty bunkies was that important to me.

Anyway, I marched over to Red prepared to play hardball. In other words, beg.

"Bro, please help me do this! I rounded up thirteen stamps. That's all I got."

Unplanned, Columbus stepped in behind me. "And I'll throw in five," he said. "Or at least I'll hook you up for that much at the canteen."

I'm a Sonata

Red sat stone-faced, allowing me time to dislike him more. "All right. Just get me three honey buns and a Mello Yello. And the thirteen stamps, of course."

I felt fleeced, but I got over it quickly. Seeing Vex three bunks down and across Broadway made me smile for weeks. Once Red dropped his sales posturing we got along fine, too. The dude knew how to play the game. Respect.

Overnights in prison could turn weird, especially the dreams. Early on I dreamt of times before incarceration, which usually provided a welcome escape. Then dreams of using the internet took over and seemed to happen every night. As time passed my dreams consisted of me in prison more often than out enjoying the world. The bummer of those could stick with me all morning, if not all day.

Many nights I slept only in blocks of two or three hours at a time, trying to find peace of mind. I never thought twice about how this affected me until the middle of one sleep-challenged night. I usually explored the a.m. radio dial when sleepless, enjoying weather forecasts from far-flung cities like Des Moines, Iowa. At least I didn't suffer a winter there, locked up or not.

I could hear broadcasts from near and far, and their signal strengths fluctuated. This made for a curious grab bag of choices. One spin across the dial produced a piano sonata – utterly incongruous as a soundtrack for my surroundings. It reminded me of the famous scene in *The Shawshank Redemption* when Defraine commandeered the prison PA system to broadcast an opera record.

The unrealistic nature of this scene struck me. In the movie, inmates stop upon hearing the music, mimic confused dogs, and smile. If that prison was anything like North Carolina in 2013, they would've stopped, all right – to bitch about the song choice. "Man, what is this bullshit? Why ain't this Tommy Dorsey or Bing Crosby?"

Anyway, the radio signal that delivered the spare piano

piece was faint but steady, even as louder broadcasts drifted in and out. Like a good conversation interrupted by a waiter that checks on the table too often. As with that, the bullying radio blather proved only temporary, and the sonata remained steadfast. This struck me as an apt metaphor for my locked-up soul; jumbled and tested, but enduring. Thinking about my spirit persevering brought a warm, genuine smile.

    This reverie began to mix with sleep-bound dreaminess because the piano piece played for seemingly twenty minutes. I fought to stay awake to learn its title, despite expecting a denial of this simple wish. Prison did that a lot. The title finally got revealed, but in Spanish. At least I'd heard the sonata before and probably will again. I hope to hear it in some fancy locale while enjoying a fine dinner, fully recovered from my journey. Perhaps I'll discern the music and then have to explain why I'm suddenly crying. I'll try to pass it off as tears of joy, but this will hardly describe it. Nothing ever will.

―――――――

I entered my third and final year of captivity in February 2014, obsessed with the thought of transferring to The Craggy Correctional Center in Asheville, as usual. Over my prison travels, I learned the place offered more charms than just being the closest camp to Atlanta and cool summers.

    This promised land also featured better food, lots of day trips into town with community volunteers, and good work-release jobs. Too bad they had reserved the highly coveted camp for inmates not bogged down by demerit points. I joined the waiting list anyway, despite my case manager telling me to not bother.

    I considered work-release to be a raw deal anyway, despite the freedom it offered. The jobs usually required heavy manual labor, and the state deducted significant amounts from paychecks to cover $600 for monthly rent, a daily "transportation fee," and court-ordered garnishments. Most workers ultimately netted a mere forty dollars a week. I refused to slave for beggar's pay. Besides, as Eugene O'Neill wrote in

I'm a Sonata

The Iceman Cometh: "You can't be too careful about work. It's the deadliest habit known to medical science."

Anyway, transferring meant leaving friends I'd made at Southern, so not moving would be okay. I felt like I started lifelong friendships, almost as if we'd gone to war together. I liked a lot of the COs, too. We bonded over a common interest in killing boredom and not getting murdered.

Still, Monday and Wednesday evenings could make me blue. Then, the intercom sounded the names of those transferring out the next morning, but never mine.

Guys that were on the list drew many visitors. Inmates he owed money to, but also dudes looking for good, cheap contraband to buy. The state didn't technically allow items like clipboards and magnets and could confiscate them during moves. If the departing inmate didn't feel like rolling the dice others enjoyed fire-sale prices or even giveaways. Southern was great for that.

One spring evening I stood in the yard juggling, radio earbuds engaged. A buddy walked up with his mouth moving. I turned down my music and tilted my head.

"I said, what camp are you headed to?"

"Nowhere," I replied. "I'm trying to get to Asheville, though."

"Well, you're going somewhere. They called your name."

My balls dropped on the spot. I recall nothing besides racing to the office where COs passed out bags to pack personal items in.

"They got you headed to Craggy, looks like," said the CO, as I tried to gain my breath.

"Hell, yeah! Asheville here I come!"

I soon learned I couldn't fully celebrate a victory, though. The honor grade camp had recently come under the management of an adjacent medium security facility, so both places were known as Craggy. Some of the guys that came by my locker told of honor grade transfers first being assigned to work at a nearby laundry facility and to live at the medium joint. Details in the paperwork provided no answers. In prison, even great bounces carried caveats.

Whatever the case, I bid farewell to friends, and hugged several of them. Hell, I almost hugged Sergeant Dellwood when I bid farewell to him in the office.

"Best of luck, Phillips," he said. "You've been a breath of fresh air around here."

I managed a "Thanks, you too," as I exited before I got teary-eyed.

The fact is, I loved Southern. I couldn't have asked for a better place to do time while waiting to get to Asheville. The warden was there to facilitate a smooth operation by respecting inmates, not punishing them. And this attitude prevailed down a chain of command that consisted almost entirely of nice people. And the camp population rarely even reached capacity, let alone overflowed. It was simply *comfortable*. I'll always look back on my time there fondly.

I slept poorly that night, wondering if I was doomed for "blowing down lint as necessary" after all. The next morning was still a joyous occasion, though. No miserably hot summer with no air conditioning for me. And at least only nine months remained for me to be jerked around, wherever I landed.

Warden stood near the bus, along with my old pal Portis and another cool CO. I suspected Warden had triggered my unexpected transfer, but I was too choked up to ask him about it. "You're a good man," was all I could manage as we shook hands. I nodded to the other two as they wished me good luck and I boarded the bus.

The temperature read an abnormally warm sixty-eight degrees on that mid-April morning in 2014. Luckily I donned a long-sleeved shirt for the trip anyway, having noted the weather forecast. A cold front hit seven hours later as the transfer bus groaned its way up Appalachian mountains. The bus soon got colder than a county jail holding tank. And just like jail, the COs in charge didn't care. The cockpit is separated from the human cargo pen. Worse, a few jackass inmates refused to close their windows despite chattering pleas from fellow felons who failed to dress in layers.

Snow blew sideways by the time the bus approached guard

towers of the gloomy medium security campus of Craggy Correctional. Rolls of razor wire atop double fences twice as high as Southern's seemed to say "fuck you." You could feel the darkness. Minimum joints might as well feature picket fences by comparison.

Knowing the incompetence of prison administration, I always feared an accidental assignment to one of these places. And this one promised "soiled linen rooms." This time I pretty much expected to hear my name called to disembark into hell.

The rear exit door opened. A frigid wind swept in, plunging the bus' temperature even farther. A gruff CO barked out names to exit, in random order. Many of my hapless inmate brethren stepped outside and into line. The wind chill matched the cold glares intake guards shot at the new arrivals. The bus slowly emptied, but I remained. My spirits rose with each name called. Then: "Phillips!"

The bottom dropped out of my stomach. I could only chuckle ruefully, unable to even curse. The system may have finally beaten me. I slowly rose and moved down the aisle. Some asshole changing seats for no clear reason cut off the aisle.

"Yo, I gotta get out the door!" I snapped.

A fellow Phillips glared back at me. "Me, too."

He stepped out and I watched the guard at the door confirm his number. Phillips joined the group outside. I sat back down and felt like I'd gotten a Porsche Panamera for Christmas.

I'd been chatting away back at the bus transfer depot when they called the names for Craggy, just like the guys I bitched about two years earlier. Had I known another Phillips was on board we could've chatted. Perhaps found kin in common to blame for our fuck-up gene.

I watched from the safety of the bus as sixteen unfortunates endured a sergeant's lecture before finally being marched inside. Yours truly Phillips was among five dudes dropped off at Craggy Minimum, about two-thousand feet yet a world away. No fence surrounded the building, which I first assumed contained only administrative offices. Once parked we simply grabbed our bags from the cargo hold and dipped straight in the front door, no lectures or intimidation involved. Honor grade had its perks.

I felt like I'd walked into a middle school. Shiny white tile dressed up typically drab prison concrete floors. No usual jailhouse gates with bars locked away sleeping areas at night. Inmates could hang out in a grassy courtyard when they locked the chain-link gate to the gigantic main yard — the only semblance of "real" prison on the site.

Craggy Correctional Minimum, the most desirable prison camp in the state. (Imagery © 2019 Google, Maxar Technologies)

This access to an outdoor area at all hours was unique to Craggy. Most of the boisterous board games, card games, and socializing took place out there. Pretty much every night was a party, only without intoxicants and a chance of getting laid.

I'm a Sonata

With most of the loud people outside, dayroom tranquility stood a chance.

Craggy's huge common area felt like a small school cafeteria, only with a prison canteen to supply goodies and two fifty-inch HDTVs to keep inmates sedated. A wall of windows provided mountain views worthy of a resort.

The barracks areas sat two doorways and a corridor away from the dayroom instead of being next to it. Same with the bathrooms and shower rooms. Ample space separated bunks, and elbow room abounded everywhere. It felt like an inmate designed the prison or something. I stayed grinning for hours after I arrived as the snow continued and darkness fell.

The next morning I felt awe similar to seeing the Grand Canyon for the first time. The camp occupied an extraordinary hilltop setting, with a sweeping panorama of a lushly forested valley in the foreground and Blue Ridge peaks in the distance. The view out the back of Asheville's famous Biltmore House is less impressive. I nearly wept, thinking about both nature's beauty and that I'd finally reached a huge goal.

Watching stunning sunsets over the mountains from an acres-wide yard became standard for me. However, when I suffered a foul mood I sometimes found sunsets more painful than uplifting. Especially when the COs closed the yard just as the clouds began to change colors in the painted sky. Like watching the first part of a good movie and being forced to watch the rest through a chain-link fence. Also, far down the hill, in the foreground, sat the bleak, low-slung medium-security facility that reminded me of Greene. Sure this sunset is wonderful, but you're still locked up. Luckily, the animals around the place helped take my mind off of that.

A flock of ten genuine wild turkeys waddled, strutted, and preened around the yard like they weren't even in prison. Small deer frolicked on the edge of the woods at dusk. Recently arrived inmates seemed especially enthralled by them. They stood and stared as if Jesus himself had wandered out of the woods. Many guys hadn't seen significant wildlife for years.

Speaking of deer, my pal "Melty" and I enjoyed a sunset from the courtyard one evening, after the yard had closed. As we sat discussing the pros and cons of Burning Man or something, an enormous buck clopped into view not sixty yards away, far from where deer normally hung out.

"Man, that thing's fucking huge," Melty marveled.

So big I started counting the tines on his antlers.

"I'm pretty sure that's a twelve-point buck," I said.

Melty confirmed my count as I sought others to check him out. The big fella bolted away in the meantime like he knew what I was doing. As if, "I just wanted to say hello to you two, not everybody else."

Since neither Melty nor I hunt, we resumed our conversation and forgot about it. Only months later did I learn some avid hunters never see a twelve-point buck. Seeing one is as rare as a hole-in-one in golf. Too bad this got lost on two dipshits equally impressed by a nice sunset and good conversation.

Besides deer and wild turkeys, our confined souls enjoyed a cat named Freedom. He was the unofficial camp mascot and maximized his prison experience by lying in the middle of the sidewalk that led to the yard. Fucker got petted all day long. God knows why he wasn't twenty pounds overweight because he ate like a king, too. So well that he refused to eat most chow hall "meat," just like me. If I'm reincarnated as a stray cat I will set up shop at the nearest minimum security prison. Life couldn't get much better.

Freedom reminded me of Richard aka "The Earl of Rummage," my first bunkie at Craggy. Both were lovable scavengers. The Earl did his work-release as a sorter at a recycling plant. He pulled recyclables out of raw rubbish on a conveyor belt and set aside usable items to smuggle back to the camp to sell. The fifty-year-old arsonist loved this job almost as much as playing Dungeons & Dragons and listening to Queensrÿche.

The Earl unearthed the likes of clipboards, water bottles, key chains, porn mags, and wallets. He beamed upon returning from work each day despite looking like he'd chased a cat through a dumpster. He brought reclaimed goods with him only when the lenient CO shift was on duty. These good-humored guards didn't bother frisking him, and they enjoyed assessing the day's inventory.

Inmates hovered around to see which items the COs allowed to pass through as if it were a game. For instance yes to fly swatters, no to portable CD players. Onlookers guessed which items would make the cut and got the first crack at buying them. CO unofficial acceptance of benign contraband was one of minimum security's charms.

The Earl, who looked like the actor Harry Shearer, was down five years for arson. Unlike most of the cons I encountered he swore innocence and detailed his circumstances to anyone that would listen.

"Being in a motel room when the building burns down is not a crime," he usually asserted.

Reasonable people could read between the lines after hearing The Earl explain the incident often enough. Becoming oblivious during a crack binge can lead to motel rooms catching fire and lead the perp to believe he had nothing to do with it.

Finding a down-low oatmeal connection in the kitchen storeroom was my top priority upon arrival at Craggy. The lack of one meant either high canteen bills or a chronically empty stomach each evening. I eventually found an oats supplier, but at a sky-high cost of three stamps per sandwich bag full due to a mysterious lack of competition. And also, racism.

A squat, middle-aged black guy called "Shorty" was the first kitchen worker I found willing to sell to me.

"Three stamps for this little bag is way too high, man," I complained upon his first delivery. "I need a bulk rate, cuz I eat a ton of oatmeal."

"Hey, the heat's on in there. I'm getting what I can," he replied.

"Listen, you charge me a reasonable price, but I'll still tell everyone I'm paying three stamps per bag."

This appealed to his meager business sense, so we agreed on two stamps. Or so I thought. Shorty showed up a few days later with a fresh bag, but the scoundrel still wanted three stamps.

"Whoa! Two stamps bro," I exclaimed. "You agreed to that not even a week ago."

"Man, I'm telling you security in the storeroom is all over me. I hardly get what I'm getting now."

I paid him with a frown on my face, like a custy bitch that had no alternative. I soon found a different source. "Berry "stood a thick six-foot-two and could have ruined Shorty with one punch. One day he showed up at my bunk empty-handed.

"Yo man, I ain't tryin' to work Shorty's corner," he explained. "He's the oatmeal guy around here."

"Are you fucking with me? My last camp had ten guys selling oatmeal!" I practically shouted.

"Sorry man, it's Shorty's hustle."

"Well, if we're playing mafia shit," I said through laughter. "Tell Shorty you'll beat his ass unless you get to sell too!"

Berry merely walked away, staying in his meek character. I lied on my bunk and simmered, wondering how tripled oatmeal costs would affect my monthly budget. I resigned myself to the shakedown and placed an order with Shorty the next time I saw him.

"No man. The heat's too much. Can't do it anymore."

He might as well have said ten months was just added to my sentence. What the fuck was this, Greene County? I suddenly felt hungrier.

I asked around. Several of my fellow oatmeal consumers reported no supply line issues. My attempted end run around Shorty's storeroom monopoly offended him. He had frozen me out. I tried to enlist a buddy to work as my secret oatmeal go-between.

"No way. I can't risk Shorty's blacklist, bro. He's my powdered milk connect."

At first, I thought he was kidding, but he was serious as a stopped-up inmate waiting for a toilet stall. I scrambled to find a different middleman. I finally convinced a black friend of mine to buy my oatmeal. Not only could he buy all he wished, but he also enjoyed volume discounts Shorty never offered me. These black guy discounts didn't trickle down, either, because my go-between charged a recurring finder's fee.

Suddenly I felt price-gouged like a ghetto grocery store customer, and I couldn't exactly hop on a bus to find a better price. Hell, my middleman probably bought the oatmeal cheaper than he claimed and profited both coming and going. Such was life in the jungle. Soon enough Shorty shipped out, lowering both trade barriers and prices. This solved my oatmeal problem, but resting easily at Craggy still proved difficult.

CHAPTER EIGHTEEN

Christmas Came Early

Over ninety percent of Craggy inmates held jobs. I didn't want one. This was convenient because my demerit points disqualified me from any work-release gig that paid real money anyway. Easier on-camp jobs rarely became available, and I refused hard labor for pocket change on the likes of a road crew. A battle commenced.

Word was Craggy didn't waste bed space on layabouts like me. Inmates either worked, or they got sent elsewhere. This kept me on edge most of the time, terrified they would call my name on transfer evenings. So I took countermeasures.

First, I employed my patented stall tactic – work boots. The Craggy CO in charge of them was a miserable and condescending man named George. I especially enjoyed tricking him because he treated inmates like trash. His attitude matched his sickly appearance. He reminded me of a hungover cross-dresser who'd only recently removed his cosmetics. I avoided standing too close to him because he always seemed ready to vomit.

One day George tried to fit me with a pair of boots. I rejected size fifteens that fit fine. "Well, this is as big as they make 'em," he professed through his typical scowl. I didn't correct him. Being categorized as *unbootable* worked for me.

"I have a bad back anyway," I added. "I can't work a job that requires boots."

"I wish I could choose my job." George snipped as he

Christmas Came Early

re-boxed the boots. "And I got news for you: If you ain't workin' you won't be stayin' on this camp long."

This made my heart sink. Something had to give. Perhaps a solution would emerge soon when I spoke with my new case manager for the first time.

"Garrett Phillips, report to the jobs office."

I asked someone where this office was and walked over there. On the way, I scoped out a wooded ravine that ran along the road. I briefly fantasized about jumping into it and escaping because no fence kept me from doing so. I came to my senses, though, and soon stood before my inmate case manager named Corbin, who doubled as the job assignment officer.

The fortyish Corbin was blunt in his manner and his appearance reminded me of an ex-high school wrestler. He talked fast and stayed suspicious because so many conniving cons faked injuries to avoid work. Guys bitched about where they worked a lot, and also about Corbin. He seemed to sense this; to carry a chip on his shoulder.

Before addressing me he asked his office mate to reduce the volume on a boombox playing classic rock. We exchanged pleasantries, and he got to it.

"I have you down to work for Yancey County DOT"

"I'm sorry, but I can't work a physical job like that all day," I said, pointing behind my shoulder. "Bad back."

Corbin briefly looked over my file.

"Until I see a doctor report that says you can't, you'll report to this job and like it," he ordered.

"Fair enough," I chirped. "I'll see the doctor as soon as I can. But they don't have work boots that fit me anyway."

Corbin paused and tilted his head at my novel excuse. "What size do you wear?"

"Fifteen," I lied, betting he wouldn't look inside my shoe.

"Hold your foot up."

I did so. He cast a crooked gaze at my ski-like size fourteens, like a carnival worker who guessed shoe sizes instead of people's weight.

His brow rose as if to say: *yeah, those are fucking huge all right.*

He spoke gruffly: "Okay listen, get me that doctor report and tell me when your boots get here."

I nearly let on that George listed me as unbootable, but caught myself. Instead, I let CO incompetence work for me for once.

"Yeah, I'll tell you when my boots show up. And listen, sorry to be a bother. I'm really not trying to play you."

"No problem," he replied. "Keep me updated about your back and send in the next guy, will ya?"

Since Craggy is not a medical camp, I sat in front of a doctor a mere four days later. He assessed X-rays that showed spine narrowing and vertebrae problems, which exempted me from hard labor. Then he lumped me in with every other scofflaw that sought doctor's orders to avoid work.

"So I assume you want to be classified as activity level three?"

This would keep me from working, but also get me transferred to a different camp.

"Oh no, doctor," I nearly shouted. "I can work, I just can't do heavy jobs all day long."

His head tilted in surprise. "I see. I'll put you down as level two then," he said, jovially. "That should serve you fine."

Corbin summoned me to his office multiple times over the following weeks. At first, he asked about my health status and scanned for jobs that fit my limited range. Soon these visits strayed from official business, reminding me of bullshit sessions I enjoyed with Sergeant Dellwood at Southern or with the DHO mediator Holsinger.

I suspected these meetings were more for Corbin and his office mate to break the monotony of their days than to put me to work. We talked about sports, music, and current events. Both guys proved friendly despite their reputations among inmates as dicks. Corbin even talked smack about inmates and other COs. He reminded me of a girlfriend who shares way too much information about her best friend's sex life.

One day the janitor job in Corbin's small office building came open, so he offered me the gig.

"If I accept it, will I see you every day?"

"Well, yeah," he responded.

I immediately grabbed my lower back and deadpanned: "Owwwww!"

We all laughed.

Sucking up to Corbin seemed to earn me an exemption from Craggy's "all inmates must work" rule. Finding me a job became a running joke. It seemed like he didn't care either way.

"I have a car-washing opening here. What does your back say about that?'

I'd wince and reach behind me.

"Oh well, we'll find you something," Corbin said, and changed the subject to football or a Tom Petty song.

Meanwhile, practically all of my neighbors in the barracks trudged off to jobs. As I continued unemployed, they started giving me shit. Common jabs included: "Must be nice to never break a sweat," or "Every day is a weekend for you, ain't it?" I started to feel like a basic training soldier who relaxed while his peers endured drills and obstacle courses. The guilt I felt made me feel institutionalized – like I needed to fit into the system.

And speaking of that, my excessive leisure time made me think I might actually *miss* prison after I got out. Being in there wasn't exactly blissful, but I stayed reasonably happy minute-to-minute. Once I adapted to the routine, I realized that endless time to read, nap, or watch sports guilt-free isn't the worst life ever. The thought of adjusting away from this scared me, though. I wondered how quickly I could shake off my chronic laziness.

To appease my hard-working haters in the barracks, I volunteered to assist in the clothes house. They needed help on busy days and administration looked favorably on inmates that did so. This gave me both a sense of accomplishment and my pick of the best clothes and sheets for personal use. Standing there folding shirts and pairing up socks while listening to music and chatting with the fellas proved a good way to pass time. One of these guys was Louie, who became my best pal of all I met on the inside.

Louie, who Gene Hackman would play in a movie, was highly intelligent, played virtuoso guitar, and possessed a biting wit. We spent a lot of time ridiculing senseless prison rules and COs we didn't like. He could laugh at himself, too. Like about his most recent arrest, which involved scrambling across a street with a stolen TV under his arm. Heroin addiction made him do things like that.

His good humor came through as we watched football one night with my Oatmeal Middleman, who knew Louie from way back. At one point the TV showed a wide picture of the Charlotte skyline. Louie beamed with civic pride: "That's my town!"

A couple of beats passed, and Oatmeal Middleman exclaimed: "Yeah! Did you see that park bench?"

"You know, that really hurts," he said, laughing through the sentence.

Louie and I bonded as sarcastic introverts who both dodged prison jobs and read voraciously. We passed time expanding our vocabularies, keeping a list of good new words and working a "word of the day" into conversations. Our long-term goal was to read a James Wolcott *Vanity Fair* piece without trepidation. Good luck with that.

Our circumstances made certain words especially amusing. Like *venal,* which described practically everyone in prison. People naturally suspect this describes an STD, but it means "motivated by susceptibility to bribery." *Pedantic* also described our inmate brethren, because lots of them prattled on about mundane topics. Louie and I weren't dumb enough to refer to them that way, though. That would start rumors and make enemies.

Out of hundreds of words learned I somehow settled on two favorites. I love the sound of *ineffable,* which is so close to how most women think of me: un-effable. But both Louie and I declared *frottage* as the runaway winner. Its vague maritime feel makes it an ideal name for a beach cottage or a yacht, and its meaning would be perfect for a fragrance or a gay bar. Frottage!

Asheville's remarkably diverse radio options broadened my music knowledge and helped me steal time from The Man. The legendary WNCW offered a wide variety of quality music, commercial-free and unlike anywhere else I'd been in the state. My favorite of many programs was *Jar of Jam*, which broadcast five hours of various Grateful Dead concert recordings. Guessing the next song played became like being at the show since I couldn't cheat by reading setlists. I even "chased" songs as Deadheads do, thrilled to hear an *Althea* after many weeks of hoping for one.

The bizarre radio monologues of Joe Frank hit the airwaves once a week, too. My first exposure to this genius came in the middle of the night. I'd fallen asleep to music but randomly awoke to *Escape From Paradise*, Frank's fictional account of a "liberal arts" prison. Inmate activities described in this yarn included ballet and orchestra, and hearing this made me wonder if I was still dreaming. Being in prison when I heard it blew me away. My neighbors must've thought I'd lost my mind as I laughed and repeated "what the fuck is this?" aloud despite myself.

Craggy, and Asheville, offered excellent work-release opportunities. Select inmates could pursue gigs at private businesses instead of laboring at grunt jobs like pallet construction or sorting recyclables. Local volunteers escorted them on job searches, and also to church services, twelve-step meetings, or to simply bop around town for a while. Asheville is widely known as the best in the system for such privileges. A pal of mine named Donner maximized his chance at them.

Donner, around thirty, looked like a movie star. He had bright blue eyes, dark hair, and his intense workout regimen lent him a perfectly sculpted physique. But as proof that a man can't have it all, he stood only about five-foot-two. And despite – or due to – an affluent upbringing he ended up abusing substances and with serious behavioral issues like armed robbery, which triggered his eleven-year sentence. Despite this, Donner carried a superiority complex that made even me look humble by comparison. He knew everything about everything, but at least his sense of humor kept me laughing.

After nine years of behaving himself in prison, Donner landed a job at a small bakery and catering outfit. This allowed him to ditch his inmate uniform and dress like the hipster he was while at work downtown. Donner's thirtyish, somewhat attractive boss even provided him with free work transportation. His sweet position put him in a good mood 24/7, and he spread the wealth. He brought home bags full of out-of-date baked goods to share with everyone.

"Thanks for the muffin, Cookie!" guys would mumble while stuffing their faces.

"Yeah, not really psyched about that new nickname but you're welcome," he once replied, snootily.

Donner soon received different monikers.

The prison grapevine often twists details about inmate drama. When the story makes the front page of the newspaper and leads the TV news, however, the facts are more clear. Such was the case with Donner's debacle.

The news broke in the aftermath of a Christmas party Donner's bakery catered, which included both food and alcohol. Backup bottles for the bar were located near the catering setup, and called to Donner. My alcoholic pal soon gave in and became blackout drunk. No word on whether cookie and cupcake service suffered as a result.

Donner stole his boss's wallet out of the catering van and walked away, apparently to find a crack house. They apprehended him a little over a mile from his starting point, reeling and stumbling toward The Hood. Donner ended up being the first perp recorded by a body camera on an Asheville cop.

They showed an overweight police sergeant on the TV

Christmas Came Early

news demonstrating the department's new toy. He narrated the cop cam footage of our staggering inmate brother. "As you can see, this gentleman is clearly a threat to society."

This elicited a tremendous roar from the dayroom gallery that knew Donner well. The only bigger laugh I heard in prison was when a widely loathed sergeant slipped and fell while trying to subdue an inmate in front of a dozen spectators.

Melty, Donner's best friend at Craggy, told me Donner's boss had been supplying him with alcohol to fuel sexual trysts for a few weeks prior to his meltdown. "He thought he could control his drinking this time," Melty explained.

I relayed this information to Louie, who said: "Shit, she didn't need to get him drunk to fuck her. Dude hasn't been laid in eight years!"

Donner's follies earned him a sixty-day stay in the hole followed by a bunk in medium security. An escape charge added over a year to his sentence. Luckily for him, his erstwhile boss and fuck buddy refused to press theft charges, thus sparing him multiple extra years in the joint.

Donner's disaster saddened me, but I mourned only fleetingly. Thirty-two months locked up had numbed my compassion for others. Staying positive was hard enough without dwelling on myriad hard-luck cases in my midst. Pals came and went, and life went on for the callous and institutionalized.

I'm a humanist, so basically an atheist. But at Christmas time on the inside I believed. My first season there a local church donated bags of goodies for inmates. Among its contents was a calendar/day planner. I filled in my plan for January 1st: "Be incarcerated." Each day after that I wrote: "See 1/1/13."

I spent my third and final prison Christmas season in Asheville, where competing churches delivered booty. Distribution lines in the chow hall brimmed with the excitement of expectant inmates. The packages weren't exactly free, however.

The first group of visitors formed a greeting line for hand-shaking and back-patting before handing out their small bags of joy. Worse, for this introvert at least, a huge obstacle stood mere feet away from my giant bags of goodies: A wax doll of a woman smothered in cosmetics that insisted on giving each inmate a full hug. I could smell her perfume cloud from two people away, and it reminded me of the "smell good" black guys used to concealed fart smells

I held my breath when I got to her and did what I had to do. I still wonder how the next greeter in line kept a straight face after seeing mine.

About an hour later a second church group's tidings of comfort and joy arrived – no hugging required. They handed out small trash bags loaded with candy, sundries, and home-baked goodies, including chunks of fudge in four different flavors. If I remained in Asheville after my release, I'd join this church. Any congregation featuring fudge packers like this is okay with me.

This avalanche of outside goods set off a frenzy of wheeling and dealing in the barracks. I traded most of my sweets for sensible items since sugar buzzes are more important to inmates than, say, dental hygiene or pens. I stocked up on toothpaste and toothbrushes to take home less than a month later. In fact, I may still use toothpaste from this period when I accept the Pulitzer for this book. Praise the Lord.

My endless string of new prison bunkmates settled down at Craggy. I suffered only five there over an eight-month period. A couple of these tested me, though, especially a soft-spoken kid of about twenty called "Lil' Homie." He stood about five-foot-three, and his wireframe glasses and high afro reminded me of Wayne Williams, the Atlanta child killer from the '80s. Homie wasn't violent, though. He was down for dealing crack in the Asheville 'hood.

Homie suffered from what appeared to be gout, a disorder that left him mostly bed-bound. This meant he was always "home," so his loud buddies visited often. He usually slept all day and moved around in the wee hours. His metal crutches sometimes jolted me awake as they hit the bed frame, like a CO knocking it with a flashlight. Worse, Homie rarely showered and lay directly on his mattress. His sheets and blanket usually sat in a balled-up mess. I felt like I lived above a doghouse.

One day the assistant chaplain (an inmate) and five of his Church of God sidekicks appeared at our bunk. They came to ask Jesus to cure Homie's leg problems. By the time I realized this they'd closed off all paths for escape. The beseechers surrounded the bunk with their eyes closed, moaning praises of Jesus and awkwardly laying hands on the subject. I'm pretty sure interrupting an exorcism sends you straight to hell, so I stayed put.

I couldn't concentrate on reading, so I stared at the ceiling in thought. *Wait ... didn't God put Lil' Homie in this pickle to begin with? Aren't these guys criticizing God's will right now?*

This congregation broke up after a few minutes, and evidently, the healers didn't work hard enough. Homie's badly swollen feet steadily worsened. One night an ambulance took him away with acute stomach pain, too. Despite this, Homie returned to Craggy a couple of days later, where the nurse wouldn't issue a wheelchair because he "could use the exercise" of crutches.

Most observers agreed Homie's health issues were more serious than gout. Several of us encouraged him to file grievances and raise hell until they transferred him to the main hospital in Raleigh. Our crotchety old-school neighbor – who I called Bane – even pulled off a ruse to force the administration's hand.

Bane, the bathroom janitor, performed his work after midnight. He got Homie to lay on the floor with his crutches splayed out as if he'd fallen. Bane ran to COs and swore he walked in to find the dude lying there. This earned Homie an instant return to the emergency room, and hopefully a hospital bed until cured. Instead, my bunkie returned to our bunk two days later, his ailment still a mystery.

The next evening a CO and a sergeant showed up to talk to Homie. Minutes later an emergency exit door opened for the first time in months. Four firemen spilled through, wearing optic yellow helmets and knee-high rubber boots. Behind them sat a huge, militaristic emergency vehicle that could have driven through a wall. I guess prayer works after all.

These first responders seemed shocked to be there, as were the inmates to see them. Everyone exchanged WTF glances. They had arrived to remove Homie as if he was the first victim of the apocalypse, worthy of immediate quarantine and study. A couple of men in helmets prepared a stretcher next to my bunk while the other two stood looking around, wide-eyed. *So this is what it looks like in prison.*

"What the Sam Hill is this?" my neighbor Bane shouted. "This poor bastard has been back and forth in an ambulance twice in one week and now they send goddamn Storm Troopers?"

"That'll be enough of that," the sergeant snapped.

The first responders gathered up Homie, who accepted farewell fist bumps and well-wishes as they wheeled him away for good. The rumor mill suggested he got diagnosed with a rare, terminal cancer. Homie was a kind soul who deserved much better.

Bane, around sixty and a career inmate, was big and loud. The dense bastard seemed born only to drive me crazy; to provide one final test of patience before I went home. The memory of Bane will keep me on the straight and narrow. Living beside him inspired a special *Biff Bugle* edition to describe the torment. (My pretend newspaper. I mailed it to a friend, who emailed it to friends and relatives.)

Christmas Came Early

INMATE ECSTATIC ABOUT WRONG THING
More Pleased With Nemesis Leaving Than Himself

ASHEVILLE, NC – In a confounding development, notable drug war casualty and current North Carolina prison inmate Garrett "Biff" Phillips is happier about a barracks neighbor going home than about his own exit. Many observers fear Phillips has become "institutionalized," and his sanity is being questioned even more than usual.

The Bugle recently reached Phillips for comment whereupon he ranted about a fellow felon identified only as Bane. "After thirty-three months down I know about obnoxious prison neighbors," the inmate claimed. "And Bane was top five, if not the worst. A walking, talking nightmare."

Phillips appeared halted by tears before continuing. "I mean, I obsess over my countdown, but I doubt my exit day will make me happier than the day Bane left. I might've caught a murder charge if he were here one more hour."

When asked to describe Bane's faults, Phillips was at no loss for words. "First of all he was half-deaf, probably from years of running a circular saw without earplugs. He was loud, stupid, passive-aggressive, inconsiderate, smelly, childish, gaseous, dishonest, phony, and an eyesore."

Asked for specifics, America's favorite felon said, "Most agonizing was the guy's level of humor. He always went for the most obvious joke, like a white Steve Harvey or something. Basic sarcasm was lost on him." Phillips began shouting: "And this, this ... *abomination* slept six feet from me for nearly two hundred days. Upwind, no less."

The Bugle reached prison staff psychiatrist, Dr. Stan Boombotz, for comment. "Mr. Phillips has experienced a Traumatic Extended Annoyance event, which can be more damaging than solitary confinement. This is fairly common for offenders preparing for egress, and removal of an annoyance is the best treatment."

A veteran inmate who requested anonymity commented on annoying prison neighbors. "(N-words) get worn down 'cuz the motherf****** is right there, 24/7. It's aggravating as f***. Ain't much can be done."

According to Phillips, Bane was "God-fearing."

"This was a giant part of the problem. He spread his bibles and Jesus lit out on his bed and read scriptures out loud – at seven in the morning! And his hobby of crafting little crucifix necklaces crossed bounds as well."

An anonymous correctional officer reached for comment claimed Phillips emoted openly following Bane's release. "Oh, he was a-whoopin' and a-hollerin' when that old bastard left. I thought ol' Biff was gettin' out his own self!"

Asked to comment on Bane, the officer agreed with Phillips. "I was happy Bane got out too. All he did was bitch, and he kept so much s*** in his locker we'd draw straws over who had to search it. And don't even get me started about his crucifix necklace makin'."

Commenting on Bane's release day, Phillips said, "When he left, the joy was palpable, which is hard to find in here." He explained further. "Feeling anything can be difficult since my soul has been in neutral for so long. But I sure felt ecstasy that day!"

Phillips expressed concern about Bane's replacement in the barracks. "The prison gods frown upon a man that's too happy about a bad neighbor leaving. That can come back to bite you," he said. "'You gotta be careful what you wish for."

The new neighbor has proven tolerable, however. "He smokes a ton and talks too loud, but that's almost a given. At least he doesn't go shirtless all day and subject me to saggy old man boobs like Bane did."

The inmate spoke of his December 24 exit preparations and plans thereafter. "I stopped requesting a buzz haircut months ago so I don't look like an inmate when I get out. And I changed the address on my magazines, sending them to friends and family who paid for them." The felon paused, thoughtfully. "I hope at least one of them freaks out when a magazine shows up with my name on it, afraid I plan on moving in. That's a funny image."

Phillips explained his initial plan. "I'll be couch-surfing until I find my way. As long as I have a laptop to write my crazy story on, I'll be fine."

Release-day transportation will be provided by long-time Atlanta friend Ignatius J. Reilly. "I asked Iggy to rent an RV stocked with a couple of hookers and perhaps a nice crudité platter with blue cheese. You know, to hit the ground running," Phillips claimed. "I think he knows me well enough to take this request seriously. I hate ranch dressing."

Throughout my thirty-five months I assumed nothing would bother me during my final weeks. Alas, prison annoyed me all the way to the final day. Instead of thinking: *I'm almost out of here, awesome!* I more often thought: *Fuck, this is taking forever!*

Having had nothing but time to worry about it, anxiety about my future added to my negativity. No decent career awaited me, only uncertainty about what kind of work I could find as a convicted felon. Would my family truly forgive me, or wash their hands of me once I was free?

As the days wound down, I thought about the little things I'd miss. My cool neighbor Harwood, who I'd sit with on his back-corner bunk waiting for count time to pass. It felt like just shooting the breeze on a front porch in the South, in no hurry at all. I also loved sharing the thrill of watching a great televised sporting event with a couple of dozen guys in the dayrooms. And the warmth of sharing moments of kindness with both inmates and guards — reminders that nice people can be found anywhere. I started realizing how much this all meant to me.

Lookout for Shorts

Impossibly, my release day arrived. I felt like my brain had been removed, placed in a chair spinning in circles, and returned to my head. Perhaps a collision of excitement and apprehension. The thrill of being free and wondering who would lend me money so I could restart my life.

I noticed the morning paper in the dayroom. The headline stated: "NO REGRETS," referring to the district attorney who corrected my direction in life four years earlier. Asheville had voted him out the previous month and his tenure ended in a few days. I hadn't thought about my former archenemy in months. I laughed and felt an urge to thank him for the memories now that it was all over. Hell, he may have even saved my life.

Before I left, I gave my ultra-light and comfortable New Balance shower shoes to Melty. (Warden, back at Southern, allowed me to special order them ostensibly due to my large shoe size.) Most guys made do with the hard plastic prison-issue version that offered no cushioning at all. I delighted in saving Melty from this fate as we sat in the dayroom.

"Check it out, ya'll," I told bystanders. "You're about to see Melty's orgasm face."

My ultra-laid-back buddy slipped into the sandals and couldn't help but show that look. It was both glorious and hilarious.

Soon I changed into ill-fitting donated clothes because my dad failed to mail me the outfit I sent him from the processing unit nearly three years earlier. I couldn't believe pants with a thirty-eight waist barely fit when thirty-sixes used to be baggy on me.

I hugged Melty and a few others on my way out (Louie had already transferred a month earlier), with a big grin on my face. A dickhead sergeant I never liked was on duty, but I repressed an urge to tell him to fuck off. He'd just handed me $45 in cash from the state, after all.

My initial feeling upon walking out was equal parts joy and relief. It reminded me of the moment of my arrest, which combined fear and relief. My release meant moving from discomfort to normal instead of normal to ecstasy. Maybe

Christmas Came Early

I would've felt otherwise had my ride been an RV with a hooker and a crudité platter in it, but my buddy Ignatius dropped the ball on that one. The seat in his Lexus felt like a throne, however.

In the days following my glorious exit I often thought of a Marc Maron quote: "I feel bad for people who have never been addicted to anything because they don't know what it's like to really want something and then get it again, and again, and again."

Like waking up as a free man each morning, for instance.

Afterword

I didn't need a steak and lobster dinner in celebration of my release. Arby's proved decadent enough to me that afternoon. The cushioned seats of the booth felt incredible and I celebrated using a real fork instead of a spork. I also used as many napkins as I wanted. Once finished, Ignatius and I walked towards the exit. Since I'd handed my used food tray to someone for the past three thousand meals, I handed it to Ignatius without even thinking.

"What the fuck do you want me to do with that?" he asked.

"Oh, shit. I guess I'm institutionalized," I replied, laughing.

My first three weeks as a free man were spent at Ignatius' house in suburban Atlanta. PTSD and possibly too much quiet messed with my sleep. I expected to walk around in a state of bliss the whole time, but since I'd stifled my emotions while locked up, turning them on again took time. Sheer joy had to wait, at least until I found gainful employment. My friend Jamal, who bailed me out following my arrest, lent me $3,000 to get going again.

I loaded my trusty Mazda with as much as it could hold and drove to rural coastal Virginia, into the carriage house on the homestead of my uncle, Tom Lakin. He and his wife Linda supported me for seventeen months as I wrote first drafts of this book and worked as something of a farmhand.

Instead of living amid two hundred men in one large building, I lived in an area populated by roughly one hundred people per square mile. This was the perfect place for me to decompress following years of sensory abuse. A steady stream of visiting cousins and my sister Dena made me feel loved and normal again. They made being broke and humiliated more bearable.

Once my manuscript was "finished" (for the first of about ten times), I moved to Richmond. I lived with my sister first, and then on my own once I landed a job stocking snack and soda vending machines. I initially lied about my criminal record, but by the time the truth came out I had proven myself and was permitted to stay on board.

I advanced in that business, and laughed that I was in essence still a drug dealer. Back in the day I sold ecstasy and weed, and post-prison I profited from sugar-filled beverages and fat-riddled snacks. I noticed my patience for life's annoyances and my tolerance for others had risen significantly once I started working again. And committing more crimes or getting mixed up in pain pills again was out of the question.

My final takeaway seems perfectly summed up by Charles Frazier in his brilliant novel *Cold Mountain*: "And so he believed everything that had been taken out of him might have been for a purpose. To clear out space for something better."

I like to think prison created space in me for increased empathy for the less fortunate. And hopefully my entitlement complex has been corrected so that I might give more than I take. My upbringing and opportunities granted me advantages others will never know. Squandering them again would be, well, criminal.

Acknowledgements

First my Uncle Tom Lakin and Aunt Linda, who adopted me for seventeen months following my release and gave me the time, space, and support to write this book. They also accepted every collect call I made from the inside and funded my canteen account when "emergencies" hit.

Toby Martin can never be adequately thanked for his extensive largesse. Ditto Tad Mitchell and Jeff Slate. Also making my prison life more palatable were Jim Shrine, Leonard Stoehr, Tom Booker, Jim Lawless, Aunt Sally and Uncle Don Risser, Paige Risser, Kate Lakin-Shultz, Ali Blake, Sarah Hart, Kevin Merritt, Lee Taylor, Mel Herncane, and Graydon Carter.

Invaluable reading and editing assistance for this book came from Jim Shrine, Matt Ralston, Brian Sweeney, Julie Belew, Brad Landry, Kelly Colson Swann, Randy Duke, Salvatore Sodano, Gordie Vanstone, Barry Johnson, Dena Lakin, Duke Stephens, William Chandler, Garrison Scott, and a whole batch of peer critters at Scribophile.com.

Finally, fellow processing camp inmates Jason and Jordan, who shared canteen items with me knowing they'd probably never see me again to be repaid.

About the author

The Author in Atlanta, 2019

Garrett is a humanist humorist or vice versa, born and raised in Canton, Ohio. He lived nearly thirty years in Atlanta and currently lives in Los Angeles, where he created, produces, and hosts The Tree Fort Report podcast, which debuted in March of 2020.

The author formerly occupied himself as an on-air morning radio douche, stand-up comic, courier, waiter, video blog host, and chauffeur, among other follies. He attended Georgia State University and constantly wants to hit a golf ball.

www.ingramcontent.com/pod-product-compliance
Lightning Source LLC
Chambersburg PA
CBHW030219100526
44584CB00014BA/1074